The Secret Still

[In Scotland] you are not allowed to make water in public or whisky in private.

Jack House

The Secret Still

*Scotland's Clandestine
Whisky Makers*

Gavin D. Smith

Birlinn

First published in 2002 by
Birlinn Limited
West Newington House
10 Newington Road
Edinburgh
EH9 1QS

www. birlinn.co.uk

ISBN 1 84158 236 0

British Library Cataloguing-in-Publication Data
A catalogue record for this book is available
from the British Library

Typesetting and origination by Brinnoven, Livingston
Printed and bound by Antony Rowe Ltd, Chippenham

CONTENTS

ACKNOWLEDGEMENTS

Sincere thanks are due to the following for information, advice and support: Ann Abrahams; Geoff Armitage; Keith Bond; Rachel Chisholm, Highland Folk Museum; Campbell Dewar, HM Customs & Excise, Greenock; Ed Dodson; Richard Forsyth; Peter Jones; Richard Joynson; Brenda Lees, North Highland Archivist; Dr Cathlin Macauley, School of Scottish Studies University of Edinburgh; Chris McCully; Fergie MacDonald; Murdo MacDonald, Archivist, Argyll & Bute Council; John McDougall; James McEwan; Ian Millar; Ian Milne; Fiona Murdoch; Ross Noble, Highland Curator, Highland Folk Museum; Richard Paterson; Chloe Randall; Iain Russell; Jacqui Seargeant, Archivist, John Dewar & Sons Ltd; Donald Smith; Ruth Smith; Willie Strathdee; Ian Sutherland; Yvonne Thackeray, Archivist, Chivas Bros Ltd; Jim Turle; Graeme Wilson, Local Heritage Officer, Moray Council; and Alan Winchester.

I am also indebted to members of staff at the Central Library, Edinburgh; Dundee Central Library; Mitchell Library, Glasgow; National Archives Scotland, Edinburgh; National Library of Scotland, Edinburgh; and the School of Scottish Studies, Edinburgh, not to mention Hugh Andrew, Liz Short, Andrew Simmons and others at Birlinn.

Finally, thanks are due to a number of individuals who, quite reasonably, wish to remain anonymous.

INTRODUCTION

A great deal of romance has grown up around the figure of the noble Highlander, distilling without benefit of a licence in order to feed and clothe his family. Stories of the resourcefulness and ingenuity of the whisky-makers are legion, as are those concerning the brutality and incompetence of their opponents, the excisemen. The reality, inevitably, was less simplistic than the myth suggests. Not all 'home' distillers were motivated by family values, and by no means everyone in the Highlands approved of the trade in illicit whisky.

Nonetheless, this trade was, at times, vast. Successive generations of Scottish historians have failed to stress just how significant it was to the 'black' economy of the country during the late eighteenth and early nineteenth centuries, and particularly to the black economy of the Highlands and Islands.

Scottish illicit whisky-making was practised from Shetland in the north to the Borders in the south, where distilling is documented at Wester Buccleuch in Selkirkshire during the late nineteenth century. As in so many areas of Ireland and North America, illicit distilling was feasible, particularly in the Highlands, due to the remote and impenetrable nature of much of the countryside. Local availability of barley, pure water, and peat to fire the stills, also tended to influence location, yet there are also many accounts of illicit operations boldly turning out whisky in the very heart of Scottish towns and cities.

The Scotch Whisky Association notes that 'Taxation in the UK is extremely high, accounting for as much as 70 per cent of the retail price of a typical bottle of standard blended Scotch whisky', but in real terms whisky is more affordable to most British drinkers today than it has been for most of its 'civilised' history. As Ian MacDonald pointed out in *Smuggling in the Highlands*, 'the extent of illicit distillation depended in a great measure on the amount of duty, and the nature of the excise regulations. The smuggler's gain was in direct proportion to the amount of the spirit duty; the higher the duty the greater the gain and the stronger the temptation.'

In Scotland the term 'smuggler' rather confusingly referred not just to those who traded in illicit whisky, but also to the people who distilled it. Sometimes, though not always, these were one and the same. The folk who transported the product of the 'sma' stills' into towns and cities for sale were often known as 'cadgers' or 'blethermen', while the arch-enemy of the smuggler was the 'gauger'.

In Ireland and the USA they have colloquial names for illicit spirit, too. The nearest Scotland gets to 'poitin' and 'moonshine' is the splendidly evocative, though almost obsolete, term 'peatreek'. As in Scotland, illicit distilling in Ireland and North America was practised partly as a way of asserting independence, of cocking an alcoholic snook at an authority that was often perceived as unsympathetic or alien. It was also the best way of turning perishable grain into a much more durable and valuable commodity. According to John McGuffin in *In Praise of Poteen*, illicit spirit was 'the common man's best cash crop'.

Both Ireland and the USA still have thriving underground distilling operations, while in Scotland illicit whisky-making is usually considered to be a historical curiosity, a long-vanished art. Well, maybe . . .

1

A HATEFUL TAX

A hateful tax levied upon commodities, and judged not by the common judges of property, but by wretches hired by those to whom Excise is paid.

Dictionary of the English Language definition of 'excise'
– Dr Samuel Johnson, 1755

The first Scottish legislation to restrict distilling was passed in 1579, when in anticipation of a poor harvest and a subsequent shortage of grain for food, it was decreed that

> no person sal mak, brew, nor sell ony aquavitie frae the 1st day of December approach and till October 1580, under pain of confiscation of aquavitie and breking of the haill lowmes of the makaris, brewaris, and stellaris thairof. But every lord of barony, or gentleman or others of such degree may brew and stell aquavitie off thair own malt and stuff in thair own house for thair own friends

During the subsequent two centuries and more, periods of poor harvests provoked similar restrictions on whisky-making, though as in this instance, the great and the good were not expected to go thirsty!

Illicit distilling took place during periods of prohibition, but became a full-time occupation when whisky-making first attracted its 'hateful tax'. At the same time, there was also a major growth in the smuggling from abroad of gin, brandy and wine.

During the year 1643 the English Parliament imposed for the first time an excise duty on spirits. On 31 January 1644 the Scottish Parliament followed suit, passing an 'Act of Excyse', which placed a duty of 2/8 - on 'everie pynt of aquavytie or strong watteris sold within the countrey'. At the time, the Scots pint was equivalent to almost half an English gallon. This was a tax levied purely on the *amount* distilled, and took no cognisance of the strength of the 'aquavytie' in question. In the same year that spirit duty was introduced to Scotland, the English level was lowered from eight pence per gallon to two pence per gallon in order to encourage small-scale distillation.

The initial imposition of excise duty in both countries had a military imperative. King Charles I required revenue to fight for his crown, while the Scots needed money to pay for the army sent south to fight with the parliamentarian forces opposing the monarch. The history of excise legislation throughout the world is inextricably linked with financing military adventures of one sort or another. Levels of duty have been raised in order to pay for wars, though curiously, in times of peace, they have rarely fallen.

In 1688 an Act was passed which charged duty according to strength, initially only on imported spirits. This measure was quite popular with patriotic folk, until it was extended to all 'spirits of the second extraction' in 1699.

Levels of duty varied between 1644 and 1707, when tax on spirits was increased significantly in order to try to curb excessive drunkenness among the population. However, drinkers could always turn to gin, brandy and wine, which was being smuggled from abroad into Scottish ports in significant quantities. One result of the 'union of crowns' in 1707 was the introduction of English-style customs officers who set out to clamp down on smuggling.

In 1713 the English 'malt tax' was extended to Scotland, though at half the English rate. When in 1725 Walpole's Government passed an Act raising the malt tax in Scotland to 6d per bushel – in line with the English level – the brewers of Edinburgh closed down production in protest. Civil disorder broke out across Scotland, leading to the deaths of eleven people in Glasgow during June's Shawfield Riots.

One effect of the Malt Tax was to reduce the scale of ale-drinking in Scotland. It had previously been by far the most popular drink in much of the country, but after the Act was passed its price rose or its quality fell, and many people switched to drinking whisky, illicitly-distilled from malt on which no tax had been paid. Whisky soon overtook ale in popularity, and by the 1760s it was becoming a fashionable drink to rival imported spirits in the upper echelons of Scottish society. The imposition in 1780 of a high level of duty on imported wine was another factor in the increasing dominance of whisky, and therefore in the attractions of illicit distilling.

In *An Inquiry into the Nature and Causes of the Wealth of Nations* (1776) Kirkcaldy-born political economist Adam Smith wrote,

Though the duties directly imposed upon proof spirits amount only to 2s. 6d per gallon, these added to the duties upon low wines, from which they are distilled, amount to 3s. 10 2/3 (two-thirds)d. Both low wines and proof spirits are rated according to what they gauge in the wash. By increasing the duties upon malt, and reducing those upon the

Distillery, both the opportunities and the temptation to smuggle would be diminished, which might occasion a still further augmentation of revenue.

The hope of evading . . . taxes by smuggling gives frequent occasion to forfeitures and other penalties, which entirely ruin the smuggler; a person who, though no doubt highly blameable for violating the laws of his country, is frequently incapable of violating those of natural justice, and would have been, in every respect, an excellent citizen, had not the laws of his country made that a crime which nature never meant to be so.

Private distilling was legal until 1781, though it was unlawful to sell the spirit produced. When a general prohibition on distilling was imposed in March 1757, due to the recurring problem of poor harvests, the practice of selling the make of private stills burgeoned. It continued to do so until long after the ban on distilling was lifted in December 1760 and was the principal reason for the eventual prohibition of domestic distillation.

In 1758 the Commissioners of Excise in Scotland reported on 'the common people in the Highlands noting that their natural love of spirits makes them attempt distilling of them in defiance of them [the laws relating to distillation] and the officers are to watch over them: this practice is carried on to so great an excess that there are many 1,000s thro' these parts who openly transgress'.

With the ending of private distillation, excise officers were granted new powers, and could now seize stills and spirit, and destroy wash. To encourage illicit distillers to inform, there was a premium of 1s 6d payable for information leading to a seizure. This 'bounty' seems to have come in useful, as 1,940 stills were detected in 1782. It is interesting to consider how many of these were worn out items, surrendered in order to obtain reward money, which would be used to buy new condensing worms, the most complex and therefore expensive pieces of distilling equipment. In 1783 another Act was passed, which gave the excise officers power to seize not only stills and spirit, but also horses and wagons used in connection with illicit distillation.

Despite a high level of illicit distilling, the legal whisky-making industry in Scotland thrived from the late 1770s, and in 1784 the Wash Act was passed – a piece of legislation which gave Highland areas special treatment in an attempt to stimulate the legal trade. Twenty-gallon stills could be licensed at £1 per gallon of cubic capacity per year. The 'Highlands' were defined as the 'several counties of Orkney, Caithness, Sutherland, Ross, Inverness, Argyll, Bute, Stirling, Lanark, Perth, Dumbarton, Aberdeen, Forfar, Kincardine, Banff, Nairn and

Murray'. Section 45 of the Wash Act stated that 'The Commissioners of Excise in Scotland might empower such persons as they thought proper to erect and work stills in producing spirits from corn.' This applied to seventeen counties in the Highlands.

Harsher financial penalties for illegal distillation were introduced at the same time, and if these were not paid by the distiller, then the landowner of the parish in which the offence occurred was liable for the fine. Needless to say, this did not go down well with the landed gentry, nor was the Act warmly welcomed by Lowland distillers.

The Wash Act did nothing to reduce illicit distilling, as the effective limit on the quantity of spirit that could be legally distilled was widely ignored, and the product of the Highland stills continued to be highly desirable in the Lowlands.

In 1785 new provisions were made which prohibited export of Highland whisky from the area, and increased the size of still allowed to a maximum of 40 gallons. The amount of malt that could be used was, however, still restricted to 250 bolls per distiller, and no parish could have more than two stills. Landowners were no longer to be held responsible for the fines of distillers, but distillers had to be reputable people, with an annual poll being conducted among the landowners to elect two distillers to hold licences in each parish. The licence fee was increased to £1 10s, and the Highland area was redefined to exclude some of the more fertile parts of its southern periphery.

The following year, the Scotch Distillery Act lowered the Highland licence fee to £1 4s in an effort to encourage more illicit distillers north of 'the line' to take out licences and therefore cut the amount of whisky being smuggled into the Lowlands. Duty was calculated on still content rather than gravity, which meant that the faster one could distil, the greater the element of profit.

Soon the Lowland distillers began to develop techniques of rapid distillation in new, broad, shallow stills in order to compete with the large-scale London distillers. It was said that stills were constructed which could work off the spirit in no more than three minutes! While the poor quality of the resultant spirit was not important if it was to be rectified and used in gin production, as whisky it was harsh and characterless, and encouraged even greater smuggling of high quality, 'small still' whisky from the Highland area into the Lowlands. One excise officer noted that 'the licence system had made it impossible for the small distiller to work as a licensed distiller: he therefore worked as an unlicensed distiller'.

The area of the 'Highlands' was again amended in 1787 (Act 37, G.III., cap.102, sec.6), when the boundary between 'Highland' and 'Lowland' was defined as

A certain line or boundary beginning at the east point of Loch-Crinan, and proceeding from thence to Loch-Gilpin; from thence along the great road along the west side of Lochfine, to Inveraray and to the head of Lochfine; from thence along the high road to Arrochar, in the county of Dumbarton, and from thence to Tarbet; from Tarbet in a supposed straight line eastward on the north side of the mountain called Ben-Lomond, to the village of Callander of Monteith in the county of Perth; from thence northeastward to Crieff; from thence northward to Ambleree and Inver to Dunkeld; from thence along the foot and south side of the Grampian Hills to Fettercairn, in the county of Kincardine; and from thence northward along the road to Cutties Hillock, Kincardine O'Neil, Clatt, Huntly, and Keith to Fochabers; and from thence westward by Elgin and Forres, to the boat on the River Findhorn, and from thence down the said river to the sea at Findhorn, and any place in or part of the county of Elgin, which lies southward of the said line from Fochabers to the sea at Findhorn.

The 1787 Act also introduced duty of 30 shillings per gallon of still content in the Lowlands, and 20 shillings in the Highlands. The lower Highland level was established partly in the vain hope of reducing illicit distilling, and partly in recognition of the fact that the poorer quality grain of much of the Highland area yielded less spirit than that of the Lowlands.

In 1795 the outbreak of war with France led to a trebling of duty, and there were subsequently further increases. The Napoleonic Wars caused a major recession in Britain, and in the Highlands many legal sources of income such as crofting, fishing and droving were badly affected. As a result, the money made from illicit distilling became a lifeline for many families, and the craft flourished accordingly.

Duty was increased north of the Highland Line, rising to £6 10s in 1797. In the same year, as a result of pressure from the major Lowland distillers, an intermediate region between the Highland and Lowland areas was introduced, where duty was £9 per gallon. The area ran northeast from Crinan in the west to the existing Highland Line at Elgin, and was partly designed to stamp out smuggling along the Highland–Lowland boundary. Four years earlier, legal distilling within two miles of the boundary had been prohibited with the same purpose in mind.

As duty levels on legal distillation were raised, the illicit trade became even more attractive as an occupation. Legal distilleries such as Ardbeg on Islay went bankrupt because of the increases in duty coupled with illegal activity nearby, while in Campbeltown virtually all distilling was of the illicit variety. Even on the small island of Tiree there were two legal distilleries until the early 1790s, when both were forced out of business, though the island continued to produce its fair share of whisky thereafter.

In 1797 a government committee was set up to study the state of distilling in Scotland. The major Lowland distillers were lobbying for an end to the lower level of duty payable in the Highlands and complaining about the quantity of spirit smuggled across the Highland Line. In order to strengthen their case, the Lowland distillers seem to have exaggerated their plight in evidence presented to the committee during 1797 and 1798. John Stein, a prominent member of the famous Lowland distilling dynasty, commented that 'the Highland Exemptions as it is called, *has been grossly abused* . . . It is proved by the Daily Use and Consumption of Highland Spirits in most of the private Families in Edinburgh, which any good judge can easily identify'.

Regarding illicit distilling, Stein declared:

> It is not confined to great towns or regular manufacturers, but spreads itself over the whole face of the country, and in every island from the Orkneys to Jura. There are many who practise this art who are ignorant of every other; and there are distillers who boast that they make the best possible whiskey, who cannot read or write and who carry on the manufacture in parts of the country where the use of the plough is unknown and the face of the exciseman is never seen. Under such circumstances, it is impossible to take account of its operation, it is literally to search for revenue in the woods or on the mountain.

David Cassell of the Kepp distillery near Gargunnock in Stirlingshire claimed that he was unable to sell any of the 15,000 gallons of whisky he produced in the locality of his distillery because of the prevalence of smuggled Highland spirit, and that he was forced to send all of it to Glasgow for sale. He reported regular cartloads of whisky defended by Highlanders armed with pistols and cudgels passing through the nearby village of Kippen.

In 1799 the committee issued a report recommending that the system of licence fees be continued, but that much closer excise supervision of the processes of distilling should be implemented. The committee also suggested the abolition of the Highland Line due to its ineffectiveness, criticised the courts north of the line for doing so little to combat illicit distillation, and castigated landowners for so frequently condoning it.

As a result of the committee's report, some changes were made, with duty outwith the Highlands being doubled to £108 per gallon of still capacity, while within the Highland area it remained at £6 10s. A lower rate of duty was introduced for whisky distilled from bigg, or bere, as its yield was considerably lower than that from malted barley.

The committee's findings also led to increased excise manpower in the most active smuggling areas, with Elgin having five officers in place by 1812, where there had been none at the time of the committee's report. Two officers had served in the Argyll North and South collections in 1793, and this was subsequently increased to seven.

In February 1799 a body of hard-pressed Scottish distillers presented a petition to the House of Commons in which they praised the Licence Act of 1786, as a result of which 'hawking and smuggling have been annihilated, Spirit Dealers have been left in the pursuit of an honest profession'. They also pointed out, however, that a recent addition of a shilling's tax per gallon on spirits, on top of the licence duty, meant that 'Hawkers and smugglers have returned to their former occupations, and thus are the natural customers of the Petitioners supplied with spirits from the old sources, to the ruin of the Petitioners'.

The closing years of the eighteenth century saw a number of very bad harvests, which led to a severe shortage of grain in much of the Highlands, and consequently periods of distilling prohibition. In 1801 the Lord Advocate wrote to the principal Highland landowners, asking for their active support in suppressing smuggling, and sometimes landowners went so far as to evict persistent smugglers.

Dr John Leyden observed in his *Journal of a Tour in the Highlands and Islands of Western Scotland* (1800) that

> The distillation of whiskey presents an irresistible temptation to the poorer classes, as the boll of barley, which costs thirty shillings, produces by this process, between five and six guineas. This distillation had a most ruinous effect in increasing the scarcity of grain last year, particularly in Isla and Tiree, where the people subsisted chiefly on fish and potatoes.

Several years later, pressure was again put on landowners to take the matter of illicit distilling seriously, with harvests being particularly poor in 1807, 1808 and 1816, leading to a consequent shortage of grain. The situation was exacerbated by a lack of peat to fire stills, both legal and illegal, during years when it could not be cut and dried due to bad weather.

> I have . . . by my influence and admonitions suppressed illicit distillation in a very extensive Highland district, my own property, which affords every facility for this pernicious practice . . . I will never sit on the bench as a Justice of the Peace at an Excise Court, where I have not the alternative of either acquitting a miserable half-fed, half-naked wretch (as many such come before me) or making the penalty less than £20.

> – *Angus Mackintosh of Inverness-shire, April 1813*

Although Lowland distillers almost certainly tended to exaggerate their difficulties at times, a number of distilleries were driven out of business by illegal distilling during the early nineteenth century, and in at least one documented case a legal distiller abandoned his trade and went 'underground'. In *The Making of Scotch Whisky*, Michael Moss and John Hume cite the example of the McFarlane family, who ran the Glenluig distillery near Arrochar in Dunbartonshire. When it was forced to cease trading around 1812 the McFarlanes set up a joint illegal distilling venture with farmer John Campbell, whose Coilessan farm enjoyed a usefully remote location on the shores of Loch Long. Presumably the trade they developed with Glasgow was very extensive, as they were fined no less than £600 when convicted of illicit distilling in the spring of 1813 – a far larger amount than was usual for such cases. They were also evicted from Coilessan farm.

Faced with large-scale illicit distillation, many legal Highland distillers became convinced that if the Highland Line was abolished and they were allowed to import grain from the Lowland area and sell their whisky there in return for paying the same level of duty as the Lowland distillers, illegal distilling would be greatly diminished. Not surprisingly, the Lowland operators were less enthusiastic about the idea, fearing competition from the invariably superior Highland product.

In 1814 a series of measures were put in place, largely at the behest of the powerful English distilling lobby, which did nothing to aid a Scotch whisky industry already struggling in the wake of an economic slump in the years after the Napoleonic Wars. Levels of duty were raised, stronger washes – better suited for making spirit for rectification than good whisky – became compulsory, and the use of wash stills with less than 2,000 gallons' capacity in the Lowlands and 500 gallons in the Highlands was made illegal. Highland distillers were dismayed by the scale on which they must now distil in order to operate within the law.

Colonel David Stewart of Garth in *Sketches of the Character, Manners and Present State of the Highlanders of Scotland* (1825) wrote:

> It is evident that this law was a complete interdict, as a still of this magnitude would consume more than the disposable grain in the most extensive county within this newly drawn boundary; nor could fuel be obtained for such an establishment without an expense which the commodity could not possibly bear. The sale, too, of the spirits

produced was circumscribed within the same line, and thus the market which alone could have supported the manufacture was entirely cut off. Although the quantity of grain raised within many districts, in consequence of the recent agricultural improvements, greatly exceeds the consumption, the inferior quality of this grain, and the great expense of carrying it to the Lowland distillers, who, by a ready market, and the command of fuel, can more easily accommodate themselves to this law, renders it impracticable for the farmers to dispose of their grain in any manner adequate to pay rents equal to the real value of their farms, subject as they are to the many drawbacks of uncertain climate, uneven surface, distance from market, and scarcity of fuel. Thus hardly any alternative remained but that of having recourse to illicit distillation, or resignation of their farms and breach of their engagements with their landlords. These are difficulties of which the Highlanders complain heavily, asserting that nature and the distillery laws present insurmountable obstacles to the carrying on of a legal traffic. The surplus produce of their agricultural labour will therefore remain on their hands, unless they incur an expense beyond what that article will bear, in conveying so bulky a commodity to the Lowland market as the raw material, and the drawback of prices on their inferior grain. In this manner, their produce must be disposed of at a great loss, as it cannot be legally manufactured in the country. Hence they resort to smuggling as their only resource. If it indeed be true that this illegal traffic has made such deplorable breaches in the honesty and morals of the people, the revenue drawn from the large distilleries, to which the Highlanders have been made the sacrifice, has been procured at too high a price for the country.

Aeneas MacDonald (*Whisky*) wrote in characteristically colourful style about the years after the 1814 Act:

Now dawned the heroic age of whisky, when it was hunted upon the mountains with a price on its head as if it were a Stuart prince, when loyal and courageous men sheltered it in their humble cabins, when its lore was kept alive in secret like the tenets of a proscribed and persecuted religion. If whisky has not degenerated wholly into a vile thing in which no person of taste and discernment can possibly take an interest, it is because its tradition was preserved, by men whose names ungrateful posterity has forgotten, during years when the brutal and jealous Hanoverian government sought to suppress in the Highlands this last relic of the ancient Gaelic civilization. It is an extraordinary thing that, while Jacobite loyalty has found its bards, this loyalty to a thing far more linked with Highland history than a Lowland family ever could become, has not yet been sung.

In April 1816 the Chancellor of the Exchequer received a petition from five of the principal Lowland distillers in which they noted that because of the strong washes now required by law 'the quality of the spirits made renders them almost wholly unsaleable, and co-operate, with the high duties, to encourage illicit distillation'.

As legal distilleries failed, and production fell, so the amount of duty received by the Government also dropped. In order to maximise revenue, the Scottish Excise Board pushed for the implementation of its long-held belief in the abolition of the Highland Line, the legalisation of stills as small as 50 gallons in the Highlands, and permission to use weaker washes. By this time, the Lowland distillers were so keen to see an end to large-scale smuggling that they agreed with the proposals, which also included the provision for landowners to make serious efforts to suppress the illicit trade, and gave greater powers to the excise service. It was clear that duty would also have to be lowered if there was to be any realistic hope of significantly curbing illicit distilling, and in November 1816 duty was duly cut by one-third. The Small Stills Act embraced the principal proposals favoured by the legal Highland distillers and the Scottish Excise Board, allowing stills of a minimum of 40 gallons' capacity, abolishing the Highland Line and legalising weaker washes to increase the quality of the product.

The washes were still too strong to produce spirit that could really compete in terms of flavour with the smugglers, however, and the rules governing their strength were regularly broken, though in 1818 weaker washes were allowed under a new Act. Two years later, the Sikes hydrometer was issued to excise officials, making it easier for them to make accurate assessments of the gravity of washes.

In 1817 duty on bere and barley was equalised, and 1819 saw the level of duty doubled. This, along with a general feeling that the permitted strengths of washes was too high, meant that the anticipated glut of applications for distillery licences failed to materialise. Illegal distillation began to rise again, and the number of licenced distilleries in the Highlands fell from fifty-seven in 1819 to forty-two in 1823. In 1820 there were almost 5,000 prosecutions in Scotland for illicit distilling, and two years later the figure rose to 6,278.

Captain Hugh Munro of Teaninich distillery at Alness in Easter Ross wrote to J.A. Stewart Mackenzie of Seaforth in 1818:

> The distillery has not been at work for two months, and it will be a few weeks before it commences; indeed the state of the country as to illicit

distillation, and the unaccountable supineness of the Excise to put a stop to it, makes it doubtful if at the present from the limited sales of spirits whether it is advisable for the legal distillers to go.

In the early 1820s, good-quality, smuggled Highland whisky sold for between 6s and 7s per gallon at something like 20 degrees over proof. By comparison, harsh, legal grain spirit cost 8s per gallon at seven degrees over proof, the highest strength allowable by law. Closer to 'source' the good stuff could be had much more cheaply, perhaps for as little as £3 for a ten-gallon cask or anker. It was hardly surprising that the Highland spirit was in great demand.

By this time, however, many Highland landowners were becoming less tolerant of illicit distilling on their property, as improved transport networks meant that they could make handsome profits by selling their own legally distilled whisky, or their grain, in the Lowlands. There was also a feeling of unease at the increasing lawlessness associated with illicit distilling, in addition to which many landowners were embracing agricultural improvement, seeing their estates as more overtly commercial enterprises than they had in the past.

In 1820 the fourth Duke of Gordon – a very influential and wealthy figure, with large estates in Inverness-shire, Aberdeenshire and Banffshire – made a speech in the House of Lords in which he reflected the views of many of his noble colleagues with estates in the north of Scotland. He promised that if the Government would expand upon the legislation of 1816 and 1818 and make it more favourable for illicit distillers to become legitimate, then he and his fellow landowners would undertake to uphold the law as diligently as they could, and evict anyone convicted of illicit distilling.

The result of Gordon's speech was the setting up under the chairmanship of Lord Wallace of a Fifth Committee of Inquiry into the Revenue in 1821, and the following year this led to the Illicit Distillation (Scotland) Act. An important element of this Act was the introduction of more severe penalties for illicit distilling. Smugglers caught in possession of whisky were to be fined £200, as was anyone apprehending using an ungauged still or obstructing an excise officer in his work. The penalty for using an unlicensed still was £100, and landowners who allowed illicit distilling to be practised on their property were liable to a fine 'not exceeding £100, nor less than £20'. The penalty for assisting in illegal whisky-making was £30 or a six-month jail sentence for a first offence, and double that for any subsequent misdemeanour.

Excise officers no longer needed warrants from justices of the peace in order to confiscate casks and wagons and other articles associated with illicit distilling activities, and they also received financial rewards for their detections, which helped to boost the morale of the service considerably. Significantly, the power of justices of the peace to fine offenders according to their means was removed. Too often in the past they had appeared to be in sympathy with smugglers, and fines imposed had frequently been derisory.

With Britain no longer at war it was possible to contemplate reducing duty to more reasonable levels, which would immediately have the effect of making illicit distilling less lucrative and therefore less attractive. The quality of much legal whisky had also greatly improved by the early 1820s.

In 1823 the most far-reaching piece of excise legislation in British history was enacted. The Excise Act of that year was based on the findings of the committee chaired by Lord Wallace, and was designed to encourage and support the legal distilling industry in Scotland. Duty was cut to 2s 5d a gallon, a historic reduction of more than 50 per cent, and a minimum still size of 40 gallons was confirmed. 'Thin' washes, to produce high-quality whisky able to compete with illicit spirit, were also sanctioned. In order to encourage distillers to use malted barley rather than raw grain, to help their product compete with illicit distillers in terms of flavour, a rebate – or drawback – of 1s 5d per gallon on malt was introduced. This allowed the distiller to reclaim some of the duty paid, which partially compensated for the higher cost of malt compared to raw grain. The licence fee was set at £10 per annum, and the concept of duty-free warehousing was developed. All distillers were able to export whisky to England and abroad, though a minimum of 80 gallons per shipment was stipulated.

The Act was very successful in stimulating the legal trade in reasonably priced, high-quality whisky, and thereby significantly undercut the market for illicit spirits. The bare statistics show the dramatic growth in legal whisky production. In 1823 there were 111 licensed distilleries in Scotland, but no fewer than 263 two years later. Three million gallons of whisky was produced in licensed distilleries during 1823, and no less than 10 million gallons in 1828. Inevitably, however, a number of the legal distilling ventures set up in the aftermath of the Excise Act were soon to collapse, sometimes due to lack of commercial experience, under-funding, trading fluctuations or even too much competition in certain areas. In the Highlands, there had been forty-two licensed distilleries in 1823, a figure which grew to 107 in 1826, but the following year the number dropped well below a hundred once again.

The extent of growth in legal distilling during the years immediately following the Act seems to have been an unexpected bonus as far as the authorities were concerned, since in their First Report in 1857 the Commissioners of Inland Revenue noted 'a most surprising increase of legally made spirits. In 1820 the quantity made in the United Kingdom, which was retained for home consumption was 9,600,000 gallons. In 1826 it was 18,200,000.' They went on to note that 'We may assert here generally, that the beneficial effects of the change in the great object of suppressing illicit trading were found in both divisions of the kingdom to surpass the most sanguine expectations.'

Writing of the 1823 Act, James M'Laren, Collector of Excise for Aberdeen, noted: 'The effect of it was very good indeed; that Act was the first thing that gave a turn to it [illicit distilling]; that Act enabled the small capitalist to commence business; and many of those formerly engaged in illicit distillation began as legal distillers.'

Captain William Fraser of Brackla distillery, near Nairn, observed that

> It is not the Excise who have suppressed smuggling, for there are miles in which there are no Excise; but it is the fine quality and low prices of the spirit which the distillers bring into the market that have alone prevented illicit distillation. But even then, if it were not the low price of barley of the last and the present crops, my opinion is there would not be half a dozen legal distilleries in the whole collection – the difference in the price of a barrel is nearly equal to that additional sixpence.

Fraser's 'additional sixpence' was the 'malt drawback', the purpose of which was, according to a report of 1832,

> to induce persons of limited capital to embark in the trade, and to erect *small* distilleries in the Highlands and other districts then infested with illicit distillation. The indulgence thus proposed enabled the distiller to make malt spirits at the *same rate* of duty as those made from mixed grain, and . . . they could be produced by the legal trader similar in quality and flavour to those made by the smuggler, and with this regulation, *combined with a low rate of duty*, it was expected that the legal would supplant and undersell the illegal distiller.

Fraser's fellow ex-army officer Captain Hugh Munro of Teaninich wrote during the 1830s of the effects of the Act:

> Since 1795 I have resided in this county, engaged in farming pursuits. From that period of time, until 1817, I may say that all the proprietors and farmers of this county were in the habit of openly disposing of the

barley raised on their farms to the smugglers, for there were only one or two small distilleries in this country...In the year 1817 the proprietors and the Commissioners of Supply of Ross, were convinced of the injurious effects of illicit distillation, and did, at a county meeting, enter into resolutions, which were published, tending to abolish smuggling and encourage the erection of distilleries. That, accordingly, three or four were built, one in particular, by several gentlemen combining, and the Teaninich distillery was built by me on my own property; yet it so happened that the illicit distillers commanded the grain market of the country, and the resolutions were not effectively carried into effect; smuggling still existed, and the success of the distilleries disappointed the expectations of those who carried them on. The partnership of one was dissolved, with a loss of £500 to each proprietor concerned. Two others were soon given up: but I continued to struggle on; and when the favourable Distillery Laws took place in 1823, with the drawback of 1s. 2d. per gallon on malt, to the extent of two gallons per bushel, an extraordinary change was soon perceived; smuggling was greatly suppressed, and for one gallon that was permitted in the country from my distillery, previous to 1823, there were, from that time till 1830, an increase of from thirty to forty times the quantity permitted and consumed in the country, and, at a later period, the smuggling was confined to some Highland glens.

In the immediate aftermath of the 1823 Act the excise service was diligent in its duty, destroying distilling equipment, burning bothies and requesting the eviction of smugglers by landowners, many of whom no longer saw the economic advantage of showing leniency towards smugglers, either in their roles as landlords or as justices of the peace. Fines increased dramatically, with the average in the county of Inverness rising from £1 before the Act to £7 13s. The number of convictions in magistrates' courts stood at 4,563 in 1823, but fell to 2,433 the following year. In 1825 the figure was 873, and by 1832 it had been reduced to 296. The 1847 statistic of sixty-four had been whittled down to a mere six in 1874.

Moss & Hume make reference to a case reported in the *Glasgow Herald* of 2 January 1824 to illustrate the harsher financial penalties being handed out to convicted smugglers after the passing of the Act. The report describes the discovery of an illicit still of 90 gallons' capacity in the village of Eaglesham by officers from the Paisley Excise Office. The still itself, along with a 300-gallon mash tun, three 280-gallon wash tuns, a cooler, 46 pounds of malt and some 200 gallons of fermented wort, were destroyed, and the two smugglers apprehended were each fined £60.

By the mid-1830s, illicit distilling was a spent force in terms of its economic impact, despite the Government's steady increase in duty. In 1825, tax stood at two shillings and four pence per Imperial gallon. The following year it rose to two shillings and ten pence, and in 1830 it reached three shillings and four pence. 'Illicit distillation and private malting . . . are in a great many parts quite abolished' – noted Colonel Alexander Campbell, excise commissioner, in 1830. There were, however, people, some of considerable social standing, who mourned the old days . . .

It is asserted that the rage for the use of whisky is still increasing, while to our sad experience we know that its quality is deteriorating among us. It is no longer the pure dew of the mountain that issued from the bothies of our free traders of the hills, healthful and as exhilarating as the drops which the sun's first rays drink up from the heathbell of the Cairngorms, but a vile, rascally, mixed compotation which fires the blood and maddens the veins without warming the heart, or, like the old, elevating the understanding.'

– Letter from Major Cumming Bruce, published
in The Inverness Courier, *April 1831*

In parts of Aberdeenshire which had long been hotbeds of smuggling, some justices of the peace dismissed illicit distilling cases without hearing the evidence after the passing of the Excise Act. In November 1824 it was decided by the Lord Advocate that if JPs failed to apply the law properly, then all smuggling cases within their jurisdiction would be heard in Edinburgh's Court of Exchequer. Sixty-six cases were referred to Edinburgh in 1824, with thirty-one convictions resulting. Fines were high, often up to the maximum level of £100.

It was necessary for the magistrates of Elgin to be instructed in October 1824 to apply the highest permissible fine to anyone found guilty of 'trespass . . . against the Act', but the following month a very poor offender was only fined £5 by an Elgin court. The local magistrates listed a dozen recent cases, two of which involved impoverished families each with seven children, and eight others also involved poverty-stricken families. Two, they noted, concerned bridegrooms making whisky for their weddings, a situation which seems to have offered sufficient mitigation for them to suggest a maximum £5 fine!

The magistrates promoted an amnesty for anyone handing in illicit stills, and even went so far as to return the fines of any recent offenders surrendering their distilling equipment. They were keen, however, to demonstrate that those individuals flouting the law and profiting handsomely from illicit distilling would receive stiff penalties if apprehended. Accordingly, in July 1825, one Alexander Murdoch of Dallas, near Forres, was convicted of 'conveying spirits without a permit' and fined £50.

Not surprisingly, there was great intimidation of newly licensed distillers in the wake of the 1823 Excise Act, most famously concerning George Smith in Glenlivet (see *Speyside*). It is recorded that in 1825 the Banks o' Dee distillery was burnt down by illicit distillers or their sympathisers, though the precise location of the Aberdeenshire distillery is not known. In Glenlivet, the smuggler John Frazer was guilty of an arson attack on at least one new distillery, and it was some four years after the passing of the Act before concerted efforts by excise officers and the military finally succeeded in virtually ending illicit distilling in the glen by the likes of Frazer and other noted smugglers such as Alexander Mackenzie of Claggan. In 1827 Braemar and Corgarff castles were upgraded to provide barracks for the Light Dragoons, whose main purpose was to help eradicate the remnants of the illegal trade.

Smuggling continued to be a sufficiently serious problem in parts of the Highlands as to warrant the stationing of revenue cutters in the Beauly Firth in the east and around Oban in the west – each with a crew of up to thirty men – in order to assist the revenue officers on the ground in trying to put down continued smuggling along the length of the Caledonian Canal.

One often-overlooked effect of the dramatic reduction in illicit distillation following the 1823 Excise Act was the depopulation of many glens. Evidence for this can be found in the *Statistical Account of Aberdeenshire* (1843), where it is noted that

> While this infamous and demoralizing practice prevailed, population increased through the facilities by which families were maintained among the hills and valleys on its profits. But no sooner was this system put down, than the effect appeared on population. Fewer marriages than formerly now take place, and a considerable number of families, formerly supported by illicit distillation, have been obliged to remove to towns and other parishes; a good many families also, have emigrated to America.

Later examples of illicit distilling cases had a novelty value and attracted a considerable degree of press attention. James Gray, a farmer, of Midtown, Carnie in Aberdeenshire, appeared in court in Huntly on 5 February 1875, charged with 'having in his possession, or in an apartment under his sitting room, all the utensils and vessels required in the manufacture of exciseable liquors, and with having a quantity of low wines'. When an excise officer from Huntly called on Gray during routine inquiries he had discovered some apparently home-distilled spirit in two jars, along with a wash tub. A thorough search of the property yielded a trap door leading into a cellar under the sitting room, in which were 'a copper, two large tubs – one containing wormwood – and two black pigs with some sort of spirit in them'.

Gray was fined the modest sum of £40, an amount which his local Member of Parliament, William McCombie, persuaded the Chancellor of the Exchequer not to increase, as was his right in cases where the fine seemed unduly low. McCombie stressed that Gray had never been in trouble before and was of limited financial means. Gray may have escaped with a small fine, but his landlord, the duke of Richmond and Gordon, terminated his lease on Midtown from Whitsun of 1875.

Illicit distillation may now be said to exist only among a few isolated evaders of the law; but they are unable to continue their operations for any length of time, and soon get discovered by the revenue authorities. The true smuggler of old exists no longer; he belongs to a bygone age, when what is now considered to be a crime was looked upon as justifiable evasion of undue laws. With all their faults one cannot but admire the smugglers of old, who had in their veins much of the pluck and daring that has been, and still is, the backbone of the British race.

– Alfred Barnard, 1887

There was a brief resurgence of illicit distilling when repeal of the Malt Tax Act occurred in 1880. For the first time a whisky-maker could buy malt rather than be forced to make his own – a process which took up to three weeks, and left him vulnerable to detection by the excise authorities. Previously malt could only be made by licensed maltsters.

Ian MacDonald took a very moralistic view of illicit distilling, and one quite clearly influenced by his former role as an excise officer. Writing in his Prefatory Note to *Smuggling in the Highlands* (1914), MacDonald observed that there had been a revival of illicit distillation in the Highlands 'especially over wide tracts of Inverness-shire, Ross-shire and Sutherlandshire' during the 1880s, and that this informed the tone and content of some of the following text, much of which had originally been presented as a speech to the Gaelic Society of Inverness in 1886.

For some time prior to 1880 illicit distillation had been practically suppressed in the north, and the old smugglers were fast passing away; but with the abolition of the Malt Tax, the reduction of the Revenue Preventive Staff, and the feeling of independence and security produced by the Crofter's Act, came a violent and sustained outburst of smuggling which was not only serious as regards the Revenue and licensed traders, but threatened to demoralise and impoverish the communities and districts affected. The revival among the youth of a new generation of those pernicious habits which had in the past led to so much lawlessness, dishonesty, idleness and drinking was especially lamentable.

In their efforts to suppress this fresh outbreak the Revenue officials were much hampered not only by the strong, popular sentiment in favour of smuggling and smugglers, but also by the mistaken leniency of local magistrates, and by the weak, temporising policy of the Board of Inland Revenue towards certain sportsmen who claimed exemption for their extensive deer-forests from visits by the Revenue officials . . . Fortunately matters have much improved since 1886; smuggling is again on the decline, almost extinct, and will soon, it is hoped, be a thing of the past in the Highlands.

There can be no doubt that smuggling, when successful, is profitable in a pecuniary sense. Barley can be this year bought for 23s. a quarter, from which can be obtained some 14 or 16 gallons of whisky, which can be sold at 18s. or 20s. a gallon. Allowing for all contingencies, payment of carriage, liberal consumption during manufacture, and generous treatment of friends and neighbours, some £8 or 10 can be netted from an outlay of 23s. This is no doubt a great temptation.

Following the 1880s 'outbreak' there was another flurry of illicit distillation in the years after the passing of the 1915 Immature Spirits Act which introduced a compulsory maturation period of two years. This led to a shortage of whisky and a consequent price rise, followed in 1920 by an increase in duty to £3 12s 6d per proof gallon. By the mid-1930s illicit distilling was again quite a serious problem, and was dealt with by the full force of the law. A celebrated case took place in Keith (see 'Speyside') in 1934, while other seizures occurred in areas with long smuggling traditions such as Auchindown near Dufftown and the Garioch district of Aberdeenshire. Illicit distilling survived through the years of the Second World War, when there was a great shortage of legal whisky, and consequently a vast rise in prices for what was available.

Writing of illicit distilling in 1906, historian A.J. Beaton (*The Social and Economic Condition of the Highlands of Scotland since 1800*) noted: 'the practice can never be suppressed so long as there is so high a duty on whisky' . . .

2

GOING UNDERGROUND

Having taken an initial look at the history of excise legislation in Scotland it is time to leave behind the world of parliament chambers and legal documents and go out among the hills and glens to get some fresh air. It is time to see how the illicit distillers operated, how they attempted to outwit the forces of law and order, and to examine the curious interaction between them and their 'betters'.

The malting is generally carried on by a distinct class, by the dealers in grain themselves; and the wash is manufactured in a rude hut in some retired or concealed spot poorly provided with a few casks and tubs. The remainder of the apparatus consists of two or three casks to receive the spirit and of a still, generally of eighteen gallons in capacity and with a very short worm and tub; the great command of water rendering a long one unnecessary. Sometimes a hut is erected to protect the still from the weather; but it is frequently set up in the open air, under some bank or rock which permits a stream of water to be easily introduced into the tub.

– John MacCulloch, The Highlands and
Western Isles of Scotland *(1824)*

Finding the right location for the still or distilling bothy was crucial to the success of any illicit whisky-making enterprise. Caves, and particularly sea caves, were popular, and stills were sometimes set up in the middle of bogs to prevent anyone unfamiliar with the territory from gaining access. Small islands also provided a degree of security, and in one instance the tell-tale smoke from distilling was hidden because the still was worked in conjunction with a nearby limekiln. According to Ian MacDonald in *Smuggling in the Scottish Highlands*, 'At the Falls of Orrin the bothy smoke was made to blend judiciously with the spray of the falls so as to escape notice.' It was also quite common for distilling smoke to be piped into the chimney of a nearby croft house. Another trick was for it to issue from below burning heather or a heap of smouldering peats.

Gamekeepers, ghillies and even animals presented a threat to bothies – the smuggler McPherson had his bothy in the Aultmore Glen destroyed by a cow falling through the roof! It was not unknown for bothies to have separate sleeping areas and even larders, so that men did not increase the risk of detection by coming and going from the site during distilling.

Sometimes, of course, it did not matter how careful the distiller was in choosing the best place in which to carry on his craft, as someone, or something, would give him away. Dr John Mackenzie (in *Highland Memories*) recounts the story of a pair of excise officers following a trail of barley which was obviously leaking from a sack. Suddenly, the grain trail stopped on a hillside. The gaugers dug around until they discovered the entrance to a bothy. One of them proceeded to conceal himself inside and his colleague filled up the entry so that it appeared undisturbed. When the unsuspecting distiller entered his bothy he was immediately grabbed by a pair of gauger's hands, while the second officer came up behind him and prevented his escape. The final scene of the drama was played out in Dingwall courthouse.

Alfred Barnard wrote that 'Morewood [Samuel Morewood, *An Essay on the Inventions and Customs in the Use of Inebriating Liquors*, 1824] mentions the instance of a person who had constructed a distillery so artfully

that it eluded the vigilance of the most expert officers of Excise, though known to have long existed in the neighbourhood. A determined gentleman of this department resolved to find it out at all hazards, and, on one moonlight night, unaccompanied by any person, he followed a horse led by a peasant, having a sack across the back of the animal, which, he suspected contained materials for this mysterious manufactory. When the horse had arrived at a certain place, the sack was removed from his back, and suddenly disappeared. The officer made his observations, returned to his residence, and having procured military assistance, repaired to the place where the horse had been unloaded, all was silent, the moon shone bright, the ground was unmarked by any peculiar appearance, and he was almost inclined (as well as those who accompanied him) to think that he laboured under a delusion. Perceiving, however, some brambles loosely scattered about the place, he proceeded to examine more minutely, and on their removal, discovered some loose sods, under which was found a trap door leading to a small cavern, at the bottom of which was a complete distillery at full work, supplied by a subterraneous stream, and the smoke conveyed from it through the windings of a tube that was made to communicate with the funnel of the chimney of the distillers' dwelling-house, situated at a considerable distance.

On occasions, methods of concealment had to be devised at short notice. During the early 1900s, one crofter at Advie, near Grantown-on-Spey, close to where Tormore distillery was built half a century later, received an unexpected visit from a local excise officer, 'acting on information received'. Seeing the approaching gauger he hid his still under a mound of straw in an outbuilding, and placed a broody hen on a nestful of eggs on top of it.

From *The Recreations of Christopher North* (1842):

Christopher North was the pen name of novelist, poet and editor John Wilson (1785–1854), a friend of the Wordsworths while living in the Lake District, and later, in Edinburgh, a contributing editor to the influential Blackwood's Magazine. He also occupied the Chair in Moral Philosophy at Edinburgh University from 1820 until his death. The following extracts nicely illustrate his general belief in the nobility of the peasantry, and his sentimental view of whisky smugglers and smuggling.

Writing of being near Loch Etive in Argyllshire, North proclaims:

See! – a faint mist dissipating itself over the heather! There – at work, shaming the idle waste, and in use and want to break even the Sabbath-day, is a STILL!

Do we look like Excisemen? The crutch has indeed a suspicious family resemblance to a gauging-rod; and literary characters, like us, may well be mistaken for the Supervisor himself. But the smuggler's eye knows his enemy at a glance, as the fox knows a hound; and the whispering group discern at once that we are of a nobler breed. That one fear dispelled, Highland hospitality bids us welcome, even into the mouth of the malt-kiln, and, with a smack on our loof, the Chief volunteers to initiate us into the grand mysteries of the worm.

The turf-door is flung outward on its lithe hinges, and already what a gracious smell! In we go, ushered by unbonneted Celts, gentlemen in manners wherever the kilt is worn; for the tartan is the symbol of courtesy, and Mac is a good password the world over between man and man. Lowland eyes are apt to water in the peat-reek, but erelong we shall have another 'drappie in our e'e,' and drink to the Clans in the 'unchristened cretur.' . . .

And these figures in men's coats and women's petticoats are females? We are willing to believe it in spite of their beards. One of them absolutely suckling a child! Thank you, my dear sir, but we cannot swallow the contents of that quech. Yet, let us try. – A little too warm and rather harsh; but meat and drink to a man of age . . .

. . . and as the old soldiers keep tending the Worm in the reek as if all were silence, the male-looking females, and especially the he-she with the imp at her breast, nod, and smirk, and smile, and snap their fingers, in a challenge to a straspey – and, by all that is horrible, a red hairy arm is round our neck, and we are half-choked with the fumes of whisky-kisses. An hour ago, we were dreaming of Malvina! and here she is with a vengeance, while we in the character of Oscar are embraced till almost all the Lowland breath in our body expires.

And this is STILL-LIFE?

Dismissing as nonsense the objection that smuggling is immoral, causing idleness and dishonesty, North goes on:

> Smugglers are seldom drunkards; neither are they men of boisterous manners or savage dispositions. In general, they are grave, sedate, peaceable characters, not unlike elders of the kirk. Even Excisemen admit them, except on rare occasions when human patience is exhausted, to be merciful. Four pleasanter men do not now exist in the bosom of the earth, than the friends with whom we are now on the hob-nob. Stolen waters are sweet – a profound and beautiful reflection – and no doubt originally made by some peripatetic philosopher at a Still. The very soul of the strong drink evaporates with the touch of the gauger's wand. An evil day would it indeed be for Scotland, that should witness the extinguishment of all her free and unlicensed mountain stills! The charm of Highland hospitality would be worn and withered, and the *doch an dorras*, instead of a blessing, would sound like a ban.

Ian Macdonald described an excise raid on a distilling bothy in the north-west Highlands in *Smuggling in the Scottish Highlands*. The details of the distilling operation are fascinating, and it is interesting to compare the ex-gauger's intrepid, upstanding officers with those so often portrayed by 'the other side' in folk history.

> One of the most complete detections and seizures made in my time took place in Achnalt deer forest. The Beauly officers discovered a quantity of malt and a bothy in course of construction in Coulin Forest, between Kinlochewe and Torridon. On an early return visit they found that the bothy was still unfinished, the inference being that the smugglers had become aware of their first visit and had taken alarm. Careful searching failed to discover the malt, and the officers suspected that it had been conveyed across the hills to Achnalt, a considerable distance. The Dingwall officers, under pretence of fishing, visited the locality, and after two days' searching, discovered the bothy in full

working order in a very lonely spot high up in Achanalt forest. There being only two officers, one said to the other, 'Is it quite safe to enter the bothy? There may be several smugglers, perhaps the worse of drink; they may murder us and bury us in the moss!'

'Well,' replied the other bravely, 'I am quite prepared to go.' To prevent escape a rush was made to the bothy, where two men were found busy, the still being on the fire running low-wines. Addressing the more elderly man, one of the officers said, *'Bha sibh fad' an so!'* *'Bha, mo thruaighe, tuilleadh is fada!'* was the sad reply. ('You have been long here!' 'Yes, alas, too long!') Pretending help was near, the officers requested the smugglers to get ready for proceeding to Dingwall. But this they resolutely refused to do, evidently guessing, as time passed, that more officers were not forthcoming. Seeing they were only man for man, and that friends might at any moment come to visit the smugglers, the officers concluded that discretion was the better part of valour, demanded the men's names and addresses, which subsequently proved to be altogether false, placed all the utensils and materials under seizure, and allowed the smugglers to go. They fled like deer over the bogs and rocks, and were soon out of sight. The bothy contained a copper still, stillhead and worm, and a complete set of the usual utensils. There was no whisky, but the receiver connected with the still contained a quantity of low-wines, and there were several vessels containing worts ready for distillation. The smugglers had actually cut and dried peats for their sole use, erected a kiln with perforated iron plates to dry their malt, and set up rollers to crush it. They had a sleeping bothy, with beds full of dried grass for beds and some blankets. Small quantities of tea, sugar, bread, butter and 'crowdie' (dried curds) were found, and several herring hung up drying in the smoke of the still-fire. At some distance from the bothy was a heap of draff, to which the deer had a well beaten track. Having demolished all that could be destroyed, the officers conveyed the still, head and worm to Auchanalt Station, where they arrived in the gloaming, tired and wet, but quite pleased with their exploits, regretting only that they were not able to bring the smugglers also. The smugglers must have been at work for months in their extensive establishment, and the officers afterwards learned that on their way to the station they had passed close by the spot where a cask of whisky was buried in the moss.

According to *The Statistical Account of Scotland*, compiled during the 1790s, illicit distillers in the Highlands and Islands often operated in groups, owning the equipment on a communal basis. Certainly, tenants operated distilling 'co-operatives' in Lewis, Easter Ross and Kintyre. This meant that if there was a successful excise raid on the still, the capital cost of replacing lost items was shared. In a whisky-making co-operative venture the fines handed out in court to any of the group caught in the act of distilling would also be divided, and therefore much more easily paid. Distilling operations could be moved from one location owned by a member of the group to another in order to make the excisemen's lives even more difficult. Another advantage was that there were enough pairs of hands to carry out all the various stages of whisky-making without any one individual being absent from his normal routines for so long that suspicion was aroused.

Set against these attractions, of course, was the perennial problem that the more people who knew the location of the still, the more people there were to let potentially incriminating information slip out in unguarded or boastful moments.

In *Still Life With Bottle* (1994) the celebrated cartoonist Ralph Steadman created a gallery of bizarre, fictitious and very funny cartoon smuggling characters. They included Blind Bag Crieff Mogran, whose unfeasibly large sporran was used to transport illicit whisky, Laughing Jack McShagbasket – 'the Che Guevara of bucket-shop peatreek peddling', Gay Gordon Fanbuggery, who was raised as a boy because 'his' parents already had twelve daughters, and compulsive 'grass' Ledrum Snitty from St Kilda. Sometimes, just sometimes, it is difficult to work out whether or not they are based on real people. Certainly Steadman's excise officers appear to be real, including Ian MacDonald ISO, author of *Smuggling in the Highlands*, but then again did the stylish, white-cloaked, pipe-smoking exciseman Cyrus Culbokie really set light to a thousand acres of grouse moor while trying to light his pipe in a strong wind.

Time would fail to tell how spirits, not bodies, have been carried past officers in coffins and hearses, and even in bee-hives.

– Ian MacDonald

Concealing the distilling equipment and actually producing spirit unmolested by the forces of the law was one thing, but if 'the cratur' was to be sold rather than consumed by the distillers and their close friends and family, the perils were really only just beginning. Death, real or feigned, was often exploited by smugglers wishing to move cargoes of spirit. The most famous story of this type concerns Magnus Eunson of Orkney (see 'In From The Cold'), but there is no shortage of others.

John Munro, also known as John Dearg (Gaelic for 'Red John'), was an illicit distiller and also a 'middleman' in Invergordon, Ross-shire. His ship's chandlery business provided good cover for his main business of distilling and distributing illicit whisky. One day Dearg had a large amount of whisky casked and hidden in cellars beneath his house, ready to be taken to Invergordon harbour, when he received word that the excise officers were in the area and due to arrive and search his premises very soon. A travelling tailor was working in the house at the time, and Dearg persuaded him to pretend to be the corpse of his brother in return for a boll of malt. A boll was 4 to 4½ bushels of grain, weighing some 140 lbs. In liquid form it was the equivalent of 256–285 pints. The tailor was duly placed on a table positioned over the trapdoor to the cellar, covered with a sheet, and the household assumed 'mourning roles' as the excisemen knocked at the door. The tailor chose that moment to demand two bolls or he would give the game away. Dearg agreed, and the officers were forced to leave him and the family to mourn in peace, despite their conviction that he was one of the ringleaders of smuggling in the area. The whisky was duly transferred from the house to a waiting boat as planned, and shipped across the Cromarty Firth to the Black Isle and on to Inverness. It was some time later that the excise officers discovered that John Dearg did not have a brother.

In many smuggling tales, funeral corteges were put to good use. One involves a smuggler called Sandy and an excise officer who was a fellow Highlander, and usually quite tolerant of Sandy's illicit activities. On one occasion, however, he decided that matters had gone too far, and he warned Sandy that from then onwards he would be pursuing him vigorously.

'Weel, I'll gie ye a chance then,' says Sandy. 'On Friday I'll bring in a firkin o'whusky under your very eyes on the north road between Beauly and Inverness, some time atween 9 a.m. and 5 p.m.'

Friday duly arrived, and the excisemen had the route under close observation. Every cart carrying hay, wood or turnips was thoroughly searched, but there was never so much as a sniff of whisky. Finally a funeral cortege appeared, with a line of slow-moving carts following it. Suddenly, one of the carts filled with oats pulled out and made a dash past the cortege, only to be stopped by the gaugers, who proceeded to search it. They found nothing, and the cart was allowed to go on its way.

When 5 p.m. arrived, the excisemen gave up their vigil, since Sandy was considered a man of his word, who would play by the rules of the 'ploy'. Later in the evening, the excise officer and Sandy met, and the exciseman told Sandy that he did not mind a trick being played on him, but that Sandy had broken his word. 'Man, I trusted you,' said the gauger.

'I kept my word,' said Sandy. 'I brought the whusky alang the north road atween 9 a.m. and 5 p.m., just as arranged, and it's in Inverness noo.'

'Have ye any witnesses?' asked the gauger, suspiciously.

'Aye,' replied Sandy, 'there's yersel. Man, ye took yer hat off tae it.'

After the death of his mother, Edinburgh city official Archie Campbell took her body back to her Highland birthplace for burial. Not wanting to waste the return trip with an empty vehicle he filled it with illicit whisky. As usual, nobody searched a hearse. Campbell told his friends on his return, 'I took away the mortal remains, but brought back the spirit.'

It is claimed that a mock funeral was used by smugglers operating between Meiklour and Coupar Angus in Perthshire to avoid a waiting group of gaugers in the years just after the 1823 Excise Act. The story goes that the local undertaker was so pleased with the whisky he received for the use of his hearse that this became a regular sideline for him. One imagines, however, that at some point John Anderson, the Supervisor of Excise based in Coupar Angus, must have noticed a suspicious correlation between anticipated seizures of spirit and interments in the local community.

It is said that funeral cortèges were regularly used as cover for whisky being transported from the wild Braes of Glenlivet area into Dufftown, and that a hotel proprietor in Stirling would send a hearse into the Highlands to rendezvous with smugglers when his supply of peatreek was running low.

Staying one step ahead of the gaugers meant being wily, and on one occasion a group of smugglers was due to run a large amount of spirit into Inverness along the shore of Loch Ness when they were warned that the excise officers had got wind of the venture. They painstakingly assembled a cargo of casks filled with herrings on the west side of the loch, and rowed them to the east bank with a pretence of great secrecy. The excisemen duly pounced, and the smugglers defended their cargo with vigour. A considerable amount of blood was spilled before the smugglers were captured and taken to Inverness gaol. In the meantime, the illicit whisky was moved to Inverness by road along the west side of the loch without interruption. When the sheriff duly tried the smugglers he asked them why they had defended their legitimate cargo of herrings so vigorously. They replied that they had only been protecting their property from a vicious attack, and despite the fact that he clearly knew exactly what had happened, the sheriff was forced to acquit them.

The hazards associated with illicit distilling were various. One Cabrach distiller on Speyside hid his still on the moor in such haste as the excise officers approached that he forgot its exact location, and never did recover it. Similarly, casks of whisky must have been hidden in a hurry and lost forever, or recovered years later. Perhaps this was the way in which it was discovered that maturation in oak casks was so beneficial for whisky.

The 1934 Christmas number of the *Northern Scot* newspaper carried the following story, recounted by John E. Murray:

> A preventive man, braving the severity of a moorland snow-storm in the hope of making a capture in a north-eastern district noted for smuggling, encountered a local character whom he knew to be an inveterate smuggler.
>
> 'Weel, Geordie, where is your still?' asked the gauger.
>
> 'A dinna ken masel' this year,' replied the wit. 'There's sax fit o' moss on the tap o' her an' sax fit o' snaw on the tap o' that. Fin' her for yersel'.'

It is claimed that Robert Louis Stevenson based the pirates in his novel *Treasure Island* on illicit distillers at work around Braemar in the 1880s. The 'real' Long John Silver was a miller in the town who supplied them with barley.

For a long time, the distillation and distribution of illicit whisky has been regarded principally as a male occupation. Women, it is acknowledged, played a useful, though supportive, role. For example, they would warn of the imminent arrival of excise officers in a smuggling community by hanging out prominent items of washing. This practice would be repeated in crofts through the glen as each wife saw the previous signal. Children would then be dispatched to warn fathers who were distilling that the gaugers were on their way.

In practice, it seems that women actually played a much fuller part in Scottish whisky smuggling than has often been assumed. The first person convicted of illicit distilling – during the sixteenth century – was a woman, Bessie Campbell, and during the eighteenth century widows and other single women in Kintyre certainly made whisky in their own right.

Throughout the Highlands and Islands where farmers were illicit distillers, the actual process of whisky production was often the responsibility of maids and other female servants. Perhaps they were considered more expendable than the menfolk if they were caught in the act.

In his 1861 novel *Glencreggan*, the English rector and writer Edward Bradley stated that as much as ten shillings per week could be earned by a full-time illicit distiller – a large sum indeed. Bradley also observed that such distillers married young as a woman's role in the venture was almost essential. The basic distilling work, he wrote, was done by women 'fit for, or employed in nothing else'.

Whatever their distilling prowess, women were certainly skilled brewers of ale in Scotland. Until the eighteenth century the craft was an almost exclusively female preserve, and a record of Aberdeen brewers for 1509 lists 153 names, only one of which is male.

'Sarah of the Bog', as she was known, worked an illicit still in Knapdale, a remote area of the Western Highlands to the north of the Kintyre peninsula. She assumed the guise of a witch to prevent her neighbours from asking too many questions about her activities. They even gave her gifts of grain and peat in the hope that she would put in a good word for them with the devil, but in fact they proved very useful in her distilling activities. Sarah died one night when she drank too much of her own product and fell into her fire. She is *not* a Ralph Steadman creation!

Redoubtable women intimately involved in illicit distilling included Helen Cumming of Cardow, Janet Macpherson of Achlochrach (see 'Speyside'), and Jean Anderson of Dundee (see 'Central and Eastern Scotland'), but many others played ingenious and invaluable roles in smuggling enterprises.

In the remote and now abandoned Caithness crofting settlement of Badryrie, near Loch Stemster, an illicit still was operated by the MacGregor family during the second half of the nineteenth century. One winter night a sudden fall of snow prevented the men of the house from returning home from their distilling bothy in case the excisemen traced their footsteps. Realising what had happened, the distiller's wife proceeded to drive a herd of cattle along the route between byre and bothy in order to obliterate all footprints. The men were then able to return in safety. On another occasion, Mrs MacGregor had just fed the cattle in the byre adjoining the croft house with the draff left over from distilling when two excise officers walked in. Pretending not to notice them, she threw a bucket of ashes from the fire in their direction, and the light peat dust stopped them in their tracks long enough for the cattle to clean the evidence from their trough.

According to Ian MacDonald,

> A good story is told of an Abriachan woman who was carrying a jar of smuggled whisky into Inverness. The officer met her near the town and relieved her of her burden.
>
> 'Oh I am nearly fainting,' groaned the poor woman, 'give me just one mouthful out of the jar.'
>
> The unsuspecting officer allowed her the desired mouthful, which she cleverly squirted into his eyes, and she escaped with the jar before the officer recovered his sight and presence of mind.

At one time whisky was made on the small island of Pabbay, off Harris, and one day an excise officer arrived without warning at a particular croft where he strongly suspected illicit distilling to be taking place. The woman of the house grabbed a cradle and put a ten-gallon jar of whisky into it, wrapped in the clothes of a baby. When the gauger entered the room, the woman was crooning to the whisky and he was none the wiser.

Another Pabbay tale concerns a woman whose husband was filling bottles of illicit whisky when the excisemen approached. As they entered the house the wife leapt into bed and began moaning and crying as though in labour. The man asked the gaugers to stay with her while he went to get help, but they dashed out, saying they would rather go themselves than stay. While they were away looking for a midwife, all the whisky and bottles were hidden, so that on their return there was not a hint that anything untoward had been taking place. The 'mother-to-be' seemed much calmer, too!

The following story comes from the archives of the School of Scottish Studies in Edinburgh and is a transcription of a recording made in Gaelic in 1974 by Donald Morrison. It refers to Mull during the first few decades of the nineteenth century.

> Uisgean was a great place for that. There was a man, his name, history records it, Murdoch MacCormick, he made whisky, and he made it at the end of the house, in the barn – it was connected with the house. And some way or another he had the fire there and the smoke was coming into the chimney of the house and they were going up, you see, and they couldn't detect it. Everything was closed during the night. However one day he was thatching the house and he had two small kegs on the kitchen floor for to send away to Ireland. Well, they would

be leaving with the sailing smack about one o'clock in the morning. It was during the night, you see, that they had to sail away. But the cutter, the cutter men were after them – that was the excisemen. And he got a sign. They had a sort of sign language. If you would see the cutter men coming – they were afloat and they were ashore – I would warn you by some way. That [sign with fingers], that was one man, and if it was like that [different sign], it was a crowd.

However they came and he seen them coming and the two kegs were on the floor . . . And it was in these days the fire was in the centre of the floor and a hole at the top to let the [smoke] and a chain coming down to hold the pot. And he said to his wife, 'Take one of them kegs and jump into the bed there and throw the clothes over you, and put the keg between you and the wall, and hum away at it, croon to put it to sleep, and I will manage the other.' And he got a hold of the other and he rolled the chain round it, whatever way, and he put it up till it reached – the roof wasn't very high – and he choked the hole and then the house was all smoke. And the men came in and she was lying in the bed and she was humming . . . a crooning song to the keg . . . And the woman faced the wall and she turned to her man, and the exciseman was sitting and talking, and she asked him, 'What man have ye got in there?'

He said, 'The king's men.'

She said, 'It doesn't matter whether you are the king's men or the duke's men. If you don't shut up, if you waken on me the child, that's bad with teething fever, I'll take the tongs to you.' And then the gaugers, they walked out, and they got free, they didn't ask. And they took the black pot with them to Canada, according to history, if it's true, and he was making whisky in the woods in Canada.

The island of Eigg is the setting for an anecdote concerning a distilling operation that was situated in a cave at the foot of the cliffs by the shore. Today the place remains known as Uamh a' Bhriuthais – the Cave of the Still. One day, Neil MacQuarrie, the distiller, got word that the excise officers had landed on the island and were making for his house, where he was likely to be caught red-handed with a cask full of whisky. He hid the cask under the bed and asked his wife to get into the bed. When the gauger came into the room Neil told him that his wife had just given birth to a child two days previously, and the gauger duly apologised for bothering her and left the house, unaware just how close he had been to the illicit spirit.

There are Gaelic and English versions of the song 'Yowie Wi' The Crooked Horn' ('The Ewe With the Crooked Horn'), dating back at least to the eighteenth century. The yowie, or ewe, is not, of course, an actual sheep but an illicit still, with the 'crooked horn' being the

worm. It is claimed that the wives of illicit distillers would sing the
song to warn their husbands of the approach of excisemen. We can
only speculate on whether the 'ewie' of the song was captured by excise
officers or stolen by a neighbour or passer-by who chanced upon it.

Were I but able to rehearse
My ewie's praise in proper verse,
I'd sound it out as loud and fierce
As ever piper's drone could blaw.

The ewie wi' the crookit horn,
A' that kent her micht hae sworn
Ne'er was sic a ewie born,
Here aboots or far aw'.

I neither needed tar nor keel
To mark her upon hip or heel;
Her crookit horn it did as weel
Tae ken her by amang them a'.

Chorus

She never threatened scab nor rot,
But keepit aye her ain jog trot,
Baith to the fauld and to the cot,
Was ne'er sweir to lead nor ca'.

Chorus

When ither ewies lap the dyke
And ate the kail for a' the tyke,
My ewie never played the like
But stayed ahint the barn wa'.

Chorus

I lookit aye at even for her,
Lest mishanter should come owre her [mishanter = misfortune]
Or the fumart should devour her [fumart = polecat]
Gin the beastie bade awa'.

Chorus

Yet Monday last for a' my keeping
I canna speak it withoot greetin' – [greetin' = crying]
A villain cam when I was sleepin'
And stole my ewie, horn an a'.

Chorus

I socht her sair upon the morn, [socht = sought, sair = sorrowfully]
And doun beneath a buss o' thorn [buss = bush]

I got my ewie's crookit horn,
But my ewie was awa'!

Chorus

But when I had the loon that did it, [loon = rascal]
I hae sworn as weel as said it,
Though a' the world should forbid it,
I wad gie his neck a thraw. [thraw = twist]

Chorus

For a' the claith that we had worn [claith = clothes]
Frae her and hers sae aften shorn,
The loss o' her we could ha'e borne,
Had fair strae-death ta'en her awa'. [strae = natural]

Chorus

But silly thing tae lose her life
Aneath a greedy villain's knife;
I'm really feart that oor guidwife
Sall never win aboon't ava'. [win aboon't ava' = get over it at all]

Chorus

Oh all ye bards benorth Kinghorn, [benorth = to the north of]
Call up your muses, let them mourn;
Our ewie wi' the crookit horn,
Is frae us stown and felled an' a'.

As Derek Cooper noted in *The Whisky Roads of Scotland*, 'As illicit distilling increased, whisky became the currency of the country.' Many rents were paid in whisky, and it was not uncommon for landowners to supply barley to tenants whose land would not sustain its cultivation. Once converted into spirit it was given back in lieu of monetary rent, or sold to smugglers who took it into towns to sell on. The leftovers from the mashing process – known as draff – were invaluable to crofters as a high-protein feed to sustain their cattle through the winter months.

There was, then, for many Scottish landowners something of a dichotomy between their moral and legal duty as establishment representatives to suppress illicit distilling and their commercial desire to obtain rent from their tenants, rent which could often only be paid on the proceeds of whisky-making. The fact that smuggling flourished to such a great extent in the decades before the 1823 Excise Act had much to do with the fact that many landowners and other authority figures either turned a blind eye to illicit distilling or actively encouraged it.

Very frequently smugglers raised the wind to pay their fines, and began work at once to refund the money. Some of the old lairds not only winked at the practice, but actually encouraged it. Within the last thirty years, if not twenty years, a tenant on the Brahan estate had his rent amount credited with the price of an anchor of smuggled whisky, and there can be no doubt that rents were frequently paid directly and indirectly by the produce of smuggling.

– Ian MacDonald

It is also important to bear in mind that to be convicted and even imprisoned for smuggling had no real social stigma in the early nineteenth century. The distillers were not criminals as such, but debtors, and their time in jail was not usually too arduous. Indeed, they were given 6d per day as a maintenance payment.

As Ian MacDonald observed,

As a rule, spirits were distilled from the produce of their own lands, and the people being simple and illiterate, ignorant alike of the necessity for a national Exchequer, and of the ways and means taken by Parliament to raise revenue, they could not readily and clearly see the justice of levying a tax upon their whisky. They drew a sharp distinction between offences created by English statute and violations of the laws of God. The law which made distillation illegal came to them in a foreign garb. Highlanders had no great love or respect for the English Government.

MacDonald also noted that the Highlanders' old habit of legally distilling for domestic use at one time must have influenced their attitudes towards illicit distilling.

Taking a pragmatic approach to the problem, Rev. David Dunoon of Killearnan in the county of Ross-shire wrote in his 1796 contribution to *The Statistical Account*, 'Distilling is almost the only method of converting our victual into cash for the payment of rent and servants; and what may in fact be called our staple commodity. The distillers do not lay the proper value on their time and trouble, and of course look on all, but the price of barley and the fire added to the tax, as clear profit, add to these the luxury of tasting the quality of manufacture during the process.'

Inevitably, many justices of the peace were landowners with at least a tacit sympathy with illicit distillers. In 1819 more than one-quarter of the 4,201 cases heard in justice of the peace courts were dismissed. Sometimes the magistrates' sympathy was quite blatant, as in a court case heard at Poolewe in the Western Highlands. Three McLeods were charged with assaulting a party of gaugers during a raid on their still, and when found guilty they asked for time to pay the fine. A week later it was duly paid, by cheque, which was a rare enough occurrence, but in this instance the cheque was drawn on the bank account of the local JP!

In similar vein, Alfred Barnard offers a rare example of humour in his otherwise rather earnest *Whisky Distilleries of the United Kingdom* when chronicling the distilleries of Campbeltown.

> A capital story is told of an aged woman who resided near Hazelburn. She was of a rather doubtful character and was charged before the Sheriff with smuggling. The charge being held proven, it fell to his lordship to pronounce sentence. When about to do so he thus addressed the culprit, 'I daresay my poor woman it is not often you have been guilty of this fault.'
>
> 'Deed no Sheriff,' she readily replied, 'I haena made a drap since youn wee keg I sent to yersel.'

An article in volume XXXII of the *Transactions of the Gaelic Society of Inverness* concerns the chief of the Clan MacNab, Fransai Mor Mac an Aba. MacNab was a justice of the peace, but tended to have a liberal view of illicit distillation as practised in the Callander area of Perthshire. On one occasion he even went so far as to obtain a key so that a smuggler could swap a cask of whisky 'evidence' seized in a raid for one of water. When the case came to court the contents of the cask were tested, and MacNab, feigning righteous indignation, dismissed the case and had the excise officer involved charged with contempt of court.

Another example of smugglers colluding with authority figures is recounted by the excise officer Malcolm Gillespie (see 'The Gaugers' Story'). Gillespie recalled an occasion when he apprehended a notorious smuggler called Grant and his two sons with a cart-load of illicit whisky en route to Stonehaven one night. Grant warned Gillespie that the whisky was destined for a Stonehaven JP, and that he would surely lose his job with the excise service if the spirit was seized. The said JP duly tried the case two days later, and while the whisky was confiscated, the official took the unusual step of returning the seized horse and cart to the Grants, and the even more unusual one of finding the excise service liable to pay the costs of the case.

Justices of the peace were not always so obliging, however. An old man in the Highlands appeared before the local magistrate charged with illicit distilling. He had been apprehended with a still in his possession, though he was adamant that he never used it. Nonetheless, the magistrate insisted that so far as the law was concerned, possession of the equipment necessary to distil was enough to secure a conviction.

'If that's the way of it, I'd like you to take several cases of rape into account when you pass sentence,' said the Highlander.

'Are you telling me you are guilty of rape, then?' asked a somewhat bemused magistrate.

'Not at all,' replied the defendant, 'but I have the necessary equipment.'

Quoting from his uncle Dr John Mackenzie's manuscript *Highland Memories* in *A Hundred Years in the Highlands*, Osgood Mackenzie wrote:

> Even so late as then, say 1820, one would go a long way before one met a person who shrank from smuggling. My father never tasted any but smuggled whisky, and when every mortal that called for him – they were legion daily – had a dram instantly poured into him, the ankers of whisky emptied yearly must have been numerous indeed. I don't believe my mother or he ever dreamed that smuggling was a crime. Ere I was twenty I had paid £1,000 for the 'superiority' of Platlock, at Fortrose, to make me a commissioner of supply and consequently a Justice of the Peace, and one of the about thirty or forty electors of the county of Ross; and before it had occurred to me that smuggling was really a serious breach of the law, I had from the bench fined many a poor smuggler as the law directs. I then began to see that the 'receiver' – myself, for instance, as I drank only 'mountain dew' then – was worse than the smugglers. So ended all my connection with smuggling except in my capacity as magistrate, to the grief of at least one of my old friends and visitors, the Dean of Ross and Argyle, who scoffed at my resolution and looked sorrowfully back on the happy times when he was young and his father distilled every Saturday what was needed for the following week. He was of the same mind as a grocer in Church Street, Inverness, who though licensed to sell only what was drunk off the premises, notoriously supplied his customers in the back shop. Our pastor, Donald Fraser, censuring this breach of law, was told, 'But I never approved of that law!' which was an end to the argument. He and the Dean entirely agreed that the law was iniquitous and should be broken.
>
> Laws against smuggling are generally disliked. People who if you drop a shilling would run a mile after you with it, not even expecting thanks, will cheerfully break the law against smuggling. When I was young everyone I met from my father downwards, even our clergy, either made, bought, sold or drank cheerfully, smuggled liquor. Excisemen were planted in central stations as terrors to evildoers, but they seemed to stay for life in the same localities, and report said that

they and the smugglers were bosom friends, and that they even had their ears and eyes shut by blackmail pensions from the smugglers. Now and again they paraded in the newspapers a 'seizure of whisky', to look as if they were wide awake; wicked folks hinted that the anker of whisky was discovered and seized when it was hidden in the gaugers' peat stack! This saved the gauger much trouble searching moors and woods for bothies and liquor. I was assured that one of our old gaugers, when pensioned off, retired rich enough to buy a street in a southern town, and I believe the story was quite true. Indeed, in my young days few in the parish were more popular than the resident gauger. Alas! When the wicked Commissioners of Excise went in for 'riding officers' and a squad of horrid coastguard sailors with long, iron-pointed walking-sticks for poking about wherever earth seemed to have been lately disturbed, it ended all peace and comfort in smuggling, for these rascals ransacked every unenclosed bit of country within their limits each month; accordingly, the gauger soon began to be the most detested of men.

On the watershed between Strath Bran and Fannich, I have been in a bothy with regularly built, low stone walls, watertight heather thatch, iron pipes leading cold spring water to the still-rooms and such an array of casks, tubs, etc., was told that gaugers never troubled their owners.

***

Many smugglers constituted a sort of recognized corporation, claiming a rank second to that of the landowners, and bearing themselves as the *petite noblesse* of the community. In church they occupied as a body the front pew of the gallery which was spoken of as the 'smugglers loft' and this not sneeringly but with a feeling of respect. The illegality of their employment was forgotten or disregarded in a neighbourhood where persons of all ranks were openly and unscrupulously their customers.

– Prof. J Walker

***

Writing of excise officers' attempts to make seizures, Ian MacDonald observed that,

It has been stated how frequently the officers failed to find the stills. This is explained by the importance and value of that utensil, especially when made of copper, and the great care taken to remove and conceal it when not in active use. It is the invariable practice of smugglers who distil at night to remove the still from the bothy to some secure place in the morning. The following story, told to me by the Rev. Dr Aird of Creich, is a good illustration of the ingenuity exercised to secure the still from seizure. The Nigg smugglers were frequently at work in the caves of the North Cromarty Sutor, which are difficult of access, and the officers could never succeed in finding the still. 'Where think you,' asked the Doctor, 'did the rascals hide the still?' I replied I could not guess, knowing how cunning and resourceful smugglers were as a rule. 'Under the pu'pit!' chuckled the doctor. But, I asked, how did they obtain entrance to the Church? The beadle must have been in collusion with them. 'Of course he was, the drucken body!' answered the doctor.

There can be no doubt that 'good, pious' men engaged in smuggling, and there is less doubt that equally good, pious men – ministers and priests – were grateful recipients of a large share of the smuggler's produce. I have heard that the Sabbath work in connection with malting and fermenting weighed heavily upon the consciences of these men – a remarkable instance of straining at the gnat and swallowing the camel.

– Ian MacDonald

Irish landowners tended to tolerate illicit distilling, just like their Scottish counterparts, and the Irish Church also had an ambivalent attitude towards the trade in poitin. Some priests during the first half of the nineteenth century made most of their income from blessing illicit stills.

In many instances, of course, the clergy did oppose the illicit trade. A popular story concerns a Highland minister's meeting with a parishioner who was a noted illicit distiller. The churchman told the smuggler that what he was doing was wicked, but the distiller replied indignantly, 'I alloo nae swearin' at the still and everything's dune decently and in order; I canna see ony harm in't.'

Joseph Mitchell was employed as Chief Inspector and Superintendent of Highland Roads and Bridges, and in his *Reminiscences of My Life in the Highlands* (1883–84) made reference to illicit distilling:

> There was a romance about it. The still was generally placed in some secluded spot, in the ravine of a Highland burn, or screened by waving birch and natural wood, so that the smoke of the fire could scarcely be observed. There were scouts placed around, often three or four savage-looking men, sometimes women and boys.

Mitchell also recalled meeting up with a smuggling convoy in Glenmoriston when he was a young man, noting some twenty-five ponies tied head to tail, and each with a pair of whisky-kegs on its back. When his identity as *'e mac Mitchell, fear a' rthaid mhoir'* (the son of Mitchell, man of the high roads) was established by the dozen smugglers, he was offered a dram from a snuff box with no lid and allowed to pass on his way. The smugglers knew his discretion could be assured, even though he was from a family of some social standing.

Thomas Guthrie (1803–1873) wrote in his autobiography about his boyhood in Brechin, and the following refers to a time a decade before the 1823 Act.

> They [smugglers] rode on Highland ponies, carrying on each side of their small, shaggy but brave and hardy steeds, a small cask or 'keg' as it was called, of illicit whisky, manufactured amid the wilds of Aberdeenshire or the glens of the Grampians. They took up a position on some commanding eminence during the day, where they could, as from a watch-tower, descry the distant approach of the enemy, the exciseman or gauger: then, when night fell, every man to horse, descending the mountains only six miles from Brechin, they scoured the plains, rattled into villages and towns, disposing of their whisky, and as they rode leisurely along, beating time with their formidable cudgels on the empty barrels to the great amusement of the public and the mortification of the excisemen, who had nothing for it but to bite their nails and stand, as best they could, the raillery of the smugglers and the laughter of the people . . . Everybody, with few exceptions drank what was in reality illicit whisky – far superior to that made under the eye of the Excise – lords and lairds, members of Parliament and ministers of the gospel.

Even more exalted personages drank it, as revealed by Elizabeth Grant of Rothiemurchus in her *Memoirs of a Highland Lady* (1898). Referring to King George IV's visit to Edinburgh in 1822, she recalled:

> One incident connected with this time made me very cross. Lord Conyngham, the Chamberlain, was looking everywhere for pure Glenlivet whisky; the king drank nothing else. It was not to be had out of the Highlands. My father sent word to me – I was the cellarer – to empty my pet bin, where was whisky long in wood, long in uncorked bottles, mild as milk, and the true contraband gout in it. Much as I grudged this treasure it made our fortunes afterwards, showing on what trifles great events depend. The whisky, and fifty brace of ptarmigan all shot by one man, went up to Holyrood House, and were graciously received and made much of, and a reminder of this attention at a proper moment by the gentlemanly Chamberlain ensured to my father the Indian judgeship.

In reality, it seems unlikely that the king had ever even heard of Glenlivet, let alone insisted on drinking it. More plausible is the theory that Sir Walter Scott, enthusiastic choreographer of the whole slightly ridiculous event, had suggested to his monarch that Glenlivet was *the* stuff, and that it would impress his Scottish subjects if he asked for it by name.

The following story, told me by the late Rev. John Fraser, Kiltarlity, shows the persistence which characterised the smugglers and the leniency with which illicit distillation was regarded by the better classes. While the Rev. Mr. Fraser was stationed at Erchless, shortly before the Disruption [the formation of the Free Church of Scotland, in 1843], a London artist, named MacIan came north to take sketches for illustrating a history of the Highlands, then in preparation. He was very anxious to see a smuggling bothy at work, and applied to Mr. Robertson, factor for The Chisholm. 'If Sandy MacGruar is out of jail,' said the factor, 'we shall have no difficulty in seeing a bothy.' Enquiries were made, Sandy was at large, and, as usual, busy smuggling. A day was fixed for visiting the bothy, and MacIan, accompanied by Mr. Robertson, the factor, and Dr Fraser of Kerrow, both Justices of the Peace, and by the Rev. John Fraser, was admitted into Sandy's sanctuary. The sketch having been finished, the factor said, '*Nach eil dad agad Alasdair?* ' ('Haven't you got something, Sandy?') Sandy having removed some heather, produced a small keg. As the four worthies were quaffing the real mountain dew, the Rev. Mr Fraser remarked, 'This would be a fine haul for the gaugers – the sooner we go the better.'

– *Ian MacDonald*

As well as the practical consequences of illicit distilling, there were also moral implications to consider, and during the nineteenth century in particular there was no shortage of commentators to lament the harm being done by smuggling.

I must now advert to a cause which contributes to demoralise the Highlanders in a manner equally rapid and lamentable. Smuggling has grown to an alarming extent, and if not checked will undermine the best principles of the people. Let a man be habituated to falsehood and fraud in one line of life, and he will soon learn to extend it to all his actions. This traffic operates like a secret poison on all their moral feelings. They are the more rapidly betrayed into it, as, though acute and ingenious in regard to all that comes within the scope of their observation, they do not comprehend the nature or purpose of imports levied on the produce of the soil, nor have they any distinct idea of the practice of smuggling being attended with disgrace or turpitude. The open defiance of the laws, the progress of chicanery, perjury, hatred, and mutual recrimination, with a constant dread and suspicion of informers – men not being sure of or confident in their next neighbours – which result from smuggling, and the habit which it engenders, are subjects highly important, and regarded with the most serious consideration and the deepest regret by all who value the permanent welfare of their country, which depends so materially upon the preservation of the morals of the people.

– *Col David Stewart of Garth,* Sketches of the Character, Manners and Present State of the Highlanders of Scotland *(1825)*

Ian MacDonald was in no doubt as to the pernicious effects of illicit distilling on the morals of the people involved, and he gave us an example in *Smuggling in the Highlands.*

I know of three brothers on the West Coast. Two of them settled down on crofts, became respectable members of the community, and with care and thrift and hard work even acquired some little means. The third took to smuggling, and has never done anything else; has been several times in prison, has latterly lost all his smuggling utensils, and is now an old broken-down man, without a farthing, without sympathy, without friends, one of the most wretched objects in the whole parish. Not one in a hundred has gained anything by smuggling in the end. I know most of the smugglers in my own district personally. With a few exceptions they are the poorest among the people. How can they be otherwise? Their's is the work of darkness, and they must sleep through the day. Their crofts are not half tilled or manured; their houses are never repaired; their very children are neglected, dirty, and ragged. They cannot bear the strain of regular steady work even if they feel disposed. Their moral and physical stamina have become impaired, and they can do nothing except under the unhealthy influence of excitement and stimulants. Gradually their manhood becomes undermined, their sense of honour becomes deadened, and they become violent law-breakers and shameless cheats. This is invariably the latter end of the smuggler, and generally his sons follow his footsteps in the downward path, or he finds disciples among his neighbour's lads, so that the evil is spread and perpetuated. Smuggling is, in short, a curse to the individual and to the community.

3

PEATREEK PRODUCTION

The romantic notion persists that illicit whisky, distilled in the Highlands, was far superior in character to the products of many legal stills. Certainly, some excellent illicit spirit was distilled, and at times some very poor spirit poured out of the shallow, overworked stills of the Lowlands, but by and large the popular view is surely a myth.

Equipment was primitive, hygiene was not a primary consideration, and all the processes of production were necessarily carried out in as much of a hurry as possible. Every minute spent making whisky increased the chances of detection. Similarly, maturing the spirit once produced in order to render it more palatable was a luxury the smuggler could rarely afford. Colonel Alexander Campbell noted in a report about illicit distilling in Argyllshire written in January 1814 that within six weeks of harvesting barley in parts of the Highlands' 'public houses were selling whisky distilled from it'.

As the Irish writer, passionate republican and Olympian drinker Brendan Behan put it, 'No matter what anyone tells you about the fine old drop of the mountain dew, it stands to sense that a few old men sitting up in the back of a haggard with milk churns and all sorts of improvised apparatus cannot hope to make good spirit.'

Regarding the relative merits of legal and illegally distilled whisky, Ian MacDonald noted that while in the past it may have been the case that illicit spirit was sometimes superior to the legal drink,

> this holds true no longer; indeed, the circumstances are actually reversed. The Highland distiller has now the best appliances, uses the best materials, employs skill and experience, exercises the greatest possible care, and further, matures his spirit in bond – whisky being highly deleterious unless it is matured by age. On the other hand, the smuggler uses rude, imperfect utensils, very often inferior materials, works by rule of thumb, under every disadvantage and inconvenience, and is always in a state of terror and hurry, which is incompatible with good work and the best results. He begins by purchasing inferior barley, which, as a rule, is imperfectly malted. He brews without more idea of proper heats than dipping his finger or seeing his face in the water, and the quantity of water used is regulated by the size and number of his

vessels. His setting heat is decided by another dip of the finger, and supposing he has yeast of good quality, and may by accident add the proper quantity, the fermentation of his worts depends on the weather, as he cannot regulate the temperature in his temporary bothy, although he often uses sacks and blankets, and may during the night kindle a fire. But the most fatal defect in the smuggler's appliances is the construction of his still. Ordinary stills have head elevations from 12 to 18 feet, which serves for purposes of rectification, as the fusel oils and other essential oils and acids fall back into the still, while the alcoholic vapour, which is more volatile, passes over to the worm, where it becomes condensed. The smuggler's still has no head elevation, the still-head being as flat as an old blue bonnet, and consequently the essential oils and acids pass over with the alcohol into the worm, however carefully distillation may be carried on. These essential oils and acids can only be eliminated, neutralised, or destroyed by storing the spirits some time in wood, but the smuggler, as a rule, sends his spirits out new in jars and bottles, so that the smuggled whisky, if taken in considerable quantities, is actually poisonous. Ask anyone who has had a good spree on new smuggled whisky, how he felt next morning. Again, ordinary stills have rousers to prevent the wash sticking to the bottom of the pot and burning. The smuggler has no such appliance in connection with his still, the consequence being that his spirits frequently have a singed, smoky flavour. The evils of a defective construction are increased a hundred-fold, when, as is frequently the case, the still is made of tin, and the worm of tin or lead. When spirits and acids come in contact with such surfaces, a portion of the metal is dissolved, and poisonous metallic salts are produced, which must be injurious to the drinker. Paraffin casks are frequently used in brewing, and it will be readily understood that however carefully cleaned, their use cannot improve the quality of our much-praised smuggled whisky. Again, the rule of thumb is applied to the purity and strength of smuggled spirits. At ordinary distilleries there are scientific appliances for testing these, but the smuggler must guess the former, and must rely for the latter on the blebs or bubbles caused by shaking the whisky. On this unsatisfactory test, plus the honesty of the smuggler, which is generally an unknown quantity, the purchaser must also rely. This is certainly a happy-go-lucky state of matters which it would be a pity to disturb by proclaiming the truth. Very recently an order came from the South to Inverness for two gallons of smuggled whisky. The order being urgent, and no immediate prospect of securing the genuine article, a dozen bottles of new raw grain spirit were sent to a well-known smuggling locality, and were then dispatched south as real mountain dew. No better proof could be given of the coarseness and absolute inferiority of smuggled whisky.

Much of it, on the contrary, was better than the products of the licensed distilleries, for it was made in parts of the country where the science of distilling, like the art of playing on the bag-pipes, was an immemorial tradition, and where the qualities of water and soil favoured it.

– *Aeneas Macdonald*

The fact remains, however, that the spirit was often rendered more palatable by various additives. Osgood Mackenzie (*A Hundred Years in the Highlands*) quotes his uncle reminiscing about *his* father and whisky-drinking in the early nineteenth century.

On the sideboard there always stood before breakfast a bottle of whisky, smuggled, of course, with plenty of camomile flowers, bitter orange-peel, and juniper berries in it – 'bitters' we called it – and of this he had a wee glass always before we sat down to breakfast, as a fine stomachie.

After supper:

a rummer tumbler, hot-water jug, milk-jug, sugar-bowl, and whisky-bottle, with sufficient wine-glasses, were placed on the table. My father put just one glass of 'mountain dew' into the rummer, then sugar, then one toddy ladleful of milk. Though the 'dew' would be coarse and fiery, its toddy was made essentially mild as cream; only nowadays I would advise drinking the milk without the 'dew'.

Bere – a four-rowed barley – was favoured for distilling purposes in much of the Highlands. In 1811 it was said to take up half the crop acreage of the Hebrides. It was also popular in the far north mainland counties of Sutherland and Caithness, and on Orkney, where it was used for many years at the legal Highland Park distillery. In Campbeltown, bere was utilised on a regular basis well into the second half of the nineteenth century.

The grain was popular because it would grow and ripen successfully on comparatively poor soil and in a damp climate, and required only seaweed as manure. It also ripened up to three weeks earlier than other cereal crops, an important factor in locations without an abundance of dry, sunny weather. The disadvantage of bere was that it yielded less fermentable sugar than barley, and therefore ultimately produced less alcohol.

Apparently, considerable amounts of the precious bere were lost during 'home' malting, due to the necessarily crude methods employed by illicit distillers. They steeped it in ponds and burns before spreading it to dry in haphazard fashion on any suitable surface considered unlikely to be detected. Careful temperature control and meticulous attention to turning 'the piece', as the malting barley is called, were luxuries unknown outside legal distilleries.

When handling bere, professional maltsters often insisted that they could not tell the difference between it and barley. This was very convenient, as bere was taxed at only 9d per bushel, whereas barley was taxed at 2s per bushel, due to its superior efficiency for distilling purposes.

According to a recipe for corn whiskey in Leon W. Kania's *Alaskan Bootlegger's Bible*, 'The corn [10lb] is placed in a feed sack and buried in the warm moist center of a manure or compost pile for about ten days. When the sprouts are about a quarter inch long, the corn is fully "modified" or malted.' Thankfully, Kania's recipe continues with the instruction to 'wash the corn in a tub'.

As Macdonald observed, accurate fermentation control was always a problem, whether making whisk(e)y illegally in Scotland, Ireland or the USA, and inefficient fermentation would certainly affect the final flavour of the spirit. A handy fermentation hint came from an old-time moonshiner in deepest Alaska, where the cold of winter made it difficult to keep fermentation going. The yeast simply stopped working if the temperature dropped too low. The Alaskan distiller reckoned that if you mixed a quarter stick of dynamite into the mash it would 'kick start' the fermentation process. The only problem was that nitroglycerin gives severe headaches to anyone inhaling its fumes, and so the hangovers from 'dynamite whiskey' were even more severe than usual.

In the County Mayo town of Crossmolina, in the west of Ireland, a police raid on a house during the 1970s led to the discovery of a barrel of wash being heated by an electric blanket!

Former Inspector-General of Excise in Ireland Aeneas Coffey noted that illicit distillers in the north-west of Ireland, whose methods would be very similar to those in Scotland, 'generally fermented not more than one sack of grain at a time; they made weak wash of it, fermenting in a short time and distilling it off rapidly, making about ten or twelve gallons of illicit spirit with it and before the individual made any more he generally brought it to market.'

It is interesting to look at the manner in which legal distillation was carried out in the early eighteenth century, as this reflects the methods used by illicit distillers up to a century later. In his book *The Compleat*

Distiller (1705), W.Y. Worth writes:

> Put your . . . pump into the Back in which it [the wash] is, directing
> your Spout to that Still which you design to charge; . . . and then filled
> so high as the upper nails, let down your Head on the Still; but put
> not the Beck or Nose as yet into the Worm; . . . the Still being charged,
> proceed to the making of your Fire, . . . until it begin to boyl, as a Pot
> going over; then you must set the Pipe of the Head into the Worm,
> and as it begins to drop and run a small stream into the Can, then
> immediately must you throw damping under the Still, which is, the
> Ashes that fall under your Grate and kept wet for that end, for if you
> should not do so, it would boyl over into the Worm, and so stop and
> foul the same . . . your Still being in a good Temper, you must begin
> to lute all fast with a paste made of Whiting and Rie-flower: you must
> exactly lute round the Neck of your Still, . . . so must you also paste the
> Pipe and Worm, wherein it goes; that is to say, exactly to close the Joint:
> you must also observe so to govern your Fire, that you bring your Still
> to work so, as that the Stream may run the bigness of a large Goose or
> Turkey Quill; . . . it must be continued till all the strength is off . . . thus
> are you to proceed in your first Extraction.

According to Worth, the 'low wines' from the first distillation would
be re-distilled after being left 'to lie for ten to fourteen days to enrich
themselves'. The distiller would add water to samples taken from the
early run, 'cutting' to allow the spirit to flow into a clean receiver
when it ceased to become clouded by the water. Once the spirit began
to turn cloudy again the receiver would be removed and replaced by
another vessel.

George Smith in his *A Compleat Body of Distilling* (1738) wrote:

> You must carefully observe . . . that the faints, or after-runnings, come
> not off and run into your Cann along with your other goods. To avoid
> this inconvenience, you must often be viewing them in a glass or vial,
> especially towards the latter end of your distillation, for then your
> goods, which before looked clear and limpid as rock-water, will now
> put on, or turn to an azure or bluish colour . . . whenever you perceive
> the colour to alter, shift your Cann, and place another under the end
> of your worm for the reception of the said faints; which must be kept
> separate from your proof goods.

An old moonshiner from Blairsville, Georgia, told *Mountain Spirits*
(1974) author Joseph Earl Dabney, 'You run them singlin's 'til as long
as they got any strength in 'em, then you put your hands under the
worm, rub 'em and inhale. When they smell right sour, the alkihol's
out. It's ready to change boils, and you refill the pot with those
singlin's for a doublin' run.'

Another method of telling which was the 'good stuff' is described in
Malachy Postlethwayt's 1751 *Universal Dictionary of Commerce.*

> Take a long phial, half-filled with the common proof spirit of the malt-
> distillers, and give it a smart stroke with its bottom against the palm of
> the hand, and there will appear, on the surface of the liquor, a chaplet
> or crown of bubbles, which will disappear in a clear strong manner;
> that is, it will first remain awhile, and then go off by degrees, without
> breaking the bubbles or rising into larger; and when the bubbles go off
> in this manner, the spirit is vulgarly said to be proof.

An old southern moonshiner who worked without the benefit of a
hydrometer, like most Scottish illicit distillers, told Joseph Earl Dabney,
'If it's high proof – say 115 to 120 – a big bead will jump up there on top
[of the whiskey] when you shake it. If the proof is lower, the bead goes
away faster and is smaller. Hand a mountain man a pint of whiskey and
the first thing he'll do is shake it. The longer those beads stay on there
the higher the proof.'

The chemist Professor M. Donovan visited an illicit distilling bothy
in Ireland and described it in his 1830 book *Domestic Economy.* His
description is one of the most detailed that we have, particularly
regarding the actual mechanics of how illicit distilling was carried out.
Although his example is Irish, Donovan could just as easily have been
describing distilling in a bothy in the Scottish Highlands.

> The distillery was a small thatched cabin. At one end was a large turf
> fire kindled on the ground and confined by a semi-circle of stones.
> Resting on these stones, and over the fire, was a forty gallon tin vessel,
> which answered both for heating the water and the body of the still.
> The mash tun was a cask hooped with wood, at the bottom of which,
> next the chimb, was a hole plugged with tow. This vessel had no false
> bottom: in place of it the bottom was strewed with young heath; and
> over this a stratum of oat husks. Here the mash of hot water and ground
> malt was occasionally mixed for two hours; after which time the vent
> at the bottom was opened and the worts were allowed to filter through
> the stratum of oat husks and heath. The mashing with hot water on
> the grains was then repeated and the worts were again withdrawn. The
> two worts being mixed in another cask, some yeast added and the
> fermentation allowed to proceed until it fell spontaneously, which
> happened in about three days.
>   It was now ready for distillation and was transferred into the body,
> which was capable of distilling a charge of forty gallons. A piece of soap
> weighing about two ounces was then thrown in to prevent it running

foul: and the head, apparently a large tin pot with a tube at its side, was inserted into the rim of the body and luted with paste made with oatmeal and flour. A lateral tube was then luted into the worm, which was a copper tube of an inch and a half bore, coiled in a barrel for a flakestand. The tail of the worm where it emerged from the barrel was caulked with tow. The wash speedily came to the boil and water was thrown on the fire: for at this period is the chief danger of boiling over. The spirit almost immediately came over: it was perfectly clear; and by its bead, this first running inferred to be proof.'

According to Donovan, the still was deliberately constructed from inexpensive materials:

The body of this still cost one pound; its head about four shillings; the worm cost twenty-five shillings; the mash-tun and flake-stand [to hold the worm] might both be worth twelve shillings. The whole Distillery was, therefore, worth about three pounds; and it is purposely constructed on this cheap plan, as it holds out no inducement to informers or Excisemen.

Donovan proceeded to explain how pailfuls of cold water were thrown into the worm tub with great force, so that the cold water penetrated to the depths of the tub, and kept the worm working efficiently. The 'singlings' were collected in a period of some two hours, and four batches of singlings were assembled and re-distilled. Although Donovan describes the spirit as having an excellent flavour, and claims that it could have passed for legal whiskey that was three months old, he described the flavour as obviously influenced by the fusel oils which were carried over from the still due to rapid distillation.

The distiller used a mixture of three-quarters malt and one-quarter raw corn, and Donovan gave an intriguing insight into the way in which he would make his malt. Having steeped a sack of barley and then spread it on a floor until germination began, the smuggler would take the bag of malt along with a bag of untreated corn to a kiln:

The raw corn was spread out on the kiln; but during the night when the kiln owner had retired to rest, the raw corn was removed, and malt spread on, dried, and replaced by the raw grain before day. The owner of corn drying on a kiln sits up all night to watch it. In this way, the discovery was eluded, and the malting completed.

Having made his whisky, it was important for the illicit distiller to dispose of his waste with due caution. If the draff was simply poured into the nearest burn then bits of barley husk could stick to rocks, and might act as an obvious pointer for sharp-eyed excise officers trying to trace stills. Sometimes, the draff was carried uphill from the still, and poured onto the ground. A farmer's herd of cattle would be rounded up and driven to the spot, where they eagerly ate up all the draff. Once every trace had gone, the cattle were returned to their fields, the farmer none the wiser.

> There was a bothy above Gartalie [in Glen Urquhart], where cattle used to be treated to draff and burnt ale. The bull happened to visit the bothy in the absence of the smuggler, shortly after a brewing had been completed, and drank copiously of the fermenting worts. The poor brute could never be induced to go near the bothy again.
>
> – *Ian MacDonald*

Traditionally, barley was the principal ingredient in poitin, as it was in Scottish 'peatreek', but gradually cheaper ingredients such as molasses, treacle, beet, potatoes and sugar have taken over, though barley and malt are still used by some distillers. One of the last illicit Speyside distillers, active until very recently, insisted on using barley, claiming he was buying it to perk up his hens. (See 'Speyside'.) Not only is barley more expensive, but less suspicion tends to be aroused if someone buys a couple of sacks of potatoes than if he tries to buy a trailer-load of barley.

According to one Belfast-based former illicit distiller, interviewed by John McGuffin during his research for *In Praise of Poteen* (1978), 'you could use potatoes or any kind of fruit but if you wanted to make it taste like really good whiskey, malt was best'.

In terms of the practicalities of distilling, gas burners came to replace the 'live' flame, which meant that distilling could take place indoors, and worms were replaced by condensers, just as in most legal distilleries.

In 1994, to celebrate the 500th anniversary of the first written record of Scotch whisky distilling, the Whyte & Mackay company set out to produce spirit as similar as possible to that made half a millennium earlier. This whisky must have been very close in character to that made by the best of the later illicit distillers.

A small, portable, rudimentary copper still was constructed, and basic malting and fermentation processes were carried out, along with the sort of simple mashing process that would probably have been employed 500 years previously. The grain used was a mixture of modern barley varieties and some bere.

Whyte & Mackay master blender Richard Paterson described the spirit produced as 'not as sophisticated or smooth as we produce today – a bit cloudy, for example – but it has an aroma that is very definitely typical of new spirit off a modern still. It has a rich, complex, peppery aroma with a hint of cereal, which is reflected on the taste. However, the spirit needs time to reveal its true character which would come through after a period of maturation in wood as we do today.'

4

THE GAUGERS' STORY

If the bold, Highland smuggler is popularly the hero of the illicit distilling fable, then the dastardly figure of the 'gauger' is surely its villain.

An unbending upholder of unjust excise legislation, and worse still, often a Lowlander or even an Englishman, the gauger was never going to get a good press in Highland folk history. As Philip Morrice put it in his *Schweppes Guide to Scotch* (1983), 'Like all tax collectors in history, he had no natural allies, save the government of the day which left him to execute its unpopular duties.'

> The exciseman was 'obnoxious to the old, and a terror to the young; no one would satisfy his enquiries, and few were willing to render him service, even for payment'.
>
> *– Samuel Milligan, Supervisor of Excise, Stirling*

Excise officers faced enormous handicaps when trying to execute their 'unpopular duties'. Invariably, they had a far less intimate knowledge of the local terrain and people than the illicit distillers, and when lairds, clergymen and even justices of the peace also often appeared to be on the side of the smugglers, their cause frequently must have seemed quite hopeless. The threat of violence was very real, and excise officers were sometimes kidnapped and held for weeks to prevent them giving evidence in smuggling trials. Financial rewards for the gauger were meagre, to say the least. As Philip Morrice noted, 'He was expected to make his living from the proceeds of the take which he shared with the exchequer, and from which he had to meet all his expenses, including sometimes costly legal fees.'

From 1816, excise officers did not have to pay out of their own pockets in order to obtain military assistance or help from revenue cutters, which encouraged them to make greater use of those resources. However, soldiers were often quite half-hearted in their support of the gaugers when called upon for help, particularly as many of them quietly enjoyed a drop or two of illicit whisky while stationed in the Highlands.

Excise officers sometimes ended up in front of the magistrates themselves for assaulting smugglers they were pursuing, and occasionally were even charged with murder. In November 1789, Fife excise officer John Black was convicted of murdering a whisky smuggler he had shot near St Andrews.

Why does any accident happening to a gauger give general pleasure – far more so than an accident to a policeman? I have heard of a Strathglass gauger being quietly murdered. It was known he would on such a day and hour be riding to where he knew a bothy was in full work. One part of the road wound round a corner where a step missed would probably land horse and rider one hundred feet below in a horrid rocky ravine. As he came round the corner a woman rose up from the side of the road and suddenly threw a gown over her head in an apparently innocent fashion to shelter herself from the wind, the horse instantly lurched over into the ravine, and both it and its rider soon died from the accident (?) to the sorrow (?) of the smugglers.

– Dr John Mackenzie, Highland Memories

Physical assault went with the job, and incidents such as that reported by the officer who apprehended Duncan MacPherson of Auchindoir in October 1815 were far from uncommon. MacPherson was so displeased by the seizure that, as the officer reported, 'he threatened me with immediate death if I offered to destroy any more, at the same time beating and bruising me to the effusion of blood, so far as medical aid was necessary'.

A gauger on the Cabrach was killed by a bullet allegedly intended for his horse, and a farm servant by the name of Adam Gordon was tried for his murder, though he was ordered to be released by the judge on the third day of the trial after refusing to make any statement in court. Popular belief was that a schoolmaster by the name of Robertson was the real culprit. In October 1817 a supervisor of excise called George Arthur was killed near Campbeltown during a fight with smugglers. Two men were subsequently arrested, but released due to lack of evidence. Excise officer Dugald Cameron failed to return from a trip into the Stirlingshire hills in search of smugglers during 1820, and was presumed to have been killed by them.

Not surprisingly, excisemen were often tempted to take bribes from smugglers in return for leaving them unmolested. It is recorded that in Ross-shire meat, cheese and whisky were given to excise officers' wives by the spouses of whisky smugglers, while one collector of excise in Inverness was actively involved in the illicit distilling business himself.

In Ireland, too, collusion between the forces of law and illicit distillers was common, with rewards being paid to Royal Irish Constabulary officers for equipment seized. In 1902 one Irish Member of Parliament claimed that to his certain knowledge the same still had been seized 200 times!

Around 1918, RIC officers regularly raided Inismurray Island – off the coast of Sligo – in search of poitin, and they would take with them letters and parcels for the islanders, with whom they were on friendly terms. These sometimes contained orders for poitin from the mainland and supplies of barm, treacle and yeast for its manufacture. When news of a forthcoming police raid reached the island all the poitin and stills would be placed into one boat, which would then be rowed out to the west of the island for a spot of 'fishing' which tended to last until the RIC party had set sail for home after another fruitless search.

The first recorded use in English of the term 'gauger' occurs in 1483 – 'All the Vessels of Wine . . . shall . . . be well and truly gauged by the King's Gauger', and in *Scotch Whisky* (1950) J. Marshall Robb recorded that 'Legislation . . . passed in 1657 was the foundation of the Excise control of manufacture, various powers were given to officers, including the power to gauge vessels'. Sir Robert Bruce Lockhart in *Scotch* (1951) noted that 'Culloden was to bring in its train an invasion of excisemen, known locally as gaugers, because their main task is to gauge the amount of spirit produced, and a mass of crippling legislation including a rise in the duty.'

Although often thought of today as no more than a colloquialism, 'gauger' was an official title until 1831, when it was renamed 'division officer' or 'ride officer'. The division officer had a round of duties in an urban area, which was termed a 'walk', while his rural counterpart, the ride, or riding, officer, patrolled a 'ride'. The most celebrated riding officer of all time was Robert Burns.

In 1834 an officer's salary was £100 per year, and riding officers had an incentive not to totally destroy the illicit trade, even if they could have done so. They needed the bonuses paid to them for seizures made in order to supplement their meagre salaries. It was in their interests to allow smugglers to prosper for a while before raiding their operations, and then leave them undisturbed for a time before returning. In that way, the smugglers did not become totally disheartened, and give up.

At the top of the Excise hierarchy was the collector, who was paid up to £600 per year, and was in charge of a collection. This was sub-divided into districts, each controlled by a supervisor. Districts were sub-divided into divisions. The best that an ambitious gauger could hope for was to be promoted to supervisor, as very few went on to become collectors.

The supervisor's salary in 1837 was £200, and he was the key figure who could make a significant difference to illicit distilling, as it was his job to see that the officers 'on the ground' were doing their work efficiently and were not being bribed. If illicit distillers could get a supervisor on their side, then their operations would undoubtedly thrive.

The excise service tended to be hopelessly over-stretched in terms of manpower, and was often treated with contempt by illicit distillers. According to a 1799 parliamentary report on the subject of 'The Distilleries of Scotland', when a supervisor of excise came upon one Walter Adams working two illegal stills near Castle Huntly in the Carse of Gowrie, between Perth and Dundee, he was simply told to go away, though perhaps not as politely as the report may imply. So unimpressed was Adams with the might and authority of the excise service that he was cheerfully distilling again the following day when the supervisor arrived with a force considered large enough to apprehend him.

R. Carrick, collector of the excise at Inverness, was charged in 1803 with dereliction of duty while supervisor of the Forfar district two years previously. His defence is revealing.

> The detections I made were indeed great and such as astounded the whole country and I had the thanks of the lieutenancy and country Gentlemen given to me at Coupar Angus in open court . . . By doing my duty zealously I brought myself into considerable Sum of arrears for the King's part of fines and seizures *which these very exertions had realized* . . . The expense of a party of from 12–20 men upon excursions of this nature for days and nights upon one survey, was no easy burden for me to bear; besides many a time being in danger of my existence, private Distillers being the set of desperate people moving often from one part of the county to another . . . It's well remembered how I followed and traced them out from my own District to the Woods of Perth. At Scone I made a discovery with one of them under ground, and below the very floor of Malthouse . . . This unfeeling miscreant of a private distiller was fined £50 but even here my share was totally consumed by defraying the expense of a party from Forfar and Cupar to support me in making the detection.

Carrick's remarks are very reminiscent of comments made by the most famous nineteenth-century gauger, Malcolm Gillespie. Gillespie's fame is due, principally, to his posthumous memoirs, which give us one of the few 'gauger's-eye views' of the situation as he saw it with regard to smuggling in the Highlands during the early years of the nineteenth century. He also remains one of the few excise officers to have been hanged.

Gillespie was born in Dunblane, Perthshire, and entered the excise service in 1799. His first posting was to Prestonpans, where officers oversaw the production of salt, which at that time was taxed. He made his mark there by detecting a considerable amount of fraud, and subsequently was promoted, being made a revenue officer at Collieston in Aberdeenshire – an area to which he had requested a transfer.

Again, he did well in this post, and in 1807 was moved to Stonehaven, where he was notably successful in combating the thriving trade of smuggling goods by sea. In 1812 he was transferred inland to Deeside – to the Skene Ride – which covered a large area between the valleys of the rivers Don and Dee, and there his battles with the whisky smugglers really began in earnest.

One evening in August 1814 Malcolm Gillespie was attacked by four men after stopping a cart carrying some 80 gallons of illicit whisky. He was badly beaten in the assault, but when he fired a shot it attracted nearby residents who rushed to his aid and helped detain the four smugglers, two of whom were later imprisoned for periods of nine months and one year. Later in life, Gillespie said that this was the most savage assault to which he had been subjected in his entire career.

Early in 1816 Gillespie bought a bull terrier, and trained it to seize horses by the nose, forcing them to rear up and spill the contents of the carts they were pulling. As Gillespie himself put it, the dog was taught to 'seize the horses one by one, till by tumbling some, and others by dancing, in consequence of the pain occasioned by the hold the dog had of them by the nose, the Ankers were all thrown from their backs'. The bulldog was a valuable asset until it was shot and killed by a smuggler at Carlogie.

Gillespie appears to give the lie to the popular image of the gaugers as bumbling incompetents, often in cahoots with the smugglers, or keen for a quiet life. He was totally fearless in his pursuit of smugglers, confiscating the best part of a hundred gallons of spirit after a particularly bloody fight with a vicious smuggler – 'a strong, hardened desperado named Hay' – in the Woods of Drum near Kintore in July 1816. During the encounter, Hay's face was badly gashed by Gillespie's sabre, while a second excise officer somehow managed to shoot himself in the groin – no less than three times. Hay was arrested and sentenced to a year's imprisonment.

Apart from intercepting smugglers on the move, Gillespie also enjoyed great successes in detecting illicit stills. One near Skene had a capacity of 50 gallons, and was 'so constructed that a person even of no ordinary penetration could scarcely be able to find it out, although within a few yards'. Along with the still, some 300 gallons of wash were also confiscated.

In March 1824 Gillespie was seriously wounded in a fight with a group of Glenlivet smugglers in Inverurie, though ten carts full of spirit – containing a total of 410 gallons of whisky – were seized when the officer and one assistant tackled some thirty men en route to Aberdeen. Hopelessly outnumbered, Gillespie still pressed on with his duty, being saved when the rest of his officers arrived, backed by local militiamen. He described the encounter as consisting of 'bloody heads, hats rolling on the road, the reports of alternate firing and other noise, which resembled more the Battle of Waterloo than the interception of a band of lawless desperadoes'.

Malcolm Gillespie faced a problem familiar to almost all excise officers – he was paid a very modest salary, and effectively made a living from the proceeds of his seizures. He did, however, have to pay his men, and feed and arm them out of his own pocket, not to mention give them bonuses for seizures made. Considerable sums of money also changed hands between excise officers and informers, and again Gillespie was forced to meet the cost. The proceeds of the sale of all equipment and spirit captured were divided equally between the exchequer and the officer involved, before all the officer's expenses as outlined above were deducted from his half. Gillespie detailed one successful seizure which actually left him out of pocket to the not inconsiderable sum of between £30 and £40.

The end result was that even such a highly effective officer as Gillespie became seriously in debt, with a wife and children to support. In his pamphlet *The Memorial and Case of Malcolm Gillespie* (1828) he noted:

> captures of the greatest magnitude are attended with very great expenses; for in a country where the inhabitants are almost wholly connected with the illicit trade, it is difficult to find a person among them who can be prevailed upon to give information against his neighbour and nothing short of the Officer's Share of the Seizure can induce the informant to divulge his secret. It has principally been in this way that that I have involved myself in debt.

In 1827 Gillespie was arrested for forging Treasury Bills, and was found guilty at Aberdeen Circuit Court of Judiciary in September of that year. As forgery was a capital crime, he was executed on 16 November 1827.

While awaiting trial he wrote his pamphlet in jail, partly as a plea for clemency, perhaps, and partly because he felt ill-used, having achieved so much yet still ended up in serious debt. At any rate, there is no reason to question Gillespie's facts and figures. He stated that he could point to forty-two wounds on his body inflicted in the line of duty, and itemised all the seizures of spirit he had made in his twenty-eight-year career. The total came to in excess of 20,000 gallons, not to mention more than 60,000 gallons of wash, 407 stills, 165 horses and half as many carts. Certainly, he seems to have been poorly rewarded for his diligence.

In his *The Origin of Glenlivet Whisky, With Some Account of the Smuggling*, serialised in *The Distillers' Magazine and Spirit Trade News* during 1897, J. Gordon Phillips presented a contrasting view of Gillespie. He called him 'the notorious Malcolm Gillespie', noting:

> so much was he detested by the Glenlivet smugglers that I remember one who stated that the biggest disappointment he ever got in his life was when he could not go to Aberdeen to see Gillespie hanged.
>
> Gillespie was the best-hated gauger in the north-eastern counties. He was forever in difficulties himself, and he showed none of that generosity which was a common trait in many of the excise officers. On the contrary, he hunted all over the country, seizing whisky wherever he got the chance, and if rumour is correct, he did not often destroy it, and the Revenue was little the better for what he had seized.

According to Phillips' account of Gillespie, his fabled dog was not a bull-dog, but 'a large black retriever . . . more feared than Gillespie himself . . . Malcolm Gillespie cared neither for God nor man, and he was said to be selfish and brutal with women, but he loved his dog passionately'.

The smuggler whose great regret was not seeing Gillespie hang was John Macgregor, described by his acquaintance Phillips as 'one of the last of the old smugglers of Glenlivet, and one of the best of them'.

On one occasion Macgregor performed a great feat of daring when he was caught by a party of excisemen and dragoons with a cargo of smuggled whisky at the Spittal of Glenshee, between Blairgowrie and Braemar. Macgregor was seated on a horse between two dragoons, with his arms and legs tied, and the party set off to take their prisoner back to Blairgowrie, with Macgregor at the rear of the column. He was able to free his loosely-bound hands without being observed, and took a knife from one of his pockets just as the convoy approached the 'Brig o' Calley'. Although the brig was some 60 feet above the waters of the Ardle, Macgregor leant down and cut the rope binding his legs, knocked both dragoons off their horses, and threw himself over the parapet of the brig into the river below. Although he injured his ankle, Macgregor survived the leap remarkably well, and hid beneath the roots of an old tree, so that the excise officers decided he must have drowned and been swept away by the water when they carried out a perfunctory search.

As Phillips noted, 'In after years John took to the much less exciting occupation of catching moles, but I remember he often went searching for a cask he buried in haste and forgot the spot. He used to say to me that if he could only discover the spot he would give me a gallon or two out of it. He was sure it would be very well matured lying so long.'

John Macgregor also recounted an occasion when he was part of a large convoy taking illicit whisky between 'the Brig o' Don and the Granite City', when it was ambushed by Gillespie and his men. A fierce fight ensued, but in the end the gaugers got the better of it, seizing seventeen horses and thirty-five ankers of spirit. Just one anker and one horse were saved from the clutches of the excisemen.

Macgregor recalled of Gillespie:

> Well, he was a curious customer that same gauger. He said to me as cool as if nothing particular had happened, 'You have got the worst of it this time, but I am afraid I have winged one of your men, if not more.'
>
> 'Well, I'm thinking I have made one of yours feel a sair bit,' said I.
>
> 'Oh,' he answered, 'that is the fortune of war, but I hope you did not kill him. You know that would mean a hanging business, and I would not like to see a decent man like you hanged.'
>
> The infernal scoundrel to use such language to me after destroying my whisky and taking my horses. Little did he know how close to the gallows his own neck was.

Prompted by Phillips, John Macgregor did grudgingly admit that Gillespie personally cleaned his head wound and dressed it for him. 'Ay, it's true enough but small consolation that was. He dressed the wound and gave me a good dram o' my ain whisky, I suppose. At any rate it never paid duty more than mine, that I make sure of.'

Another Gillespie story is a variant of the old smugglers' standby of pretending that there was disease in the house where a still or spirit was thought to be concealed. On this occasion the 'body' of a wanted smuggler was laid out when Gillespie entered the dwelling. Hearing the world 'smallpox' he hurriedly took a couple of pinches of snuff, which was believed to help prevent infection. Recognising the smuggler, and becoming suspicious, Gillespie placed his snuff mull under the nose of the 'corpse', which promptly sneezed violently. Gillespie was supposedly so amused by the episode that he did not report it – highly unlikely one would have imagined, knowing the zealous nature of the man. Instead, he shared the smuggler's whisky with his men, feeding their horses on the malt prepared by the smuggler, Stuart, for his next brew.

According to John E. Murray, writing in the 1934 Christmas number of the *Northern Scot* newspaper, 'Gillespie, it may be of interest to mention, was eventually found guilty of poisoning his housekeeper. He was sentenced to death and was, it is believed, the last person to be hanged on the open-air gallows at Aberdeen.'

The facts of the hanging may be true, but the nature of the crime, of course, is not.

Gillespie may have been a famous – or infamous – gauger, but Robert Burns was the most celebrated Scottish excise officer of all time. However, his relationship with the excise service, by which he was employed in the Dumfries area from October 1789 until his untimely death in 1796, was ambiguous to say the least. It was Burns who penned the oft-quoted lines 'Freedom and whisky gang thegither! – /Tak' aff your dram!'

In his 'Epistle to Dr Blacklock' (October 1789) he wrote:

But what d'ye think, my trusty fier,
I'm turned a gauger – Peace be here!
Parnassian queans, I fear, I fear,
　Ye'll now disdain me!
And then my fifty pounds a year
　Will little gain me.

Elsewhere, Burns described himself as 'a paltry exciseman', and considered the job an 'insignificant existence in the meanest of pursuits, and among the vilest of mankind'.

Despite his apparent ambivalence towards the excise service, Burns took to the job well, proving an able administrator, and no 'soft touch', as many folk in the Dumfries area might have imagined when they heard that a poet was joining the service. Alongside his name in excise records is the comment 'The poet, does pretty well'. He was earning £70 a year when he became ill, and had to take sick-leave, having previously acted on a temporary basis as a district supervisor to cover another officer's illness. Following his death, Burns' widow, Jean Armour, received an excise pension until she died in 1834.

In 'The Author's Earnest Cry and Prayer', Burns voiced a protest at oppressive excise legislation, addressed to 'The Scotch Representatives in the House of Commons'.

Paint Scotland greetin owre her thrissle; [greetin=crying]
Her mutchkin stoup as toom's a whissle: [stoup=flagon, toom=empty]
An' dam'd Excisemen in a bussle,
　Seizin' a stell,

Triumphant crushin't like a mussle
    Or limpet shell.
Then on the tither hand present her,
A blackguard smuggler, right behint her,
An' cheek-for-chow, a chuffie vintner, [chuffie=fat]
    Colleaguing join,
Pickin' her pouch as bare as Winter
    Of a' kind coin.

Is there that bears the name o' Scot,
Ut feels his heart's bluid rising hot,
To see his poor old mother's pot
    Thus dung in staves, [dung=smashed]
An' plunder'd o' her hindmost groat
    By gallows knaves?

In 1792, while serving in the excise service, Burns had some fun at the expense of his colleagues in the song 'The De'il's Awa' wi th' Exciseman', composed while he was keeping watch on a brig in the Solway Firth, suspected of involvement in the smuggling trade.

The Deil cam fiddling; through the toon,
And he's danced awa' wi' th' Exciseman,
And ilka wifie cries:- 'Auld Mahoun,
Ach, I wish you luck o' the prize man!'

The Deil's awa', the Deil's awa',
The Deil's awa' wi' th' Exciseman!
He's danced awa', he's danced awa',
He's danced awa' wi' th' Exciseman.

We'll mak' our maut, and we'll brew our drink,
And we'll dance, and sing, and rejoice, man,
And mony braw thanks to the muckle black Deil,
That's danced awa' wi' the' Exciseman.

Chorus

There's threesome reels, and there's foursome reels,
And there's hornpipes and strathspeys, man,
But the best dance ever tae cam' tae the land
Was – the Deil's awa' wi' th' Exciseman.

Chorus

Another song involving a gauger and the Devil is traditional:

I know that young folk like to hear a new song
Of something that's funny and not very long

Concerning an exciseman, the truth I will tell
Who thought one night he was landed in hell.

The exciseman went out for to look for his prey
He met two or three smugglers upon the highway
And gauging their liquors they had got to sell
The exciseman got drunk for the truth I will tell.

He got so drunk that he fell to the ground
And like a fat sow he was forced to lie down
Just nigh to a col pit the exciseman did lie
When four or five colliers by chance passed by.

They shouldered him up and they carried him away
Like a pedlar's pack, without any delay
And into a bucket they handed him down
This jolly exciseman they got underground.

The exciseman awoke in a terrible fear
Up started a collier, says 'What brought you hear?'
'Indeed Mr Devil I don't very well know
But I think I am come to regions below.'

'O what was you then in the world above?'
'O I was a gauger and few did me love
But indeed Mr Devil the truth I will tell
For since I got here I shall be what you will.'

'O then' said the collier 'it's here ye'll remain
Ye'll never get out of this dark cell again
For the gates they re shut and they'll bind you secure
All this you must suffer for robbing the poor.'

'O Mr Devil have pity on me
I'll ne'er go a-robbing the poor you shall see
If you would look over as you've done before
I'll ne'er go a-robbing the poor anymore.'

'Then give us a guinea to drink with demand
Before you get back to a Christian land'
'O yes Mr Devil!' The gauger did say
'For I long to get back to see the light of day.'

After visiting Cameronbridge distillery at Windygates in Fife during
the mid-1880s, Alfred Barnard wrote that

> Kennoway, a mile and a half from the works, is a delightful place situated
> at the head of a romantic glen, the sides of which are rocky and precipitous,
> containing numerous caves, the haunts of smugglers and marauders of
> a bygone age. Many a tale of daring and bold adventure is told by the

inhabitants, and it is said that at one time some revenue officers were blind-folded and taken into the caves, where they were compelled to swear that they had been inside, but had seen nothing illicit.

Ian Milne, retired excise officer of Keith, spent fourteen years as a distillery-based officer, operating at some thirty distilleries. He worked mainly in the eastern area of Speyside, but also served at Cameronbridge. He offers an interesting variation on the common illegal practice of 'grogging the cask' – that is adding water to an apparently empty cask and swirling it around in order to extract the remaining whisky:

If you apply heat to emptied casks you can actually get up to a couple of gallons of spirit out of them, and it's pretty strong – between cask and normal bottling strength. During the hot summer of 1976 one of the men at Cameronbridge was going back in the late evenings when it was dark and just turning the emptied casks over to collect the spirit that had come out by the heat of the daytime sun. What was pretty blatant was that he took a market stall in Livingston and was selling it from that before the Customs & Excise caught up with him!

On the same theme, I was told at Cameronbridge that years before, one winter, the stillman on the night shift rolled an emptied cask into the stillhouse and propped it against the hot still in order to get spirit out. All was fine until the early hours of the morning when he went to roll it back to where it had been taken from and he discovered there had been a heavy fall of snow. If he'd rolled it back then it would have been very obvious, so, according to the story, he broke it up and burned it in the still . . .

Sometimes subterfuge was employed by excise officers intent on catching their quarry 'in the act', perhaps pretending to be holidaying fishermen or walkers, so as not to arouse suspicion among the local populace. In the USA, revenue man George Atkinson and an associate took fishing and hunting equipment into the Cumberland mountains of Kentucky in the middle years of the nineteenth century, and set up camp close to a settlement of known distilling houses. By day they fished and hunted, and by night spent time gathering evidence around the still-houses. Not only the moonshiners were favoured by the hours of darkness.

In most surviving folk stories of illicit distilling, the forces of the law are outmanoeuvred by wily and resourceful smugglers, but sometimes the excise officers outsmarted their foes. Seumas Mor McDonald of Tom-a-choachain farmed in a remote spot north of Loch Tay, between

Aberfeldy and Killin in Perthshire, during the early nineteenth century. He was renowned as a great distiller and a very wily man, whose activities frustrated the excise officers for years. An attempt at bringing in two young Lanarkshire gaugers as 'undercover' men, pretending to be walkers, backfired when McDonald got them very drunk on his whisky and they reported back to base in Killin none the wiser about the whereabouts of his still and with no incriminating evidence of any sort.

Next an Irish exciseman by the name of Kelly was brought in from Deeside where he had earned a reputation for catching illicit distillers. Kelly organised what amounted to a military operation against McDonald, involving a detachment of soldiers from Perth and many excise personnel.

They proceeded to raid the farm and search it painstakingly for a full day without result. As they were leaving, Kelly hit upon an ingenious plan. He called at the farm neighbouring McDonald's and asked the farmer, John Robertson, to bring his horse and cart, saying he had captured McDonald's still, and needed the cart to remove it to Killin. Robertson duly fetched his horse and cart, and with Kelly beside him set off to McDonald's farm. He drove past the farm itself and stopped a short distance away, just as Kelly had hoped he would. The still was soon discovered hidden in a knoll beside the track, and McDonald duly received a heavy fine for illicit distilling. After this he decided to give up the distilling game to concentrate on farming, and lived to be an old man, dying during the 1850s.

Once illicit distilling had been more or less stamped out, the role of the excise officer concerned with whisky distilling became a comparatively pleasant, and not unduly onerous, one. During the 1930s, at least one exciseman and novelist found time to spend many of his weekday afternoons at home writing books, and other officers were only very reluctantly prised from the banks of good fishing rivers and lochs.

Every distillery had at least one resident officer – 'the watch-dog of the Government', as R.J.S. McDowall put it (*The Whiskies of Scotland*) – for whom the distillery was obliged by law to supply a house. This arrangement dated back to the 1823 Excise Act, which required the provision of houses for excise officers in cases where the distillery was situated more than one mile from a market town. The excise officer was there to make sure that every drop of alcohol produced was recorded, so that duty could be paid on it, but there was usually a degree of 'give and take' between excisemen and distillers, such as in the matter of 'dramming'. The practice of 'dramming' the men – giving them measures of whisky while at work – was usually overlooked by the excise officers as it was tacitly agreed that if the workers were not given whisky in this way, then they would surely find another means of illegally obtaining it. Dramming ended with the advent of health and safety legislation, and increased observance of drink-driving laws.

John McDougall joined the old Distillers' Company Ltd as a management trainee in 1963, serving initially at Aultmore distillery near Keith, on Speyside. He went on to manage such high-profile distilleries as Laphroaig, Balvenie and Springbank before becoming a respected whisky consultant. During his time working in distilleries, McDougall encountered some memorable excise officers, including Banff's 'Mr MacDonald', who always wore a kilt to work, and was accompanied by his Afghan hound. 'He was a pleasant, helpful man', recalls MacDougall, 'but very much a throwback to the days when the excise officer at a distillery was a bit like a laird. The excise officer was still a powerful figure in the mid '60s, and the distillery tended to run to suit his personal timetable. He would arrive to oversee the accounts of spirits and everything else when he was ready to!'

At Balvenie there were five resident officers in John McDougall's time, including a Yorkshireman called Harry Carrington and a southern Englishman called Ron Pickthall. Pickthall was clearly not impressed by having a distillery manager who was younger than he was, and who had not been a wartime officer in the yeomanry.

'The two of them used to spend afternoons supposedly testing instruments,' says McDougall. 'They would draw spirit samples from casks in one of the warehouses and retire to their office to make sure their instruments were working properly. They seemed to be very diligent, because they did this quite a lot! By five o'clock if you went into their office the air would be thick with cigarette smoke, the playing cards would be out on the desk, and the sample tube would be more than half-empty.'

At Dailuaine distillery on Speyside, McDougall worked alongside the excise officer Ray Lyons. Lyons arrived early in the morning to take the whisky charge and spirit account, adding some of the new spirit to the thermos flask that contained his coffee. Like Banff's 'Mr MacDonald', Lyons was accompanied to work by a dog, in this case an Irish Wolfhound called Seamus. 'As the day wore on', remembers McDougall, 'Ray's glasses slid further down his nose and his eyes became progressively more glazed. When it was time to go home he called for Seamus, and then it became apparent why he took the dog to work. He needed it to hang onto on the steep path from the distillery up to his house!'

In his entertaining account of the four years which he spent working for HM Customs & Excise on Speyside during the mid-1970s, Keith Bond (*Memoirs of An Excise Man*) described a fellow officer who had been a guardsman in a previous life, and who had a habit of walking into doors. This was not, as Bond at first charitably assumed, because he wore his excise cap like a guardsman would and had restricted vision, but because he carried a sauce bottle on a length of string and regularly dipped it into casks of spirit.

Bond observed that a high percentage of his fellow officers on Speyside were English, with at least one 'going native' with a vengeance and wearing full Highland dress, while speaking in a broad Lancashire accent!

From Islay comes the story, by way of Bruichladdich distillery's Jim McEwan, of an unpopular exciseman at Bowmore, who was always following the men about in the warehouses, looking for minor leaks and generally being officious. 'The cooper trained his terrier to pee against the end of casks, and then watched as the exciseman reached down and put his fingers in the liquid and tasted it. "Leak," he'd shout out. "Are you sure it's spirit?" the cooper would ask. "Oh aye, it's spirit all right," the officer would reply. "See to that leak."'

Master Blender Richard Paterson – of Glasgow-based distillers Kyndal – tells a story associated with Dalmore distillery near Alness in Easter Ross. Dalmore is one of Kyndal's prize possessions, and its single malt is a significant component of the company's Whyte & Mackay blend.

According to Paterson, Major Bartlett and Captain Peter Willis were friends and fellow officers in the Territorial Army during the late 1940s, and Willis – known as 'Captain Bang Bang' because of his enthusiasm for shooting – was a Customs & Excise officer responsible for Dalmore distillery, along with nearby Glenmorangie and Teaninich.

Convinced that illicit distilling was going on in the area, Willis' great ambition was to capture an unlicensed still. Bartlett was a forestry officer who lived near Alness, and one day his forestry duties took him to a location near Ullapool, on the opposite side of the country. Suddenly, while walking in a forest, he came across an illicit still, very much in use. Knowing his friend's near obsession with the subject, he took a photograph of the still, and duly sent it to Willis with no accompanying note or other means of identification. On the back he had written simply 'guess where!'

Apparently, Willis remained forever ignorant of the fact that it was Bartlett who had sent the photo, and the latter did not admit his involvement, never disclosing the whereabouts of the still to anyone.

The first distillery on Speyside to tanker malt whisky away by road rather than allow it to mature on site had three tankers. Only two were actual road tankers, no.1 and no.2. The resident exciseman was known as 'Tanker no.3'.

Since 1983, there has been a significant degree of 'self-regulation' in distilleries, with managers assuming responsibility for measuring all yields and submitting returns to HM Customs & Excise regarding the amounts of wash and spirit produced. There are no longer resident excise officers in every distillery, holding one of the keys required to open the spirit safe – formerly the most tangible example of the excise officer's position of authority.

Robert Burns was not the only excise officer who was better known for his writing than he was for his work as a gauger. During the twentieth century, Neil Gunn and Maurice Walsh both became acclaimed novelists, with Gunn writing classic fiction such as *Highland River* and *The Silver Darlings*. He was the son of a crofter-fisherman, born in the east Caithness fishing village of Dunbeath in 1891. He entered the civil service in 1907, joining the excise branch four years later, going on to spend a decade as an 'unattached officer', travelling widely in the Highlands and Islands.

Gunn was also responsible for what remains one of the best-written and most characterful of all books about Scotch whisky – *Whisky and Scotland*. Gunn wrote what his publishers described as 'this witty, indignant little book' during the mid-1930s, at a time when the Scotch whisky industry was in the economic doldrums, and single or 'self' whiskies, as they were often known, were virtually unobtainable to the average drinker.

Gunn was a passionate nationalist and an equally passionate single malt man, who shared with Robert Burns an ambivalence about his role as representative of the Government's excise service. He considered the tax discrimination against whisky as 'so manifestly unjust that it does have the appearance of being deliberately vindictive'.

In 1921 Gunn married Daisy Frew, and two years later the couple were living in Inverness, where Gunn had been appointed excise officer at the now demolished Glen Mhor distillery, situated beside the Caledonian Canal. He remained there until 1937, when he decided to leave the security of the excise service and write on a full-time basis.

While serving in HM Customs & Excise Service, shortly before the outbreak of the First World War, Neil Gunn met and became friends with a fellow exciseman and writer, one Maurice Walsh, a farmer's son from County Kerry in south-west Ireland.

Walsh was resident officer at Dallas Dhu – where a plaque now commemorates his association with the distillery – and Gunn was sent to cover his annual leave. In a conversation with his co-biographer Francis Hart, Gunn noted 'I'd write ahead and say, "Look here! I'm coming to replace you. Kindly see that the books are all in perfect order so that there is absolutely no work to be done."'.

Once in situ, Gunn would spend much of his time fishing and shooting with Walsh, a situation that finds a fictional parallel in Walsh's best-selling 1926 novel *The Key Above The Door*. The book's narrator, Tom King, spends time on Skye, where his Irish friend Neil Quinn is an excise officer, sent to the island to cover the resident officer's summer holiday.

Attempting to persuade King to join him on Skye, Quinn writes, 'above all there is the whisky – Uiskavagh whisky, the finest whisky in the world when drunk in Skye; old as a grown man, mild as your goat's milk, soothing as a woman's hand in your hair, inspiring as a tune – a very great whisky'.

Some of *The Key Above the Door* has a Speyside setting, as have several of Walsh's other novels, most notably *The Hill is Mine*, in which Stephen Wayne from Montana inherits a Banffshire croft and falls in love with the country, not to mention the obligatory spirited and beautiful young woman. Walsh's own wife, Caroline Begg, was a Dufftown girl, and served as the red-haired model for many of his fictional heroines.

Apart from *The Key Above The Door*, which appeared in the same year as Neil Gunn's first novel *The Grey Coast*, Walsh is probably best-known for his short story *The Quiet Man*, part of his 1935 collection *Green Rushes*, which in 1952 was made into one of Ireland's most famous films, starring John Wayne and Maureen O'Hara.

Walsh did not write much about whisky in non-fiction terms, though he contributed a foreword to J. Marshall Robb's 1950 volume *Scotch Whisky*, which serves as a useful 'whisky autobiography'.

He recalled entering the excise service in 1901.

I mind well that a week before Xmas I was away down in Valentia Island at the American side of the Kerry Mountains, and looking forward to a pleasant Festival in Tralee, where, at the time, I was coortin' a nice girl – even if she was a Presbyterian. But I spent that snowy Xmas under Ben Nevis, five hundred miles away. That was where they made and matured the famous Long John . . . After that, for my sins, I was sent down among the raw grain distilleries about Alloa. Carsebridge, Glenochil, Cambus.

A spell in the breweries of Burton-upon-Trent was followed by a move to Speyside, where Walsh fell in love with 'that soberly-rolling and chimney-stalked territory . . . Three dozen of us young fellows used to gather for the distilling season from October to May: lads from all Scotland, England, Wales and Ireland, the four most quarrelsome nations in the world – but it was not blood that flowed'.

He concluded in characteristically lyrical style.

When I do get the first whiff of, say, Standfast, I see a vision. I see the long-winding valley with the chimney stalks and kiln-pagodas above the trees; I see the Fiddich and the Dullan running fast and clear over bright gravel, the bald Convals fringed with a hair of pines, big Ben Rinnes with cap atilt over the glen; I smell again the peat, the wash, and the feints, and feel the tightness of carbon-dioxide in my throat; and I see myself getting out of a warm bed in the dark of a Januar' morning. And I see a girl with red hair.

5

SPEYSIDE

Of all the areas in which Scottish illicit distilling took place, Speyside was unquestionably the most significant. Today, the whisky-making tradition remains very strong in this part of the north-east, as the region is the heartland of the legal industry, and home to around half of the country's operational distilleries.

Many of the factors that influenced the great growth of legal Speyside distilling during the late nineteenth century also go a long way towards explaining its importance as a centre for whisky smuggling. Access to excellent water supplies, good malting barley and an abundance of peat, were important, though one of the area's 'selling points' during the 1890s was its good transport links south by way of the railway network. This had been developed during the 1850s and 1860s, and before long, every new distillery was being constructed with its own railway siding.

For the illicit distillers, of course, remoteness was a prize asset, though markets for their goods in towns and cities not too far distant were also essential. Much illicit Speyside whisky found its way into Aberdeen to the east, Perth and Dundee to the south, and even as far afield as Edinburgh.

Between 1723 and 1740 General George Wade developed a series of roads linking military centres such as Fort William, Fort Augustus and Fort George at Inverness as a response to the Jacobite rising of 1715, but slightly less than a century later Thomas Telford continued Wade's work on a much larger scale, genuinely 'opening up' much of the Highlands. This facilitated the efforts of the excise officers to some extent, but the bleak and inaccessible nature of much of the country of the north-east remained, as did its reputation for severe winter weather.

The Cock Bridge to Tomintoul 'Lecht road' – built by Wade, and now classified as the A939 – which connects Strathavon with Strathdon can still usually claim the dubious honour of being the first road in Britain each winter to appear on Ceefax and Teletext road reports with the information 'closed due to snow'. The road rises to more than 2,000 feet before it drops into Tomintoul – a settlement that claims to be the highest village in the Highlands at 1,150 feet above sea level.

As well as being a hotbed of smuggling in its day, the Lecht gained a new notoriety a century after the smugglers' heyday, when in 1920 the 'Monocled Mutineer' Percy Toplis shot local policeman George Greig, while holed up in a Lecht bothy. Toplis was an army deserter credited with being the ring leader of a mutiny at an army base in France during the First World War, and he was hiding from the police on Speyside after murdering a taxi driver in Andover, Hampshire.

Just as smoke had often alerted gaugers to illicit distilling a hundred years previously, a local gamekeeper saw smoke coming from the bothy chimney and told local farmer John Grant, who summoned Constable Greig from his base in Tomintoul. Grant and Greig were shot by Toplis when they disturbed him as he slept, though both survived. Toplis fled to Aberdeen on a stolen bicycle and caught a train south, but he was killed five days later during a shoot-out with police near Penrith in Cumberland.

Inevitably, certain routes were favoured by whisky smugglers, and 'whisky roads' have exotic-sounding names such as Cairn o'Mount, Glen Clova, the Fungle and the Ladder. Many of them are now metalled roads or can be followed on foot with the aid of an OS map and a dram or two to speed the journey. For maximum authenticity, of course, the treks should be made in the dead of night, with a convoy of ponies loaded with unwieldy ankers of spirit, and the traveller should be ready to take to the heather or stand and fight at a moment's notice.

The Ladder 'whisky road' is a path from Chapeltown of Glenlivet via Strathdon and Glen Tanar to Tarfside in Glen Esk, north of Brechin, and whisky transported via the Ladder was usually destined for the Dundee or Perth areas. The Cairn o' Mount route (now essentially the B974) from the Banchory area down to Fettercairn and Brechin was another popular option for smugglers.

The Fungle path runs from Aboyne to the favoured illicit distilling centre of Tarfside, and then crossing the North Esk it is known as the Priest's Road, also being signposted as the Whisky Road. It stretches to Tullybardine and Glen Lethnot, ultimately ending near Brechin.

Another much-used route was the Beatshacht, which is now metalled but unclassified and runs over the hill via Edinvillie off the A95 near Aberlour to join the B9009 Glen Rinnes road to Glenlivet south-west of Dufftown. Jock's Road was a famous whisky run and starts south of Braemar, going through Glen Doll to Glen Clova, Kirriemuir and eventually to Dundee, while the road over the Cabrach was a popular passage from Speyside to Donside.

Corgarff Castle is a stunning building, dating from 1537 and situated more than 1,400 feet above sea level in bleak country, some ten miles south-east of Tomintoul, and close to the Lecht Road. During the 1745/46 Jacobite rising it was burnt out for the fourth time in its turbulent existence, and in 1826 one James McHardy, a local man, was granted a licence to distil in Corgarff Castle. This act of perceived treachery led, almost inevitably, to another fire, this time started by illicit distillers. A £100 reward for conviction of the arsonist was offered, but, not surprisingly, it was never claimed. It would have taken a brave man to turn in the culprits, even for so tempting a reward.

After this fire, the castle was refurbished and used as barracks for government troops, with fifty-eight soldiers from the 25th Regiment of Foot being stationed there. McHardy did nothing to improve his local standing when he took on the role of providing provisions for the garrison, along with a small cottage for use as a military hospital.

Troops were stationed at Corgarff until 1831 to back up the excisemen in their attempts to stamp out illicit whisky-making in this heartland of the craft – Glenavon and the Ladder Hills. Remarkably, their presence actually came about as a result of a popular ballad composed by a smuggler, John Milne of Glenlivet.

Milne's ballad celebrated a skirmish between gaugers and smugglers at Glennochty, in which the smugglers had emerged victorious. The ballad – which greatly exaggerated the scale and ferocity of the encounter – reached the ears of the great and the good in Edinburgh who concluded that the situation on Speyside was totally out of control, hence the military deployment.

Corgarff was strategically ideal for anti-smuggling operations. As J. Gordon Phillips observed in his *The Origin of Glenlivet Whisky, With Some Account of the Smuggling*, 'From this point they could march over the Leicht Hill into the Braes of Conglass at Blair-na-Marrow (i.e., Field of the Dead), and from that point cross into the Braes of Glenlivet. Or they could march right down Strathdon and turn west into Glennochty.'

The soldiers did not like the work, however, and Phillips recounted the story told to him by an old smuggler who, with his colleagues, was being pursued from his bothy by a party of gaugers and soldiers. The flight took the smugglers and their pursuers up the slopes of Benmore, and as the smugglers rested for a moment to regain their breath, the officer in command of the soldiers gesticulated to the gaugers and shouted to the smugglers in Gaelic 'Why don't you roll down stones on the devils?'

This suggestion was duly acted upon, while the soldiers ignored the gaugers' shouts to open fire on the smugglers. The old smuggler told Phillips, 'We afterwards heard that the officer belonged to Braemar, and that both he and the private soldiers were thoroughly disgusted with the whole thing. The smugglers of Corgarff soon found that out, and, believe me, as long as the red-coats occupied the old castle they never wanted a drop of good stuff.'

Speyside is home to what is without doubt the most famous glen in whisky history – Glenlivet. The glen is renowned for its illicit distilling, for being home to one of the world's most popular single malts, and also for the fact that its founder, George Smith, was the first man to take out a distilling licence under the provisions of the 1823 Excise Act.

Glenlivet was truly remote, an ideal place in which distillers could operate with little fear of discovery by excise officers, though it was just the highest profile of many similar, remote Speyside glens where the illicit trade was carried on. When Speyside whiskies became all the rage during the late nineteenth century 'whisky boom' it seemed that every distiller in the north of Scotland wanted to add cache to his product by putting 'Glenlivet' on its labels. During the 1880s George Smith's son, John, fought a court battle for the exclusive rights to the word, the outcome being that other distillers were allowed to use 'Glenlivet' in hyphenated form, but only Smith could use the definite article in front of the Glenlivet name.

The glen and its principal product have often been praised in literature, with Christopher North quoting the 'Ettrick Shepherd', James Hogg, as saying 'Gie me the real Glenlivet, and I weel believe I could mak' drinking toddy oot o' sea-water. The human mind never tires o' Glenlivet, any mair than o' caller air. If a body could just find oot the exac' proportion and quantity that ought to be drunk every day, and keep to that, I verily trow that he might leeve for ever, without dying at a', and that doctors and kirkyards would go oot o' fashion.'

In *Sir Ronan's Well* (1824), Sir Walter Scott wrote of Glenlivet that 'it is worth all the wines in France for flavour, and more cordial to the system besides', and it was for Glenlivet whisky that King George IV had called upon his arrival in Edinburgh two years earlier.

George Smith's family was established in the Glenlivet area by 1715, and anglicised their name from its Gaelic equivalent of Gow in an attempt to disguise their support for, and involvement in, the Jacobite rising of 1715. The popular myth is that the Smiths fled to Glenlivet as fugitives after the '45, but there is no truth in the story, though the family was staunchly Jacobite in its sympathies.

George Smith was born in 1792, and trained as a carpenter, going on to combine that trade with farming at Upper Drumin. He also continued the old tradition of adding a little illicit distilling to his other duties, as his father had done before him, though in 1816 he was turning out just one hogshead of spirit per week. Whisky-making was clearly an established element of family life, as two of George Smith's brothers were prosecuted for illicit distillation.

Many years later, Smith recalled being told by his father that prior to the mid-1790s, when new excise legislation made illicit distilling even more attractive in the Highlands, there had been very little illegal distilling in Glenlivet, though the area was to become one of the principal 'hotspots' for whisky smuggling during the following three decades. The illicit stills were usually of between 25 and 40 gallons in capacity, and according to Glenlivet man John Grant of Eskmore, 'scarcely a house but had a still . . . I have known 50 stills going at one time . . .'

Glenlivet smugglers could get 15 to 20 gallons of whisky on a horse, and one man might have two or three horses under his control. The 'real Glenlivet' was highly prized, and fetched at least a shilling in excess of more inferior illicit whiskies. Other Speyside illicit distillers would even buy Glenlivet and mix quantities with their own spirit in order to get higher prices from the people to whom they sold it.

George Smith recalled a raid in Glenlivet around 1819 which involved not just the usual excise officers but also the crew of a revenue cutter, operating quite a long way from the sea! This was at a time when the excise service was deploying more cutters in an effort to curtail illicit distilling, particularly in areas like the Firth of Clyde, though their crews also had their uses inland.

> They travelled all night, and got into the glen in the early morning. They got as far as the centre of the glen unmolested, and the gauger's eyes were rejoiced to see some forty or fifty smugglers' stills reeking away finely. But he soon saw another sight he did not like so well. The smugglers had been advised of their coming, and having collected to the number of several hundreds, suddenly made their appearance, and defied the gauger's party to molest a single still. The gauger had an idea of fighting; but the notion was banished by the cutter's men, who protested that their cutlasses and pistols were of no service against the splendid long guns with which the smugglers were armed.

The romantic view of whisky smugglers is of men armed with simple cudgels, opposing the forces of the law who were equipped with significant fire-power, but Smith's anecdote gives a slightly different view.

The dramatic story of how Smith of Glenlivet began to distil legitimately is best told in his own words, as reproduced in an 1868 interview for *The London Scotsman*.

About this time [around 1820] the Government, giving its mind to internal reforms, began to awaken to the fact that it might be possible to realize a considerable revenue from the whisky duty north of the Grampians. No doubt they were helped to this conviction by the grumbling of the south country distillers whose profits were destroyed by the number of kegs which used to come streaming down the mountain passes. The Highlanders had become demoralized through long impunity and the authorities thought it would be safer to use policy rather than force. The question was frequently debated in both Houses of Parliament and strong representations made to north country proprietors to use their influence in the cause of law and order. Pressure of this sort was brought to bear very strongly on Alexander, Duke of Gordon, who at length was stirred up to make a reply. The Highlanders, he said, were born distillers; whisky was their beverage from time immemorial, and they would have it and sell it too when tempted by so large a duty. But, said Duke Alexander, if the legislature would pass an Act affording the opportunity for the manufacture of whisky as good as the smuggled product at a reasonable duty easily payable, he and his brother proprietors of the Highlands would use their best endeavours to put down smuggling and encourage legal distilling. As the outcome of this pledge a bill was passed in 1823 to include Scotland, sanctioning the legal distillation of whisky at a duty of 2s. 3d. per wine gallon of proof spirit with £10 annual licence for any still above 40 gallons; none under that size being allowed.

This would seem a heavy burden to smuggling, and, for a year or two before, the farce of an attempt had been made to inflict a £20 penalty where any quantity of whisky was found manufactured or in process of manufacture. But there was no means of enforcing such a penalty for the smugglers laughed at attempts at seizure; and when the new Act was heard of, both in Glenlivet and in the Highlands of Aberdeenshire, they ridiculed the idea that anyone would be found daring enough to commence legal distilling in their midst. The proprietors were very anxious to fulfil their pledge to Government and did everything they could to encourage the commencement of legal distilling; but the desperate character of the smugglers and the violence of their threats deterred anyone for some time. At length in 1824, I, George Smith, who was then a robust young fellow and not given to be easily 'fleggit', determined to chance it. I was already a tenant of the Duke and received every encouragement from his Grace himself and from his factor Mr Skinner. The look-out was an ugly one, though. I was warned by my civil neighbours that they meant to burn the new distillery to the

ground, and me in the heart of it. The laird of Aberlour presented me
with a pair of hair trigger pistols worth ten guineas, and they were never
out of my belt for years. I got together two or three stout fellows for
servants, armed them with pistols, and let it be known everywhere that I
would fight for my place to the last shot. I had a pretty good character as
a man of my word and, through watching by turns every night for years,
we contrived to save the distillery from the fate so freely predicted for
it. But I often, both at kirk and market, had rough times of it among the
glen people; and if it had not been for the laird of Aberlour's pistols, I
don't think I should be telling you this story now. In 1825 and 1826 three
more legal distilleries were commenced in the glen, but the smugglers
very soon succeeded in frightening away their occupants, none of
whom ventured to hang on a single year in the face of threats uttered
so freely against them. Threats were not the only weapons used. In
1825 a distillery that had just been started near the Banks o' Dee at the
head of Aberdeenshire was burnt to the ground with all its outbuildings
and appliances, and the distiller had a very narrow escape from being
roasted alive in his own kiln. The country was in desperately lawless
state at this time. The riding officers of the Revenue were the mere
sport of smugglers, and nothing was more common than for them to be
shown a still at work and then coolly defied to make a seizure.

Smith was only once forced to use his 'hair-trigger pistols', which was
when he stopped at an inn at Cock Bridge on his way home from
a lucrative trip to the south. He was shown into a room filled with
vicious-looking characters, who eyed his bulky waistline – covering a
purse-belt bulging with gold – with curiosity. Deciding that his best
course of action would be to forestall any possible attack, he drew a
pistol and shattered the topmost peat in the blazing fire with one shot.
The other men left the room, and Smith remained unmolested.

After becoming a legitimate distiller, Smith enlarged his distillery,
and adapted it to work on more professional and productive lines. By
1826 he was producing around 100 gallons of spirit per week. In 1850
he built a new, larger, distillery at nearby Delnabo, which in turn was
superseded by the present plant at Minmore.

Initially his legal 'make' was transported overland to Perth and
Edinburgh, but later was exported by sea from the Moray coast, at
Burghead and Garmouth, where it was taken by pack-horses, which
were often escorted by Smith himself to ensure its safe delivery.

The opposition of illegal distillers to Smith was not based simply
on a belief that he was a traitor to the cause. They knew that his
legal operation would bring excise officers to Glenlivet on legitimate
business, and they certainly did not want that. From the authorities'
point of view, the idea of having a legal distillery in Glenlivet in the
wake of the 1823 Excise Act was a very attractive one. Not only was it

clearly an excellent place in which to make whisky, but there was also obvious symbolic significance in having a new, legitimate operation in the very heartland of illicit distilling country.

Nonetheless, James Skinner, factor to the duke of Gordon at Drumin where George Smith distilled, wrote in September 1826 to Gordon Castle in response to a request by his lordship for a list of tenants who were engaged in smuggling. 'I much fear there are few names indeed in the rental who are not concerned directly or indirectly in the traffic except the gentlemen who occupy farms in the lower ends of Glenlivet and Strathavon.'

Excise figures for the Elgin Collection in the year ending July 1824 relate 3,000 detections of illicit distilling, with some 400 stills working in Glenlivet and the neighbouring Cabrach and Glenrinnes areas. It was said that up to 300 bolls of barley per week were being transported from the Lowlands to the area for distilling during the latter part of 1823.

In *The Origin of Glenlivet Whisky, With Some Account of the Smuggling*, published in 1897, J. Gordon Phillips wrote: 'I have followed the course of one stream which runs down between two mountains in the Braes of Glenlivet and counted the remains of thirteen bothies, but at one time there were over twenty by the same burn-side.'

He also observed, 'It may be supposed that smuggling led to habits of intemperance, yet as a matter of fact the heaviest drinking smuggler of which I am aware was a woman. Many anecdotes are told about her. I am not going to mention her name, for she may have friends still living . . . As stated, however, the men were not heavy drinkers. Certain it is that, contrary to general belief, the whisky manufactured was vile.'

Phillips recalled a smuggling bothy on the 'Burn of the Ladder' where there was a big stone located next to a well. The alarm signal for an imminent visit by the gaugers was for someone to take another stone and knock upon the large one three times. That was heard in the bothy, and the distillers inside knew to sit tight. Writing of the 'black pots', Phillips noted, 'these vessels were manufactured in Keith, and there was often considerable difficulty in getting them conveyed to the Glen owing to the watchful eyes of the Excisemen'.

He also makes interesting observations about the smugglers' *modus operandi*, and the typical leniency shown by certain authority figures regarding cases of illicit distilling.

> They took out a licence for the making of malt, say a couple of quarters of barley, to make *beer* for themselves and their family. Instead of a couple of quarters, they would make six, or as many as they had money to buy the barley. When the Excisemen or Preventives came round and

discovered that they had infringed the law, they were summoned to appear before the Justices of the Peace at Keith, when they would be fined to the extent of half-a-crown and sometimes as low as sixpence. I have heard it related that the smugglers always liked to see the Earl of Fife and the Cripple Captain on the bench. When those gentlemen dispensed justice they were rarely fined more than sixpence, which the Earl of Fife usually paid himself. Captain Grant – the Cripple Captain – was a Glenlivet man and lived at Achorachan, consequently he had no desire to inflict heavy penalties.

Sometimes there were not lacking signs of sympathy on the part of the Revenue officers. This was more particularly the case with the regular Excisemen. They did not like the work of going searching people's barns and other places for malt. They considered that it was not their legitimate duty. The Preventives, on the other hand, were much stricter, and so earned the hatred of the smugglers and of all the people.

I commenced smuggling with my father at Milltown, Inveravon when I was a boy. We sold our whiskey to the late John Grant afterwards Distiller at Glengrant and people from Aberdeen, Perth and the South, to whom it was all sold as Glenlivet. It commanded a higher price being Glenlivet. All the smuggled whiskey made in that district was called Glenlivet. My father James Howie, who died long ago, and I started a Distillery at Dalnashaugh in the parish of Inveravon about the year 1823. We called it Dalnashaugh Distillery. We sold the whiskey as Glenlivet. We carried on the Distillery till Whitsunday 1827 when it was stopped.

– Archibald Howie, April 1883

According to a Speyside character interviewed during the mid-1950s for the archives of the School of Scottish Studies in Edinburgh, local lore insisted that there were still many kegs of whisky hidden in Strathdon and lost – waiting to be stumbled across in peat hags and moorland bogs. The same interviewee reckoned that the last illicit whisky made in Glenlivet was produced around 1900 by James Gillies and associates, and that much of the actual distilling was undertaken by women during the winter months.

Along with Glenlivet, nearby Glenbuchat in Upper Donside was traditionally another great centre for illicit distilling, sharing as it did with its neighbour the advantage of considerable remoteness. In *The Book of Glenbuchat* (1942) W. D. Simpson wrote that a still could be found in the glen as late as 1906, 'But knowing the penalty attached to such a possession, those in the secret would be slow to disclose its whereabouts'. Earlier generations had not been so timid, however. 'It is not too much to say that every man in the glen was directly or indirectly interested in smuggling, either in making whisky or in transporting it to the low country.'

By 1845, however, the local minister, Rev. Robert Scott, was able to write in the *New Statistical Account* that 'The improvements in every respect, since illicit distillation has been happily put down, are truly astonishing. The people are generally hardy, active and intellectual . . .' We should never forget, however, that the church was hardly an unbiased observer in such matters.

Glenlivet may once have had more stills than anywhere else on Speyside, but today the place with the greatest concentration of distilleries is Dufftown, to the north-east of Glenlivet. Many of the old illicit distilling tales centre on the Banffshire village and its environs, not to mention some more recent ones, too.

Take a drive from Dufftown over the Cabrach to Rhynie, and before you drop down into lush Aberdeenshire farmland you pass through some of the most bleakly beautiful terrain you are likely to encounter in Scotland. The Cabrach was a legendary haunt of distillers, and it is not difficult to see how daunting the area must have been for excise officers attempting to curtail their activities. The same applies to the journey along the B9009 through Glen Rinnes and into Glenlivet. 'The Cabrach was the last place they'd be making illicit whisky', according to a retired Dufftown distillery worker. 'That's if it's stopped there yet . . .'

Today in Dufftown, the heritage of the old-time whisky-makers remains strong. The clocktower at the centre of the village square was home to a clandestine distilling operation for many years. The distiller's bold theory was that passing excise officers would not notice the smell in a town with so many legal distilleries in production, and the liquid effluent of distilling was cunningly discharged into the town drains. Smoke was disposed of by way of a chimney that looked like a lightning conductor. The story is that the still was only discovered when an excise officer who was a keen amateur horologist eagerly climbed the stairs to the top of the tower, having noticed that the clock had stopped. He was confronted by an unmoving clock mechanism and a very lively still.

The village's excellent Whisky Museum also features a display of illicit stills of varying ages and degrees of subtlety, captured in a wide variety of locations. With the co-operation of HM Customs & Excise service the Dufftown Whisky Museum assembled this range of illicit stills for the autumn 2001 Speyside Whisky Festival, and it is now on permanent display there.

Included is a copper pot still discovered in the Mortlach distillery office, which was one of the first items acquired by the museum. The age and pre-Mortlach origins of the still are not known, but it is manufactured from a 'Greybeard' type of jug as used in the distilling industry, with a ball-cock from a toilet cistern and copper piping leading to a copper 'worm' which would have been immersed in a wooden tub with water running through it.

Simplest but most fascinating of all the stills on show is the 'Gordon Still', originally made by an Italian engineer for Major General Charles Gordon, hero of Khartoum, to distil drinking water in the desert. After Gordon's death in 1885 the still was sold off with other effects, and was ultimately seized by Customs & Excise when being used for illicit distillation of spirits.

The still consisted of the main vessel in which the wash would be heated and a worm in which either water (originally) or spirit (later) would condense before passing into a container. Unfortunately, the second container, along with the still's stand, has been lost.

There are also two 'ship' stills, one of which was recovered in September 2000 from a wardrobe in an unoccupied cabin of the Maltese-flagged vessel MV *Manley Havant*, which had docked in Invergordon with a cargo of fishmeal. During a routine search the still was discovered, producing a pleasant-tasting, blackcurrant-flavoured liquor when sampled in the receiver. The Ukrainian crew denied all knowledge of its presence.

The second was also recovered during 2000 from a ship in Invergordon during a search for drugs and contraband goods. It was probably designed to run on cheap cereal or potatoes, and was fashioned from a milk urn, connected to a condenser made out of a fire extinguisher.

A third piece of distilling apparatus was recovered at an earlier date from a ship manned by sailors from the old Eastern Bloc, and was based on the design of a Soviet Union home still. It was legal in the old Soviet Union to distil spirits for personal consumption – a practice outlawed by the 'enlightened' British Government in 1781! This apparatus is actually two separate stills, one of which is of an older design, and the pair were probably used in tandem at one time. They were almost certainly designed to distil from potatoes, and the resultant liquor was often blended with fruit and left in jars for as long as possible before consumption. As in the old days of Highland whisky-making, this gave flavour to, and took the harsh edges off, the new spirit.

To make illicit distilling in the Dufftown area even more tangible, Geoff Armitage of Highland Activity Holidays conducts guided walks up to Corryhabbie in Glenrinnes during the Speyside Whisky Festivals. The trek to Corryhabbie begins on the metalled road that leads to Glenrinnes graveyard, no more than a stone's throw from one of Speyside's most modern distilleries, Seagram Brothers' 1970s Allt a Bhainne.

'There's a ruin there which has two former barley-steeping pits', says Armitage, 'and I show people those, and just generally tell them about the olden days of smuggling. Corryhabbie is a very remote area, so there would certainly have been quite a lot of illicit distilling going on, and not just the one operation. One of the problems of trying to bring it to life is that there is very little left on the ground to show where it took place. The equipment was easily portable, and the distillers would have used heather-thatched bothies, which didn't have long lives.'

'They'd be making whisky for their own consumption and also to sell probably, until the middle of the nineteenth century, I'd say. There are stories of pony-trains full of illicit whisky going from Speyside as far as Edinburgh to sell, but I don't think that can have happened very often, and from the Dufftown area they'd not have gone much further than Elgin or Aberdeen. If you think about the economics of longer trips it doesn't really make much sense. One pony would carry two 18-gallon barrels at most, so you'd need quite a lot to make it worthwhile, and by the time you'd paid the men and fed all the ponies you'd not have a lot of profit, considering you'd be selling the stuff at less than the legal market price'.

Robbie Macpherson was the best-known distiller in the area during the eighteenth century, and it is almost certainly his home to which Armitage guides visitors. Macpherson moved with his wife Margaret to Upper Folds, Corryhabbie, probably during the 1760s or '70s, and started working a derelict croft, going on to build a primitive house on the site. He began to distil whisky, but had lots of visits from the excisemen after the passing of the 1784 Wash Act, and moved his still to a more remote part of the glen. Robbie was a rare creature in that he aged his whisky in oak casks to improve its flavour, hiding them in places dug into various hillsides. Remnants of three distilling bothies can still be seen in the area, one by the Easter Burn, and two close to Corryhabbie Burn.

Robbie and his fellow Glenrinnes distillers would smuggle the spirit they had made in winter to ports such as Banff and Buckie during the summer months in well-organised convoys, with whisky hidden among legitimate goods such as sacks of barley and bales of wool. The Glenrinnes men were warned of the imminent arrival of excise officers in the area by means of a beacon lit on Conval Hill by sympathetic folk from Dufftown, and also on Meg's Wood, a hill south of Dufftown.

On one occasion, when Robbie's still was in need of replacing, he and his friends set up a dummy distilling bothy, complete with worn equipment in situ, and one of them was dispatched to Dufftown to report finding the bothy. He was duly paid to keep watch on it with an excise officer, and after a week's employment of this nature, he had received enough money to be able to replace the worn-out still.

When Robbie was an old man and the excise officers had made it almost impossible for the Corryhabbie men to distil in safety, Donald Cameron, a crofter from The Shank in the glen, came up with an ingenious idea. His plan was to divert the water from the Corryhabbie Burn in a ditch down to the hill known as Little Laprach, where the excise officers would not suspect distilling to be taking place. The ditch was a mile in length and took several months of night work to complete, before finally a bothy was built in a hollow beside the 'new' burn. The high-quality whisky distilled in the bothy was sold widely during the next few years, and was known as 'Laprach whisky'.

Another legendary smuggling figure in the area was James Smith, familiarly known as 'Goshen'. At Ballindalloch, Glenfarclas distillery displays the actual still seized in March 1888 from Goshen in the parish of Glass by a team of revenue officers from nearby Huntly. Goshen was one of the most celebrated illicit distillers of his day, being renowned for the quality of make he produced.

He was born around 1800, and ran a croft called Stoniley, at Beldorney, not far from Huntly, where he distilled large quantities of high-quality whisky, being wily enough to avoid detection until he was a very old man.

The excise officers tried many tricks to catch Goshen, even sending in an undercover man dressed as a passing tramp on one occasion. Goshen gave the 'tramp' some soup, but was suspicious when he asked for a drop of whisky to warm him. Claiming (probably correctly) that he never kept alcohol in the house, Goshen told the tramp that a second bowl of soup would be far better for him, and the exciseman duly departed.

In old age, however, Goshen let his guard slip, allowing neighbours to watch him working at his still, but the manner of his detection was extraordinary. It did not come from some jealous fellow-distiller or a paid informant, but was wheedled out of Sir William Grant during a London dinner engagement. Grant was in conversation with a senior figure in the excise service, though he did not realise his fellow dinner guest's occupation at the time. The exciseman was intrigued to hear Grant's story of sampling Goshen's whisky while staying at Beldorney, and the result was that on 14 March 1888 a group of excise officials led by the Huntly Officer descended on Stoniley and began a thorough search of the property. A 20-gallon still and a 40-gallons mash tub were duly discovered in a carefully hidden bothy, which the party actually located by chance, and more distilling equipment and some sacks of ground malt were also found in an outbuilding.

Goshen duly appeared in court in Keith on 17 April, and was fined the modest sum of £10, largely thanks to a skilful defence lawyer who painted a picture of a poor, weak old man. Goshen's equipment was, of course, forfeited, and this event marked the end of his distilling career.

One of Goshen's descendants is octogenarian innkeeper Dorothy Brandie, who presides over the tiny, idiosyncratic Fiddichside Inn, near Craigellachie. She keeps a photograph of her ancestor on the wall of the bar, and is scornful of suggestions that any illegal whisky-making might still go on today. She makes the point that the *need* to distil has long disappeared, that, despite taxation, whisky is now affordable to the average man, which was not always the case.

⊱≈≈≈⊱

In 1922/23 *The Dufftown News and Speyside Advertiser* carried an anonymously contributed, 15-part serialisation about Donald Macpherson's life as a whisky smuggler. Although some of the events, and all of the dialogue, must of necessity be fictional, Macpherson was a real person, born around 1789 at Claggan, near Inveravon and resident in Glenrinnes, dying at Achlochrach in March 1871. It can be assumed that many of the incidents chronicled in the newspaper had been passed down in local lore through the half-century between Macpherson's death and the writing of the articles, so many of the events described probably did happen.

Much of the story is occupied with accounts of Macpherson's ongoing battle of wits with his arch-enemy, Barret, the local supervisor of excise. In the introductory episode the writer notes:

> Notwithstanding the pains, penalties, fines, and forfeitures, Donald contrived to '"mak" his wee drappie,' and if questioned as to the morality of such proceeding, his reasoning was at least quaint if not very logical.
>
> 'There's naething wrang in makin' a drappie for yersel' an' frien, but if thae billies (the excisemen) catch ye they'll gar ye pay for what ye've made an' what ye hinna, besides takin' every dish (vessel) ye hae,' and with this reasoning he was satisfied.

Donald Macpherson is described as being

a crofter, farming a small strip of land near the base of the Little Conval, a little above Lettoch wood...Donald's croft extended on both sides of the burn that flows into the river Dullan . . . nearly halfway up the side of the Conval, and in a number of places was thickly studded with trees.

Here Donald resided with his wife Janet . . . [whose] capacity for work seemed inexhaustible, and it was well nigh impossible to pass the place without finding her either washing or busy in the wash-house boiling 'neeps' for kye.

The writer then goes into great detail as to how the distilling operation actually worked and how it was concealed.

The copper in which the 'neeps' were boiled was the most wonderful article about the establishment. Situated in corner of the wash-house, and surrounded by bricks which formed a sort of rude furnace, it seemed the only useful article the room contained. A number of wash tubs in all stages of demolition littered the floor, while in a corner adjacent to that in which the copper was placed a mound of peats. A close observer might wonder why the brickwork surrounding the copper did not reach to within some six inches of its edge, but he would naturally put that down as a matter of detail. It was not a matter of detail however, but served a very useful purpose as the reader will understand further on. The peats in the corner also served a twofold purpose, for besides making a fire to boil the copper, they also concealed a hole in the wall about three feet in diameter, forming the entrance to a short passage which ran under the 'knowe' at the back of the wash-house. At a few yards' distance from the entrance this passage opened out into a fairly large cave, which ran directly under the knowe. Here were situated two wash-backs or fermenting vessels formed from two puncheons placed on their ends, and having one of the heads knocked out. From these issued the pungent odour of escaping carbonic acid gas, which showed that fermentation was actively progressing. On the floor, beside the fermenting vessels, lay a third composed of copper, and very much resembling that in the wash-house. It differed from it in this however, that instead of having the ordinary bottom, its sides were drawn into a long and tapering curve, not unlike a gigantic cow's horn. Suppose this extra-ordinary looking vessel were taken and placed in an inverted position over the copper in the wash-house, it would be found to exactly fit that part of the edge that was left bare – in fact, the fit would be found so exact that a little of the tenacious clay from the bed of the burn plastered over the join would render it air tight. The other end – the curved and tapering end – would now be found to fit a small hole in the wall which separated the cave from the wash-house. An examination of this part of the wall would reveal, right beneath the hole and in a detached portion of the cave, a hogshead on its end, with the head knocked out, and containing a copper tube coiled inside. This vessel was always kept filled with water, a supply of which reached it from the burn running in front of the wash-house.

The reader will naturally inquire as to the use of all these vessels in a wash-house, and why they have been so minutely described.

I will tell him.

The vessels from which the pungent gas was escaping were used for the manufacturing of *wash* from the wort already made in one of the apparently useless vessels on the floor of the wash-house; the vessel containing the copper spiral was a worm tub, and the copper in which Janet boiled the 'neeps for the kye' nothing else but a small still when the head (that curved portion lying on the floor of the cave) was placed in position.

As the ground on which Donald's house stood was at a considerable elevation above the surrounding fields, it was impossible to approach it without coming under the observation of Janet's lynx eye, when she would hurry down to the wash-house and pretend she was engaged in her everyday work.

'Donald Macpherson did not run the risk of making malt at the Lettoch. Not only had he no accommodation for doing so, but he found he could buy it already ground from the numerous malting bothies in the neighbourhood – especially from the mill of Auchindoun – more cheaply and with less risk to himself. This mill was situated in a particularly favoured place for carrying on illicit operations. To the north-east were the valley of the Fiddich and the outlying district of Botriphine, while the south and south-west were guarded by the dreary moorland of the Cabrach and the wooded fastness of Glenfiddich forest. The former, in particular was a favourite habitat of the smuggling fraternity, as during the winter months the frost and snow rendered the roads impassable, and therefore a thorough search of the place by Revenue Officers and their satellites, the preventive men, was utterly impossible.

One night, according to our anonymous chronicler, Donald was returning from the mill with a sack of malt, also carrying a sack of meal by way of 'cover' on the back of his pony. The excisemen had long suspected Donald of illicit distilling, and that night they were lying in wait close to his home. The pony didn't like strangers, and knowing this, Donald contrived to manoeuvre her into a position where she kicked out at one of the two gaugers as they attempted to examine her cargo. While the second gauger was helping his colleague to his feet, under the cover of darkness, Donald slipped the sack of malt over the parapet of the bridge at which he had been apprehended. He also proceeded to lament the spilling of the meal, some of which had landed on the road as the pony took exception to the exciseman's attention, and Donald surreptitiously loosened the string around the neck of the bag. Sensing that he had the upper hand, the apparently innocent Donald insisted that he would take the matter before the sheriff unless the officers would write a note for the miller, giving Donald another sack of meal at their expense. This, he said, would prove to his wife that the loss of the meal was not his fault. The officers agreed, and Donald ultimately arrived home with his malt, retrieved from the ridge embankment, along with the note for a new sack of meal, not to mention the almost full sack of meal which he had collected from the road!

Another Macpherson victory occurred on an occasion when Barret raided the Macpherson holding with a party of gaugers, intent on finding the still. Knowing that they were about to search the wash-house Janet Macpherson

> secured a quantity of pepper which she hid upon her person. On arriving at the wash-house she proceeded to fill all the empty tubs it contained with foul water from the cesspool – particularly that portion into which the stable drained, and which was largely impregnated with carbonate of ammonia. This accomplished she took a number of half-burnt peats from beneath the copper and flung them into the liquid, producing a hissing sound and a dense cloud of smoke, the stench from which was unbearable. Nor was she satisfied with this. Getting some cotton waste, which Donald was in the habit of using when fixing the head of the still, she dusted the pepper carefully over it and set it on fire. She then divided it into several pieces, which she deposited in various parts of the building, and allowed it to smoulder.

When Barret and his associates barged into the wash-house, Janet closed the door behind them, and the Macphersons waited a while before approaching the door, 'where coughing and sneezing at a great rate proclaimed the effect of Janet's drastic application to their unwelcome visitors'.

Janet duly opened the door, insisting that the officers must have let it close behind them.

> When Janet opened the door they were left in total darkness, and blinded with smoke and almost suffocated with the fumes coming from the tubs, it is little wonder they were unable to find the door. In their efforts, however, to gain this means of escape several of them tumbled over the various utensils lying about the floor, sustaining sundry cuts and bruises, and a large addition of soot and mud to their faces and various other parts of their bodies.

Donald again took the moral high ground, and was vociferous in his condemnation of the officers for causing damage in the building.

> The supervisor stormed and fumed, but all to no purpose; Donald had got the first word of the argument, and he meant also to have the last. Indeed, to a person not acquainted with the whole circumstances

it would appear that the officers had exceeded their powers and taken unwarrantable liberties with things they had no business meddling with, and Donald took care to let them understand this . . . Under the circumstances it is little wonder that Barret was only too glad to call off his men and beat a hasty retreat.

Clearly, Janet Macpherson was one of those doughty women in the mould of Helen Cumming of Cardow (see *In From The Cold*), whose contribution to the success of so many illicit distilling ventures in Scotland is frequently overlooked.

Barret was more determined than ever to catch Donald Macpherson now, and came up with what seemed a suitably cunning plan. On his way into Dufftown one day, Donald passed a stranger, apparently a tourist, who appeared to be somehow familiar. The appearance of the stranger unsettled the smuggler, and after conducting his business in Dufftown he visited an inn to see if a rare legal dram would help cure his apprehension. 'Here he found Jock Grant, who was on his way to the Lettoch to purchase an anker for distribution among the worthies of Pitglassie, among whom Donald's manufacture seemed to be in perpetual demand.'

The pair set off home, and when Donald told Jock Grant about his concerns, Grant replied 'I think I could gi'e a guid guess wha the person is, an' if I'm richt ye canna be hame ower seen. I forgot to tell ye that I heard in Dufftown the day that Barret had shaved off his beard, an' if I'm no' mista'en he was the very party ye met'.

Approaching the croft, the pair heard Janet's raised voice saying 'Gie ye a dram o' speerits, will I, an' ye'll pay me weel for it an' I'm no' to let Donald ken aboot it. Troth ye're very obliging, Mister Barret, an' when I'm sae hard up as to sell my ain conscience an' my husband I'll come to ye for advice an' the siller.'

By the time Donald and Jock Grant reached the croft Janet had deposited Barret head first in the 'meal bowie', and the pair struggled to extricate him before he suffocated. On removal,

> the upper portion of his body, face, and hair (for his hat was on a chair when Janet assisted him into the bowie) had assumed that of a miller who had not had a wash or brush for a week. Despite the gravity of the situation Donald could not refrain from a guffaw at the odd appearance presented by Barret, whose body from the waist up presented an appearance so much at variance with the remainder, which was encased in spotless black. In this he was joined by Jock Grant, who enjoyed the ludicrous appearance equally well with that of the discomfiture of the supervisor.

Once again, a potentially disastrous situation was turned against the forces of the law, as Jock Grant said, 'This is a very serious matter, entering a person's house during the owner's absence, where there are none but a defenceless woman present [here he glanced quizzically at Janet], and this, too, without a warrant, and endeavouring by bribes to entice that woman to conspire to render her husband guilty of an offence against the law. The case would have been bad enough had the woman been a stranger to Donald, but his own wife! Why, I believe any judge would at least transport, if he did not hang you for it'.

'An' noo that ye've heard the law on the subject,' added Donald, 'tak' yersel' oot o' this wi' yer claes as they are, an' dinna let me see ye aboot here again'.

And so the over-zealous Barret had to return to Dufftown in his present position a sadder and a wiser man.

The Mill of Auchindoun (or Auchindown), as patronised by Donald Macpherson, is located on the Huntly road, three miles east of Dufftown. Until the first decade of the twentieth century a number of distillers were working there. According to *The District of Moray: An Architectural Guide*, 'The Mill of Auchindoun . . . was the site of a busy co-operative of illicit distillers in Edwardian times; only rumbled by the excise after clyping by one who grudged his share of the profits.' One distiller was subsequently sentenced to three month's imprisonment, though just before the law arrived the still was dismantled and buried in a peat hag on the Cabrach. A local gamekeeper, Alec Nicol, knew where it was, and later sold it to Willie Taylor of the Speyside Cooperage in Craigellachie for £20. The last recorded arrest for illicit distilling in the Dufftown area took place at the mill in 1934, during a brief resurgence in the popularity of illicit distilling.

The tale is told of a farm at Newley, not far from Milltown of Auchindown, where an illicit still was hidden in a mill-pond during the 1920s or '30s. The pond was regularly drained under cover of darkness to reveal the distilling apparatus. Before the sun rose next morning, with a run completed, the pond was filled again, leaving no trace of the submerged still! The same Dufftown source of this story also insists that during their lifetime, what the Irish would call 'parliament whisky' was cut with the illicit stuff and sold in the bar of a well-known, remote Speyside hostelry.

Auchindoun is the subject of a lengthy anonymous ballad, written in the style of the old ballads which celebrated victories over the gaugers during the early years of the nineteenth century, though this one is thought to have been composed sometime between the two World Wars. It goes by the title of 'The Gagers' Raid on Auchindown'.

It commemorates an occasion when the local excise officers held a ball in Dufftown Hall, and the illicit distillers of the parish apparently took the opportunity to distil with something close to safety:

> The smugglers thocht this was their chance,
> To brew a drappie whisky,
> The gagers' a' bein' at the dance,
> T'wad no be just so risky.

> On gaied the pots, in gaeid the ma't,
> Oot cam the sparklin' speerit,
> An' afore the gagers' ball broke up,
> Baith stills and pigs were beerit.

When the excisemen got wind of what had been happening they mounted a large but abortive night-time raid on Auchindown and other places where illicit distilling might have been taking place.

> On Sunday night the raid began,
> Through Auchindown the motors ran,
> Excisemen and policemen, they numbered a score,
> And sic a night in Auchindown was never seen afore.

However, apart from one old man's 'great grandsire's wirm pipe' they returned to Dufftown empty-handed.

The ballad concludes, with a nod in the direction of Burns:

> Noo that's a sample o' the wark
> That's deen by oor excisemen,
> You cudna blame the deil himsel',
> For thinkin' they're nae prize man.

⁂

At Benromach distillery, near Forres, there is a photograph captioned 'An illicit still – somewhere on Speyside'. It is carefully posed, with distilling equipment laid out in neat, parallel lines, and a man of later middle age sits at a bench, his still in front of him, gas burner aflame. What is most notable is that the style of the man's coat and cap suggest he is not some nineteenth-century distiller, but that this photo could have been taken in the 1950s.

Perhaps it was taken in Keith, since the distilling town which is home to the famous Strathisla distillery seems to have been something of a 'hotspot' for latter-day unlicensed whisky-making. Newspaper reports provide two interesting examples of illicit distilling in Keith during the decade before the Second World War.

On 8 January 1934 the owner of the Gordon Arms Hotel in Keith was charged at Banff Sheriff Court with having 'between September and 29

A. The Still	L. A Pewter Crane
B. The Worm-tub	M. A Pewter Valencia
C. The Pump	N. Hippocrates bag or Flannel Sleeve
D. Water-tub	
E. A Press	O. Poker Fire-shovel Cole-rake
FFF Tubs to hold the goods	P. A Box of Bungs
GGGG Canns of different size	Q. The Worm within the Worm-tub mark'd with prick'd lines
H. A Wood Funnel with a iron nosel	
I. A large Vessel to put the Fains or after-runnings	R. A Piece of Wood to keep down the Head of the Still to prevent flying of
K. Tin pump	

OLD DISTILLING UTENSILS, 1738

Highland Bothy, The Alarm

Sandy MacGruar's Bothy, Strathglass

Whisky still, engraving after a painting by Landseer, 1827
(School of Scottish Studies, Edinburgh University)

Whisky still, engraving after a painting by Landseer, 1827
(School of Scottish Studies, Edinburgh University)

TWO SEIZURES BY THE SAME REVENUE OFFICERS C.1890
(HM CUSTOMS & EXCISE, GREENOCK)

PORTRAIT OF GEORGE SMITH, FOUNDER
OF THE GLENLIVET DISTILLERY
(CHIVAS BROTHERS)

ILLICIT STILL SEIZED FROM A SHIP IN
INVERGORDON HARBOUR, 2000

ILLICIT STILL SEIZED IN GLASGOW 1922
(HM CUSTOMS & EXCISE, GREENOCK)

STILL FROM WEST COAST OF ROSS-SHIRE
(HM CUSTOMS & EXCISE, GREENOCK)

THE OLD SMUGGLER ENTERTAINS THE "GAUGERS" DINGWALL C.1926
(HM CUSTOMS & EXCISE, GREENOCK)

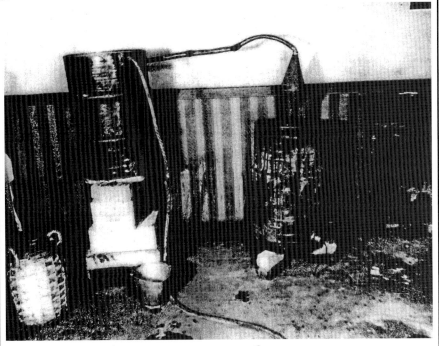

AN ILLICIT STILL SEIZED IN GLASGOW 1943
(HM CUSTOMS & EXCISE, GREENOCK)

RUINS OF THE ORIGINAL GLENLIVET
DISTILLERY AT UPPER DRUMIN, 1924
(CHIVAS BROTHERS)

A DISTILLERY WORKER SAMPLES
THE SPIRIT PRODUCED FROM THE
REPLICA 500-YEAR-OLD POT STILL
DEVELOPED AT INVERGORDON
GRAIN DISTILLERY
(KYNDAL INTERNATIONAL)

TOP.
OUTBUILDING,
ALLEGED TO BE THE
SITE OF AN OLD STILL,
SMEARISARY, MOIDART,
INVERNESS-SHIRE, PHOTO
BY IAN WHITAKER, 1959
(SCHOOL OF SCOTTISH STUDIES,
UNIVERSITY OF EDINBURGH)

MIDDLE.
FIONA MURDOCH OF
THE WHISKY SHOP IN
DUFFTOWN, SPEYSIDE,
WITH AN ILLICIT STILL
FROM THE TOWN'S
WHISKY MUSEUM

BOTTOM.
THE ILLEGAL
MOIDART MUSEUM

December 1933, in an underground cellar at the Gordon Arms Hotel, without being licensed to do so, had or used a still for distilling and rectifying spirits, brewed or made wort or wash, and distilled low wines, feints and spirits in contravention of the Spirits Act, 1880, thereby being liable to a fine of £500 and forfeiture of all materials and utensils'.

During an unrelated search of the hotel cellar, two policemen had discovered a locked door, which the landlord insisted gave access to a cupboard, but for which he did not have a key. The policemen duly forced the door, only to discover 'a copper still, with a capacity of twelve gallons, a copper worm, 15.7 proof gallons of spirit of fairly good, indeed, quite good quality; thirty-six gallons of wash, a liquid in preparation of being made into spirits; three or four gallons of low wines and feints; eighteen packets of yeast; three bushels of malted barley, and a considerable quantity of vessels and utensils for use with the still'.

Note the careful description 'fairly good, indeed quite good quality' spirit, which suggests very conscientious sampling!

The result of the trial was that the hotelier was fined £150, and a local carrier, who was charged with handling the spirit, was fined £50. This had been no still for domestic or local use – as the carrier's role had been to distribute the whisky in Aberdeen and even further afield.

Then, during the summer of 1937, one Adam Riddoch of Gateside in Keith appeared in Banff Sheriff Court on a charge of having an illicit still in his house.

Riddoch pleaded not guilty, and claimed that coils of copper tubing found by excise officers during a raid on his home were to be used in a wireless transmitter, that the purpose of a 60-gallon tank was to hold water for photographic developing purposes, and three and a half hundredweight of barley was being stored in readiness for the purchase of hens. The sheriff, in his wisdom, found the case not proven. Perhaps he was a customer . . .

The tradition of illicit distilling persisted on Speyside in the years after the war, with a farmer on the outskirts of Rothes making whisky, while Alan Winchester, manager of Aberlour distillery, recalls older workers in the whisky industry telling him that in the years immediately after the Second World War some of their colleagues were stealing wash from one of the reopened distilleries, situated not far from Aberlour.

Winchester refuses to name it, but the likelihood is that it was Dailuaine, as that was one of the first distilleries in the area to recommence distilling. 'The story', says Winchester 'is that guys were taking quantities of the wash, not to drink themselves, as often happened, but to distil. They were going out with six or seven per cent alcohol, and they set up a still at the falls above Aberlour distillery in order to distil it. They were selling it as far away as Elgin, and the ringleader was very nearly caught. He got away, and ended up as a prominent councillor in London!'

Ed Dodson, manager of Glen Moray distillery in Elgin, has an anecdote relating to the war years in Dufftown, where many troops were quartered in distilleries which had been closed down for the duration of hostilities.

'A regiment was billeted in Glendullan distillery, and one day they decided to hitch up a truck to the bars on one of the warehouses and pull them off in order to get in and take some of the whisky. They duly did this, climbed in, prised open the first cask they came to, and started to drink it. It turned out that the cask they had chosen contained some of the feints from the last run before closing. The excise would have insisted it was casked, and it would have been used for the first distillation when production began again. You can't help wondering whether they just left the rest of the whisky alone, thinking it would all have tasted like that!'

Dodson also recalls an occasion during the 1970s when an excise officer from one of the Dufftown distilleries was out for a drink with his son in the town of Keith. He asked the barman for a dram of X, from the distillery where he was based. On being told that the bar did not stock it, he became quite voluble in his indignation. Suddenly one of his fellow drinkers sidled up to him and said 'You like X then? I can get you some if you like, and the proper stuff, straight from the distillery.' 'Can you now?' replied the excise officer, unable to believe his good fortune. 'Well, I'd be very interested in that.' Too interested for the hapless 'smuggler', and the upshot was that several members of staff at X distillery were dismissed for theft of new spirit.

Ian Millar is manager of Glenfiddich distillery in Dufftown, having started work at Bell's Blair Athol distillery in his native Pitlochry in Perthshire, where he graduated to the role of brewer. Before joining William Grant & Sons Ltd at Glenfiddich he was based at the Dufftown distillery of Mortlach. Ian has many entertaining stories concerning the smuggling of spirit from legal premises.

It was customary for workers to have a metal tube or 'dog' in which to conceal spirit, and in addition to an example of a copper dog, the Dufftown Whisky Museum has a medium-sized hipflask from Mortlach distillery which would have been carried under the arm by the excise officer. Alongside that in the window display stands a vast flask that would have been used by the manager. According to Ian, 'it's so big and would have been so heavy when filled that he'd have carried it on his stomach. Presumably the manager was always fatter when he was going home on Friday afternoons for the weekend!

'When salaries got better and more bottles were legally given to staff by the companies there was less incentive to take the stuff, and more to lose if you were caught. I'd got a wife, two kids and a mortgage, so I wasn't going to do anything stupid.'

Talking about the art of smuggling whisky out of distilleries by employees, one former Dufftown distillery worker said, 'Some of it was taken to be sold, but a lot of it was really just about beating the system, it was the sport', a sentiment that perhaps echoes the raison d'être behind much of the illicit distilling that once took place.

Willie Strathdee, octogenarian former excise officer at many Dufftown distilleries, recalls a warehouseman who was working without gloves one day asking for an elastoplast for a cut from a barrel splinter. It transpired that the plaster was, in fact, to seal a leak on the rubber tube the warehouseman had concealed down his trouser leg in order to draw spirit from casks into his dog.

'The guys with the sauce bottles and the hot water bottles round their waists were fussy,' says Ian Millar. 'They'd sample a few casks before deciding what was the good stuff and taking that!'

Ian remarks that it was common practice for a slater/joiner and a plumber to work together on warehouse construction projects, and it was not unknown for such pairs of tradesmen to build hatches into the roofs of warehouses across Speyside. One was allegedly installed at a prominent distillery not unassociated with Johnnie Walker. The practice came to light when the excitement of getting into a warehouse one night proved too much for one of the hatch-builders, who had a heart attack, and subsequently died, having been discreetly removed from the premises and sent to hospital by the manager of the distillery concerned.

'Last year some guys came down in a Land Rover from around the Elgin and Lhanbryde area to get spirit out of empty casks at Glenfiddich,' notes Ian. 'And they were selling it for £5 a litre. There were 70,000 casks on site at the time, so they had plenty to go at. Apparently they were doing the same at the Speyside Cooperage at Craigellachie for a time. They cut a hole in the perimeter fence and drilled holes in the casks to drain them. We've all had to improve our security since then.'

Richard Forsyth is the third generation of his family to be involved in running the well-known Rothes-based coppersmith company of

A. Forsyth & Son (Rothes) Ltd, which works closely with the Scotch whisky industry. Richard recalls that 'there was a coppersmithing business in Rothes in the mid-1800s, and they probably made equipment for the illicit distillers.

'My grandfather, Alexander Forsyth, founded the present firm, and he was Provost of Rothes, a pillar of society, who never missed a church service, yet he was fond of a dram and was happy enough to be involved in distilling it illicitly.

'The firm's old Rothes Copper Works was in Green Street, and about 40 per cent of its work involved repair and maintenance in distilleries. This gave the men access to "substances", shall we say – low wines and feints, and maybe even wash. They would help themselves to a bucketful while doing the work in a distillery over the weekend, and then distil it in the Copper Works on Monday. This would be before the Second World War, I'd say.

'All the copper was nailed on a coke fire, and it was then plunged into a bath of water to cool it, so you had a source of heating for a still, and you could put your cooling worm into the water bath – it was almost too tempting!

'My grandfather was certainly very involved himself in this – I have his hydrometer on my office wall today. They did it more for devilment than anything else – to see how good they could make it. None was ever sold or anything like that, they just drank it.

'The old Copper Works where they were doing this distilling was directly across the road from an exciseman's house, but the town of Rothes had a permanent smell of whisky about it from the various distilleries, so he'd never notice that some of it was actually coming from the Copper Works.'

Perhaps the most recent example of illicit distilling in Scotland comes from a Morayshire crofter, who lives close to the 'whisky capital' of Dufftown, but who, unsurprisingly, wishes to remain anonymous.

'Distiller Y' is 70 years old, and gained practical experience of whisky-making when employed as a maltman in one of Dufftown's legal distilleries. His father had been brewer in another local distillery, so there was distilling knowledge and skill within the family. Y left the distillery to run the family croft, but was not inclined to leave his old trade behind altogether, and began to distil his own whisky in winter, using a copper hot water boiler and a washing machine tub, set up in a shed on the croft.

Until very recently he made whisky, and has passed all his knowledge on to his son, so that the family's distilling tradition will continue. The distilling equipment remains in place and ready to begin working again. Y distilled only for his personal consumption, not to sell, which probably explains why he was never caught.

'I would buy the barley four tons at a time', he says, 'and that would make two gallons of whisky, at about 100 proof. I'd get the malted barley without making anyone suspicious by saying it was for my hens – barley picks them up in winter when they're a bit under the weather. The yeast came from a bakery in Elgin.

'My still was nearly discovered on a couple of occasions, once by the postman who saw the smoke coming out of the shed and thought it must be on fire! My wife managed to get him away from it in time, though. I'd drink it at about 60 proof, and it was better than any of the new spirit I'd tasted in a distillery, sweeter, and better stuff altogether!'

6

THE WESTERN HIGHLANDS AND ISLANDS

If remoteness was one of the principal attractions for illicit distillers, then it soon becomes apparent from a cursory look at even a modern map of the Western Highlands and Islands why illicit distilling flourished in this vast area of Scotland. From the bleak north of the Outer Hebridean island of Lewis to the tip of the Mull of Kintyre, it was possible for smugglers to operate in comparative safety, with little likelihood of an unexpected visit from the gaugers.

Distilling on many islands was practised using oats, as barley would not grow in poor soil and with harsh climates, and even on more fertile islands such as Islay, barley only made up a small percentage of the total of grain cultivated. Distilling tended to take place when there was a good harvest, but the islands suffered from the widespread problem of a perpetual shortage of grain for food due to distilling activity.

Distilling was prohibited by the Commissioners of Supply in 1782/83, due to serious grain shortages caused by poor harvests, and all private stills in Argyllshire were ordered to be confiscated. Grain shortages brought about by the Napoleonic Wars caused further prohibitions on distilling between 1795 and 1797, and bans followed with depressing regularity well into the following century (see 'A Hateful Tax').

The Duke of Hamilton wrote to his Arran factor in 1801, declaring that 'Those persons detected illegally distilling of Grain must quit my farms as soon as may be.' This may, however, have been principally for appearances sake, as some of the duke's rent on Arran was paid in whisky, which was collected at Brodick and then smuggled across to the mainland. Rents were also commonly paid in whisky on the Seaforth estates of Lewis.

The Duke of Argyll does seem to have meant business, however, ordering that every tenth tenant on Tiree who was convicted of illicit distilling should be evicted from his property. By October 1801 fourteen tenants had been removed, but the illicit trade was so profitable that many took the risk of fines and possible eviction and carried on making their whisky.

In Ireland, a number of landowners followed the Duke of Argyll's example. In County Cork, the earl of Kingston suppressed illicit distilling to a considerable degree by inserting a clause into his tenants' leases to the effect that an illicit distilling conviction would lead to certain eviction.

Those less than charitably disposed towards the landed gentry of Scotland might suggest that the Duke of Argyll had reasons other than the moral welfare of his tenants in mind when he opposed illicit distilling. If he accepted grain 'in kind' rather than cash as rent, he could sell it for inflated prices during the years of the Napoleonic Wars. Despite attempts to persuade tenants to surrender their cereal as rent payments rather than distil it into whisky, there were 157 prosecutions in Argyllshire during 1801 for illicit distilling.

Landowners such as the Duke of Argyll created a number of small legal distilleries, which they leased to tenants, in the hope that this would remove the impetus for illicit distilling by supplying the local populace with legal whisky of decent quality. This idea seems to have been doomed to failure from the outset, however, and rarely made any significant inroads into illicit distilling.

It was often difficult to persuade tenants to take on the leases, and on Tiree the duke failed to establish a legal distillery for that reason alone. Presumably the sort of opposition from smugglers that George Smith in Glenlivet was later to encounter was one deterrent.

A letter from Neill Malcolm of Poltalloch's factor, John Campbell, dated 15 January 1805, survives in the Argyll and Bute archives:

> I ordered your Barron Officer Duncan McIntyre to go with his hatchet and cutt down the timbers of the Hutts they had in the hills distilling whisky and I went after him to see it done. I have ordered afterwards the miller of Slockavullin and Tayintluich milne not to grind any grain more of malt or else if they would not obey orders they certainly would be removed . . . there is no drop of whisky made within your estates but it is a report that some of our neighbours are making some privately by times.

Illicit distilling continued to be widespread in the West Highlands, however. Writing on 3 September 1813, Dr MacLeay of Oban noted that of all the parishes in Argyll 'we can only name one where there are not stills constantly at work in this illegal manufacture'. He estimated that in excess of 360,000 gallons of illicit spirit was being made in Argyllshire each year.

Colonel Alexander Campbell of Argyll was in no doubt where the blame lay. In January 1814 he observed that 'It is well known to every native . . . that no still can continue at work a single hour in the Highlands when it is in the interest of the Laird to suppress it.'

John MacCulloch describes an encounter between gaugers and distillers on Lismore, an island in Loch Linnhe, north of Oban, in his 1824 volume *The Highlands and Western Isles of Scotland*. MacCulloch, a geologist, was being given a ride in an excise cutter one morning when it was seen that

> beneath a rock, close by the edge of the water was burning a bright and clear fire near which sat an old man and a young girl with two or three casks scattered about. An iron crook suspended on some crude poles supported a still and the worm passed into a tall cask into which fell a small stream from the summit of the rock behind. Two or three sturdy fellows were lounging about, while the alchemist sat over the fire, in the attitude of Geber or Paracelsus waiting for the moment of projection . . . Before the boat was well in sight, an universal scream was set up; away ran the girl to some cottages which were perched on the cliff and down came men, women and children, hallooing, scolding, swearing and squalling, in all the unappreciable intonations of a Gaelic gamut; the still-head was whipt up by a sturdy virago, the malt was thrown out, the wash emptied.

Sometimes the excise officers in their cutters had a crucial element of surprise when thick mists were on the water. They would sail very quietly close to land and sniff the air for scents of distillation, before going ashore and following their noses! A cutter was stationed on Loch Lomond in 1816 because so much illicit distilling was taking place on the islands of the loch.

Stories about secreting stills in mill races to hide them from the attentions of excise officers are widespread in Scotland, but the smugglers of Loch Druing in the far north-west went a stage further and hid theirs in the loch, with floats attached to remind them of their whereabouts.

One comparatively late north-western illicit operation was that run by Hamish Dhubh Macrae of Monar, whose still continued to turn out 'the cratur' until the early years of the twentieth century.

Loch Monar is remote, even by West Highland standards, being located almost midway between Loch Carron on the west coast and Inverness in the east. Today, the loch is accessible only by an unclassified road through Glen Strathfarrar, west from the A831 by Strathglass, itself a notable smuggling haunt. During the nineteenth century it would have been a smuggler's dream, with forty hard miles of travelling up Strathfarrar from the nearest excise office in Dingwall, and no shortage of folk disposed to warn the Macraes of any imminent visit by the gaugers.

Hamish carried on the distilling business started by his father, Alister, who constructed a bothy at Cosaig close to the shore of the loch during the 1840s. The family had originally come inland from Kintail to settle at a spot near Pait Lodge. A spell in Dingwall gaol when the bothy was discovered persuaded Alister to opt for a more inaccessible place, and new bothies were duly constructed high on Meall Mor, where the young Hamish could act as lookout while his father distilled. Whisky-making and selling was virtually a full-time occupation for the Macraes, who distilled in winter and distributed the spirit in summer. Sometimes, in winter, the pair would stay in the bothy for days on end when snow fell, and there was a danger that footprints would lead the gaugers to the spot. The Macraes' whisky was sold not only to individual locals in the area, but also to several inns, a number of lairds, and at Beauly market.

On one occasion, it is claimed, a party of excisemen from Dingwall set off up Strathfarrar, determined to catch Hamish in the act of distilling, but they got so drunk while enjoying the hospitality of a house in the strath that the following morning they did not feel well enough to continue the mission, and retreated to their office in town.

Alister Macrae lived to the age of 97, perhaps due to the powers of the *uisge* he distilled, and Hamish carried on the 'family business' until around 1900, when he was prevailed upon to retire by Captain Stirling, proprietor of the Monar estate. Being the wily character that he was, Hamish decided to capitalise upon his retirement, and accepted the government's £5 'seizure' reward in return for telling the gaugers the location of his bothy, and allowing them to take away his still.

The Macraes lived in a roughly made, stone cottage on a small island in Loch Monar, which Alister had linked to the mainland by a causeway after settling there. Today the island has vanished, as the level of the loch was raised in 1959 when the Monar Dam was built to provide hydro-electric power.

∼

As was the case on the island of Islay, sea caves were used for distilling in the north-west Highlands around Gairloch and Poolewe. In one instance, a burn was diverted over a cliff to provide water for cave distilling, and in another, local smugglers got some peace from the excisemen for a while by diverting a burn in a very obvious manner over an inaccessible cave. The gaugers did not know that it was inaccessible, however, and spent several months trying to find a way in to capture the elusive still they *knew* must be operating there.

One of the more recent seizures of spirit in Scotland took place near Melvaig, situated on a remote peninsula north-west of Gairloch in Wester Ross. According to the report in the 25 December 1987 edition of the Skye-based *West Highland Free Press,* fourteen officers from HM Customs & Excise service and three police officers had descended on the area on 9 December, and proceeded to search seven properties. According to reporter Torcuil Crichton, their search involved 'digging up floorboards and searching babies' cribs'. In total the grand amount of one and a half litres of illicit spirit was recovered, with a half-bottle being discovered in the possession of North Erradale crofter Kenneth MacKenzie. No distilling equipment was found, however, and with MacKenzie insisting that the bottle was nothing more than a souvenir from days gone by, no charges were ever brought. MacKenzie was quoted as saying, 'People around here are generally law-abiding – the way the Customs officers behaved you would think we were making whisky and exporting it worldwide. We don't make a habit of drinking whisky here. I've still got the bottle from last New Year in the cupboard.' MacKenzie's grandfather had, however, been imprisoned along with five other Melvaig men for illicit distilling back in 1936, and not many bottles of whisky survive opened for a year in Wester Ross . . .

This was not quite the end of the story, for the *West Highland Free Press* inadvertently identified the wrong Kenneth MacKenzie, naming a Gairloch man as the one involved. In the next issue, the newspaper editor apologised to MacKenzie from Gairloch, noting 'He has been inundated with telephone calls requesting New Year orders of the famous dram'!

Writing in 1965, Steve Sillett (*Illicit Scotch*) speculated that the last illegal stills to have operated in Scotland were almost certainly located in the glens of the north-west Highlands. Seizures of stills took place at Gairloch during the 1930s resurgence in illicit distilling, as they did in other places with long traditions of illicit whisky-making.

In the early 1950s a bothy was discovered in Gairloch, hidden inside a peat stack. It was made of corrugated iron and wood, was some eight by fifteen feet in size, and contained a fresh water supply, along with a still made from a household hot-water tank. As it was situated on common land and was unattended when discovered by excise officers, no individuals were charged with its construction and use.

Sillett noted of the Gairloch smugglers: 'Their early-warning system is as effective as it is simple – a sheet on an otherwise disused clothes' line – and their skill in the art of camouflage unrivalled.'

Fergie MacDonald is a renowned Scottish dance band leader, 'button box' maestro, composer, physiotherapist, stalker, angler, clay pigeon marksman and hotelier, who lives in the Moidart settlement of Mingary in the West Highlands. Fergie was responsible for setting up the intriguingly titled Illegal Moidart Museum in a restored 'black house' called Cnoc Breac, close to the MacDonald family's Clanranald Hotel. The museum features replica distilling equipment, and is open to visitors during the summer months.

Fergie MacDonald is a descendant of Roderick MacDonald – known as Red Roderick or Ruaridh Ruadh in the Gaelic – and it is to him that the museum is dedicated. Ruaridh was born in the black house in the years following the Jacobite defeat at Culloden in 1746, and he became one of the best known and respected distillers in Moidart, making whisky on a small fireside still until private distilling was outlawed. It was then necessary to move the still out of the house and up the burn that ran through the croft, where it was less likely to be discovered by the gaugers. The burn became known as Ault-a-Bhuiritis – the Burn of the Still.

Legend has it that the local lairds turned a blind eye to Ruaridh's distilling activities, in return, no doubt, for a drop of the cratur from time to time. Ruaridh was also, however, a skilled poacher, and this was *not* acceptable to the landowners of the district, who forced him into exile for a number of years.

On his eventual return, Ruraidh began to distil again, but most of the product of his sma' still now found its way down his own throat. He is supposed to have been found dead by the Ault-a-Bhuiritis, killed by acute alcohol poisoning, with his faithful dog, Pibroch, guarding its master's body.

According to Fergie MacDonald, 'We know that at one time there was a line of maybe six stills around here, all within sight of each other, presumably so that warnings could be signalled if the gaugers were on the prowl. These included two at Glenuig and one on the northern shore of Loch Moidart, along with Ruaridh's.

'When I was young and my father was quite an old man we were up by the burn one day and he showed me a rock where he said the still had been located. It was almost certainly Ruaridh's, although it could have been somebody else's I suppose, as this was a hot area for illicit distilling. Ruaridh's whisky was the best, they say.'

One of the stills was by the shore near Kinlochmoidart, at a place where a burn ran into a small bay. Fergie MacDonald tells of a day when the distillers were surprised at their work by a party of gaugers, and as the tide was out they fled across the sands, pursued by the officers of the excise. 'The lads knew their way across the sands, of course, but the gaugers didn't, and soon got caught in the quick sands. "For God's sake help us," they are supposed to have cried out, "and we'll forget what we saw." I don't know what the outcome was, but I think they'd have helped them.

'The ruins of the gauger's house are still there at Caolis, between Kinlochmoidart and Glenuig, on the shores of Loch Moidart, opposite Invermoidart, and I suppose it would have been lived in until the 1860s or '70s. They said that there were always people watching that house to make sure they knew where the gauger was, and that he couldn't so much as go to the toilet without them knowing!

'Maybe they're still making whisky yet in this part of the world. They're into all the other stuff, fields of cannabis and the like, so why not? Certainly there was distilling here until just before the First World War, and one of the last people caught making whisky was a MacLean. His descendant, Angus, is still in this area.

'There are stories of folk seeing serpents and lions – hallucinating with it. They'd be drinking the stuff straight from the still, maybe with a drop of water added. It must have been like petrol!'

Long renowned for its illicit whisky, the Kintyre peninsula in Argyllshire developed into Scotland's most productive legal distilling centre during the nineteenth century. When Alfred Barnard visited Kintyre's 'capital' of Campbeltown in 1887 he christened it 'Whisky City'. By 1934 US prohibition, and a decline in quality of much Campbeltown spirit as distillers tried to satisfy the voracious appetites of the blenders, meant that only three distilleries continued to operate. Also, the remoteness of Kintyre – which had been a boon to the illicit distillers – became a serious handicap for legal whisky-makers as the twentieth century developed. In its place, Speyside began to thrive as the region favoured by blenders.

The burgh of Campbeltown's associations with whisky go back at least to 1636, when it was recorded that six quarts of 'aqua vitae' were payable by the town of Lochead (as Campbeltown was then known) as rent for Crosshill farm. Malting was established in the area by the late seventeenth century, and in 1743 there were at least twenty-one maltsters working in and around Campbeltown. When the 1792 *Statistical Account* was compiled, the Rev. John Smith noted in his entry on the parish that twenty-two licensed distillers turned out just short of 20,000 gallons of whisky per year, while a further ten stills operated in the outlying parts of the parish.

Thomas Pennant observed in 1772 that despite a shortage of bere in Kintyre, the inhabitants of the peninsula were 'mad enough to convert their bread into poison', and when there was a poor harvest in 1812 it was reckoned that more than 50 per cent of the whisky made in Kintyre was being distilled illegally. Some 20,000 bolls of grain were made into whisky per annum.

When licence duty rose to £9 per gallon in 1797 distilling was driven underground in Campbeltown as in so many parts of Scotland, and for the next twenty years there was no legal distilling in the burgh. Legitimate distilling in Campbeltown recommenced in 1817, when John Beith & Co. built a distillery in Longrow. I. Glen (*A Maker of Illicit Stills* – in volume 14, part 1 of *Scottish Studies* (1970)) makes the point that 'John Bieth' had been supplied with distilling equipment by Robert Armour of Campbeltown prior to 1817, and so assumed that the distiller had been 'keeping his hand in' until it was advantageous to switch to legal production. She also noted that other customers of Armour who went on to be associated with legal Campbeltown operations included members of the Colville, Ferguson, Galbraith, Greenlees, Harvie, Johnston, Mitchell and Reid families.

The still books of Robert Armour, detailing the construction and sale of distilling equipment for illegal purposes between May 1811 and September 1817, have survived, and form a unique record of illicit distilling. Thanks to the work of Ms Glen in interpreting material from the still books we have a real insight into the mechanics of illicit distilling during the early nineteenth century.

Robert Armour was the principal supplier of illicit whisky-making apparatus in and around Campbeltown from the founding of his plumbing and coppersmithing business in the town in 1811 until the years after the 1823 Excise Act. The plumbing business provided a legitimate 'cover' for Armour's principal trade of still-making, and the firm remained in family ownership until 1948.

Armour's equipment was sold and used in the burgh of Campbeltown, but also found its way to a wide variety of locations throughout the Kintyre peninsula. Additionally, Armour seems to have been the main supplier of stills to the smugglers of south-west Arran and the island of Gigha.

Various members of the Armour family were involved with distilling in Kintyre, both legally and illegally, from the late eighteenth century onwards, and in the wake of the 1823 Excise Act the family had associations with Meadowburn and Glenside distilleries.

The still books provide a fascinating and detailed account of what was supplied and how much it cost. The first entry, for 16 August 1811, was to Samuel Harvie, 'To a body 23 lib. To a head 6 lib. 10 oz.' This is followed on 21 August by 'To a body 13 lib. 8oz.' The grand total came to £5 6s 3d.

Ms Glen's analysis of Robert Armour's still books concluded that a complete distilling system could be provided for less than £5, this including a pot still with a capacity in excess of ten gallons. In addition to the pot still itself, Armour provided a head, arm and worm, and several sets of distilling equipment were supplied to a group of people at one address, suggesting that each individual operated their own still on the premises.

Armour's still books reveal that only one in five purchases was made by a person operating on his or her own, the remainder being sold to groups. Interestingly, the illicit distillers with whom Armour did business tended to be quite respectable members of the community, such as coopers, farmers, cobblers, wrights, butchers and innkeepers.

According to Glen, Armour produced stills in two principal sizes – using either 12–14lbs of copper or 20lbs of copper. The still books also reveal the construction of a tin still with a copper head and worm for a local widow who obviously could not afford the full copper rig. Armour charged just £1 15s, but the tin would not withstand use for anything like as long as copper, not to mention the fact that the spirit produced would almost certainly be of inferior quality. A copper still could last for up to twenty years if treated with respect.

The price of whisky during the period to which Armour's still books relate varied from just over one shilling per pint to in excess of nine shillings per pint, reflecting, Glen suggested, fluctuating grain prices, along with the quality of spirit and scale of distilling enterprises in question.

By 1822 illicit whisky in Kintyre was selling at between ten and twelve shillings per gallon, with a dramatic fall in grain prices accounting for the drop in cost due to the economic recession that followed the ending of the Napoleonic Wars. According to *The Fifth Report of the Commissioners of Inquiry into the Revenue arising in Ireland, etc. VII* (1823) the illicit whisky distilled in Kintyre was at that time transported to the Ayrshire coast for sale, and even carried in fishing vessels and coasters up the Clyde and into Glasgow. Illegal Kintyre whisky was often blended with the unpalatable products of the legal Lowland stills in order to make a whisky that would sell, particularly to the increasing numbers of Highlanders migrating to the west of Scotland to find work. Many Scots, of course, travelled much further from the country of their birth, and a number of emigrants from

Campbeltown wrote letters to their families back home from America during the mid-1820s, in which they stated that they were putting the old illicit distilling skills to good use in Ohio!

※※※

The Report from the Committee upon the Distilleries in Scotland, 1798-9 described the rural population of Kintyre as 'disorderly and tumultuous', and concluded that excise officers were regularly 'obstructed, insulted and beat'. They faced the perennial problem of lacking true local knowledge in Kintyre, just as they did in every part of rural Scotland. There were also difficulties with place and personal names among members of the service on the islands and in areas like Kintyre, as very few of them spoke Gaelic.

The Duke of Hamilton's factor, Robert Brown, grew impatient of what he saw as excise officers' incompetence or lack of commitment regarding illicit distilling in the west, and particularly on Arran, and he eventually sent a group of his own untrained men to the island. They discovered and seized more than thirty stills, while the excisemen could only account for six.

Excise officers displayed a human side at times, and the story is told of an old smuggler near the Mull of Kintyre who was caught distilling by a couple of Campbeltown gaugers. He suggested that as he had been having a hard time lately, perhaps they would allow him to throw his still into Kilbrandon Sound rather than go to court and be fined. He also pointed out that it was a very hot day, and this would save the officers having to carry the heavy still all the way back to town. It was an old still and not worth much to them if they did take it, and by doing as the smuggler suggested, they would be putting him out of business anyway. They agreed, and the smuggler duly threw all of his equipment into the sea, looking deeply unhappy as they left. A few hours later he was down on the beach collecting the pieces as the tide washed them back in, knowing the local currents well enough to be certain where they would be washed up.

※※※

Prior to visiting Glenside distillery in Campbeltown, Alfred Barnard wrote that 'our worthy landlord offered to drive us to see Saddell Castle, a place intimately connected with Campbeltown in former times, and standing in a district which used to be a favourite haunt of the smugglers'.

He also recalled that close to Glenside distillery, Robert Burns' lover 'Highland Mary' lived in a cottage overlooking the bay. 'Her father was a sailor in a revenue cutter stationed at Campbeltown . . .'

During the last [eighteenth] century and up to seventy years ago the unlawful occupation of distilling Whisky was carried on to the greatest extent, the landed proprietors rather encouraging the practice. Those found smuggling by the Excise Officers were brought before the Court of Justice and fined; but usually the judge was one of the landed proprietors, so the fines were small and many got off free. When legal distilling was first introduced the Distillers met with a good deal of opposition and resentment from the smugglers, but they managed to live it down, and owing to the quality of the product, the trade developed so rapidly that it has now become the staple article of commerce, and there are no less than twenty-one Distilleries in Campbeltown.

– Alfred Barnard, 1887

To the east of Kintyre, between the peninsula and the mainland, the isle of Arran lies in the Firth of Clyde. It was blessed with the classic illicit distilling advantages of difficult terrain for gaugers, and good supplies of water, yet it enjoyed close proximity to the ports of Ayrshire, and beyond that the lucrative markets of Glasgow.

Arran whisky was highly regarded, with John MacCulloch in *The Highlands and Western Isles of Scotland* (1824) describing it as 'the burgundy of the vintages'. There was clearly quantity as well as quality. So much illicit spirit was being made in Arran in the early years of the nineteenth century and shipped to the mainland that a Royal Navy cutter – the *Prince Edward* – was operated by the revenue service in the Firth of Clyde from 1816. The cutter was not only there to watch for Arran smugglers, but also those on the island of Bute, to the north-east. In 1816 the excise service significantly increased its overall use of 'revenue cutters', each of which carried a crew of around fifty men, all armed with cutlasses and firearms.

Also in 1816, the entire excise staff on Arran was dismissed for its apparent tolerance of illicit distilling. The Duke of Hamilton, who owned a large estate on the island, had at the very least been aware of the amount of smuggling going on. Certainly his factor, Robert Brown, had been involved in the conversion of barley into whisky for shipment to the mainland.

One particularly serious event on Arran occurred in March 1817, when the smuggler John McKinnon and his son, also John, of Kildonan in the south-east of the island, set out for the mainland with a cargo of spirits distilled by themselves and some of their neighbours, bound for Saltcoats on the Ayrshire coast. Once in the firth they were spotted by the *Prince Edward*, and just made it back to shore near Largybeg ahead of the cutter. On shore, a crowd had gathered to help unload the boat and spirit away its contents, but the excise officers got there in time to prevent this, and in the ensuing fight the two McKinnons and one Isobel Nicholl were killed by gunfire the crew of the cutter. Seeing the bodies, the locals – tenants of the Duke of Hamilton – turned and fled, taking a number of wounded men and women with them. The ankers of whisky were loaded onto the *Prince Edward* and removed by the excisemen.

In the subsequent furore, the mate of the cutter, John Jeffrey, was tried in Glasgow for assault, though many on Arran and further afield felt that the charges against him should have included murder. He was cleared of all charges, but, probably wisely, was posted away from Arran.

In the aftermath of the trial of Jeffrey, Paul Campbell of Ballymichael near Shiskine on Arran, inflicted quite serious injuries on an excise officer who discovered his still, and was sent by boat to Glasgow to stand trial for assaulting the officer. The captain of the ship *Islay* was John MacArthur, who, like most Gaels, had sympathy for the smugglers and was no friend of the excisemen. Speaking in Gaelic, which the officers could not understand, MacArthur advised Campbell that when they were close to the shore, near Glasgow, he should jump for it, despite being in handcuffs, and that he, MacArthur, would claim he was unable to stop the ship because of difficult currents. This duly happened, with Campbell subsequently joining his brother in the USA, while MacArthur was never suspected of any involvement.

One of the centres for smuggling on Arran was the area around the village of Pirnmill, in the north-west of the island, which faces the Kintyre peninsula. Towards the end of the nineteenth century, Shaunie Sillars and his sister Mary lived at High Banlicken farm, where he combined farming and distilling with a role as gillie to the duke of Montrose at his Dougarie estate. Shaunie's still was located by the burn above High Banlicken, with a good vantage point from which to see the revenue cutter from Greenock patrolling the Kilbrannan Sound between the west coast of Arran and the Kintyre peninsula. From High Banlicken the whisky was taken down a cart track to Immacher, and on down the Brae to a series of caves on the Immacher shore. From there it was just a four-mile crossing to Kintyre, where the spirit was sold, though some, according to local lore, was also available at the Immacher Inn.

One autumn day in the mid-1880s, Shaunie saw the revenue cutter heave to, and drop a small boat which landed on the shore. Shaunie whistled the pre-arranged warning signal to Mary at the farm so that she could hide the whisky which was being stored there before the excise officers arrived to search. She got it all hidden in the loft, but did not have time to remove the tell-tale ladder from the loft opening before the first officer arrived, demanding entry. He put one foot on the ladder, but Mary seized a meat cleaver and threatened to do unspeakable things with the cleaver if he tried to climb up into the loft. As she said it in Gaelic he may not have understood the words, but he would surely have understood the sentiments. The gauger dashed from the house, and rather than admit that he had been so frightened by one old woman he told the rest of the party when he returned to the cutter that he had found nothing during his search.

The principal village in the parish of Kilmory, in the south-west of Arran, is Lagg, where a legal distillery operated from around 1800 to 1837. The kiln where barley was malted still stands at Clauchaig. This was the last legal whisky-making operation on the island until Isle of Arran Distillers Ltd opened its new facility at Lochranza in 1995.

Lagg was another smuggling 'hotspot' on the island. In the Scottish Women's Rural Institute guide to Arran, the tale is told of how during the last years of the nineteenth century, the mother of the late Kate Currie (nee McKelvie) of Clauchaig was at a local ceilidh one evening where mention was made of a trip to be made to the mainland the following day with some whisky. Someone present informed the authorities, and when the smuggler got on the boat for Ardrossan the presence of a gauger among the other passengers was pointed out to him. The whisky was in a stoneware cask, and as the smuggler set off down the gang plank, closely followed by the gauger, the smuggler dropped it into the sea, then turned to the officer and said, 'You've followed it all this way, now follow it the rest of the way!'

The unnamed SWRI contributor on the Parish of Kilmory notes:

> In Kilmorie [*sic*] smuggling was not considered a disreputable pursuit and there were few if any in the parish who at some period of their lives were not engaged in some form of smuggling. To the smuggler no stigma was attached on account of his employment, on the contrary it was considered rather an honourable occupation, as exhibiting an intrepidity and art that required for the possessor a distinction in the minds of his companions. Often it was in the darkest night and in the tempestuous weather when no cruiser would or could stand the gale that in his little skiff the smuggler transported his cargo to the opposite shores of Ayrshire a distance of approximately 20 miles.

A third popular smuggling venue was Whiting Bay, on the east coast of Arran, where it is said that tales of supernatural happenings at Bocan's Bridge were invented by locals to keep away the gaugers while illicit distilling took place.

According to the Edinburgh-based whisky writer and connoisseur Charles MacLean, 'My formative years were spent at Kildonan on the south coast of Arran, where we have a family cottage. As late as 1972, I tasted whisky allegedly made locally, and I have to say it was horrible. Ian Colquhoun and a local gamekeeper, Ronnie MacDonald, had a lemonade bottle of the stuff at The Glen Farm, a very remote place at the back of Kildonan. A local farmer, Lordy MacDonald, joined us, and when he saw the bottle he insisted on trying it. He filled a glass and knocked it back as though it was normal whisky, but of course it was over strength, and within a couple of minutes of drinking it, he'd passed out. Next day, he was mowing Whiting Bay golf course, and he kept falling off the tractor, literally falling off it!'

Agricultural improvements and the construction of new roads were not popular in the smuggling districts of Arran, when they commenced around 1814. The north of the island had far fewer illicit stills than the south, with fishing being a more significant occupation, but some of the smugglers of the south of the island were very concerned that the new developments would damage their trade. Accordingly, they stole equipment being used for making the roads and demolished houses in the process of construction. Arran landowner the duke of Hamilton was furious with this behaviour, and threatened to make sure that all illicit distillers were removed from the island, though this clearly this was not a practical possibility.

It is thought that, as in Tiree, the Arran distillers had contact with their northern Irish counterparts, who sometimes distilled for them when the attentions of the gaugers temporarily became too intense.

As well as the whisky brought 'over the water' from the isle of Arran to the Ayrshire coast, there was also a significant amount of illegal distilling going on in the area around Largs in Ayrshire, which was the location of a revenue post from 1817 until its closure in the middle years of the century.

Though often occupied with the activities of Arran smugglers, the officers at Largs also found time to work closer to home, and in 1823 a still was discovered at Outerwards, just a few yards from what was then the main Largs to Greenock road, though Largs also had a legal distillery, which operated for just nine years from 1825. Records show that in the period from 1817 to 1834 the Largs revenue officers detected at least nine stills at a variety of locations, including farms and private houses in the parishes of Largs and Innerkip. Casks of illicit 'Highland whisky' were also discovered at the premises of a number of vintners, grocers and inns. A seizure at John Lyon's Waterside Farm, Innerkip, included a still, 100 gallons of wash, and a variety of casks, varying in capacity from 120 gallons to eight gallons, while a raid at Lease Muir, Innerkip, uncovered a substantial still of 50 gallons' capacity and 300 gallons of wash.

In 1834 the officer in charge of the Largs office reported that smuggling was 'of a very small extent mainly whisky from Highlands or soap from Ireland', though three years later he noted 'a considerable quantity of whisky has been landed on coast'.

Islay is the ultimate 'whisky island', with seven distilleries producing highly distinctive single malts currently in production. The oldest of these is Bowmore, which was granted a licence in 1799, but illicit distilling had long been a feature of Islay life by the time of Bowmore's foundation.

After visiting Islay during the 1880s, Alfred Barnard wrote of Lagavulin distillery that around the year 1742 'ten small and separate smuggling bothys for the manufacture of "moonlight", which when working presented anything but a true picture of "still life", and were all subsequently absorbed into one establishment, the whole work not making more than a few thousand gallons per annum'.

The first resident excise office had only arrived on the island two years before Bowmore distillery was founded, with the Campbells who owned the island previously acting as tax-gatherers on behalf of the Government. In his contribution to the *Statistical Account* (1794), the Reverend Archibald Robertson of Kildalton lamented:

> We have not an Excise officer on the whole island. The quantity therefore of whisky made here is very great; and the evil, that follows drinking to excess of this liquor, is very visible in this island. This is one chief cause of our great poverty; for the barley, that should support the family of the poor tenant, is sold to the brewer for 17s the boll; and the same farmer is often obliged to buy meal at 11.3s Sterling, in order to keep his family from starving. When a brewer knows that a poor man is at a loss for money, he advances him a trifle, on condition that he makes him sure of his barley at the above price; and it is often bought by the brewers even at a lower rate; while those who are not obliged to ask for money until they deliver their barley, receive 20s or more for it. This evil, of distilling as much barley as might maintain many families, it is hoped, by some means or other, will soon be abolished. It may take some time, however, to prevent the people from drinking to

excess; for bad habits are not easily overcome: but there would surely
be some hopes for a gradual reformation, if spirituous liquors were not
so abundant, and so easily purchased.

The establishment of a permanent excise presence on Islay meant
that, in the short term, many illicit stills were seized, and in the wake
of this the Ileachs persuaded Irish tinkers to cross to the island and
fabricate make-shift stills from boilers and large pots. According to
The Report from the Committee upon the Distilleries in Scotland, 1798–9. XI,
(1803), these and similar vessels made perfectly decent whisky, with the
report's writers concluding that the type of equipment mattered less
than the skill of the distiller in being able to identify and collect the
'heart of the run', or middle cut.

Clearly, the excise officers' initial successes on Islay were not
followed up, since the possibility of sending soldiers to the island
to aid them was mooted in 1800. The recruitment of a force of local
volunteers rendered this unnecessary, but it indicates how serious the
problem of illicit distilling was perceived to be.

Records show that the brothers Alexander and Archibald McGilvray
were outlawed in 1798 for failing to appear at a trial to answer charges
of 'maltreating the Revenue officers'. A reward of 20 guineas was
offered for their capture, but as was so often the case in such situations,
it went unclaimed.

With serious grain shortages and a ban imposed on distilling, in
March 1801 the Stent Committee – a kind of local council comprising
influential island figures – declared 'This meeting resolve collectively
& individually to use their utmost exertions for preventing any of the
grain of the Island being destry'd by illegal Distillers, and for that
purpose pledge themselves to inform agt any person or persons that
they may know or hear to be concerned in this illegal and destructive
Traffick'. One of the signatories of this document was David Simson,
founder of Bowmore distillery.

Considering the scale of illicit distilling apparently going on,
the Port Ellen-based excise officers seem to have been less than
energetic, according to records. Between May 1837 and the end of
1843 they discovered and seized just five illicit stills, with a total
of almost a thousand gallons of wash and four casks of low wines.
Most seizures took place in the same localities, too, which suggests
that the enthusiasm of the gaugers was clearly not great. They were
usually mainlanders, only too pleased to get back to 'civilisation'
whenever possible.

The remote Oa peninsula, west of Port Ellen, was a haven for illicit
distillers, and malt was stored in caves at Killeyan, while a sizeable
seizure of malt and wash took place on one occasion at Giol, a little

to the north. Stremnishmore and Cragabus were other popular haunts for the distillers.

In February 1850, with support from the revenue cutter SS *Chichester,* excise officers caught up with distillers in a cave at Lower Killeyan. They escaped, but were later apprehended, as they were all well-known smugglers. According to the excise report of the event '[the officers] were obliged to descend over a precipice about 70 feet deep and during the time they were descending the smugglers fled by some outlet among the rocks which was not easy to discover; their names are Alexander McCuaig of Upper Killain, Donald McGibbon of Lower Killain and Neil McGibbon his brother. There were also in the cave five large casks containing about 300 Gallons of wash ready for distillation which they completely destroyed.' The men were subsequently found guilty and fined £30 each. Not surprisingly all three had to opt for the alternative of spending three months at Her Majesty's pleasure in Inveraray jail.

In his 1811 volume *General View of Agriculture of the Hebrides or Western Isles of Scotland,* J. MacDonald noted that grain for whisky-making was being exported from Islay to Kintyre because the island laird Walter Campbell of Shawfield was keen to leave his tenants with nothing from which to distil illegally. Deciding that providing his tenants with good ale was another way of avoiding conversion of grain into illicit spirit, he built the only brewery in the Hebrides on Islay. This measure was only partially successful, since the people of the islands were never really converted to the merits of ale over whisky.

In 1816 Walter Campbell died, and his grandson and successor Walter Frederick Campbell was instrumental in getting a number of illicit farm distilleries to turn legal, though many were productive for only a short period of time. These operations included Daill, Lossit, Mullindry, Newton and Tallant, while the establishment of legal distilling at Laphroaig, Ardbeg and Lagavulin also dates from this period. (See 'In From the Cold'.)

Lochindaal is really an arm of the sea, expanding into the Bay of Laggan, and terminating at the Point of Rhynns on the west, and the Maol-na-Ho on the east, where it forms the capacious Bay of Laggan. The cliffs on the Maol-na-Ho rise to a great height, and in one of them is a large cave called Sloc Mhaol Doraidh, of historical and smuggling fame, many a good cask of Whisky having been removed therefrom to the coasting ships. The nefarious and immoral trade of illicit distillation used to be carried on all over the island to a very great extent, and Whisky making was formerly, as now, the staple commodity of Islay. The steady and persistent discountenance which the illicit traffic received from the proprietors of the island in the early part of the present [nineteenth] century, and the introduction of legal Distilleries, has well nigh put an end to smuggling. Along the route [to Lochindaal distillery] our driver pointed out several abandoned haunts of the smugglers.

– Alfred Barnard, 1887

On Islay, the last distillers caught making whisky in the Portnahaven area at the remote end of the Rhinns peninsula were arrested in 1911, according to local man James Macarthur, when interviewed during the 1950s.

Jim McEwan is one of the Scotch whisky industry's best-known figures, having worked in the business for thirty-nine years, thirty-eight of which were spent in the employ of Bowmore. McEwan is now production director for the revived Bruichladdich distillery, and is relishing once again living on his native island after a lengthy exile in Glasgow, while acting as international brand ambassador for Morrison Bowmore Distillers Ltd.

McEwan probably knows more about Islay and its distilling heritage than anyone else in the industry, and he says, 'When I started at Bowmore thirty-nine years ago, the old men there were in their sixties, and none of them ever talked about there being illicit distilling going on. If there had, then the guys doing it would have been folk heroes! In the old days, certainly, the Mull of Oa in the very south of the island was a place where lots of illicit distilling took place – it's very remote. For the same reasons of remoteness, I guess there would have been quite a lot of it on Jura, too. Just 200 people, no policeman or excise officers, and all those places you could operate.

'One of the last illicit stills to be worked on Islay, I think, was run by a guy called Baldi Cladach, and he had it in a cave on the Sound of Islay, which would have been useful for escape by sea if the gaugers ever came after him. This was on Dunlossit Estate land, near Port Askaig.'

According to one resident of the Dunlossit Estate, 'Baldi's still was in a cave at An Cladach, just north of McArthur's Point, and one day the gaugers came after him, so he climbed up onto the cliffs above the cave, and hid his still in the cliffs. As far as anyone knows it's still there. Just near the spot there's a bothy which has been reinstated by the Mountain Bothies Association, and is used as a mountain shelter. It's well known that at night people using the bothy often hear strange noises. It's the ghost of Baldi searching for his still.'

The small illegal still and worm on display in Port Charlotte's Museum of Islay Life reputedly came from the wild land behind

McArthur's Head, on the extremely inaccessible east coast of the island, so perhaps Baldi's ghost is too late . . .

The same Dunlossit resident also suggests that down on a remote part of the Rhinns coast there was another cave, accessed from a passageway above, that was used for illicit distilling until as late as the 1950s or even 1960s. The whisky was apparently carried out from the still in the barrels of rifles, secured against spillage with corks. The rifles were being carried ostensibly to shoot marauding deer.

Whatever the true situation with regard to illicitly distilled Islay whisky, there was certainly no shortage of illegally obtained spirit during Jim McEwan's time at Bowmore distillery. 'You realise that the designers at Heinz had whisky in mind when they came up with the Heinz salad cream bottle?' he inquires. 'It fits perfectly through the bung of an American barrel. We didn't have dogs like they did on Speyside, we used salad cream bottles – much more hygienic. We were far in advance of them . . .

'And, of course, there were wash drinkers. One at Bowmore was Fat Sam, who always wore wellingtons. One night he climbed over the sea wall at Bowmore at low tide into the tun room, and proceeded to drink wash all night. In the early morning a gauger came along, and before he could be discovered, Sam staggered up off the floor where he had collapsed and climbed hastily back over the sea wall. Unfortunately, in the meantime the tide had come in, and Sam weighed about 18 stones and was wearing Wellingtons. He was rescued by the customs officer who gave him a dram to help him recover. A customs officer giving a wash drinker a dram!

'One of the uses to which we put new spirit was in the screen washers of cars in winter, as it didn't freeze. One night we were at a dance and we ran out of whisky, so we took turns to have new spirit – at 68.5 per cent – squirted into our mouths by a car driver from his screen washer.'

On the neighbouring island of Jura there was an illicit still beside the burn at Lussagiven, where the present metalled road degenerates into little more than a track. A local man, interviewed by the School of Scottish Studies during the 1950s, said that it was well known that illicit distilling had ceased on the island by the time the road was laid down in 1914. The remains of kilns for malting barley are to be found on Jura, and one, in woods near the ruins of An Carn, is thought also to have been used to fire an illicit still.

From Jura's 'capital' of Craighouse, where today Kyndal's legal Isle of Jura distillery is located, comes the story of an excise raid on a house where two brothers who were illicit distillers lived. Hurriedly, they placed a cask of whisky beside the fire and got their elderly mother who was wearing a voluminous hooped skirt to sit on it, hiding it completely. When the excisemen arrived, the old lady invited them to search the house, which they duly did, while she calmly knitted a sock, sitting on the whisky all the time, apologising for not getting up due to her severe rheumatism.

Regarding hotel charges on the Isle of Skye, Anderson's *Guide* of 1843 noted: 'In one article only are they higher than in the mainland highlands, namely, whiskey, of which not a drop is made in Skye, either by smuggler or regular distiller.' As Talisker distillery had been founded in 1831/32 and was almost certainly not 'silent' during the early 1840s, we must treat Anderson's remarks about illicit distilling on Skye with as much caution as those concerning the legitimate trade on the island. It seems implausible that in a location with so many obvious geographical advantages, illicit whisky-making did not take place.

Certainly, more recent observers believe this to be the case. In *Spirit of Adventure* (1992) Tom Morton claims that there is a place on Skye where quite fresh scorch marks are clearly visible on a telephone pole. One would-be distiller heated a length of copper pipe and wrapped it round the pole with the intention of making a 'worm'. The bending process worked well, but once the metal cooled he realised that short of sawing down the pole there was no way in which he could remove the worm intact! A hacksaw was required to destroy the evidence . . .

According to Morton, 'There are . . . stills around to this day, from Shetland through Orkney to Skye and definitely Glasgow.'

Prior to the introduction of higher still licence fees as a result of the 1786 Scotch Distillery Act, virtually every farm on the island of Tiree had its own still. Enough whisky was made there to satisfy local thirsts and still leave some 200 to 300 gallons for export to the mainland each year. In 1790 Tiree had two legal distilleries, which used coal and grain shipped over from the mainland, in addition to locally-grown barley or bere. When the Duke of Argyll began his crackdown on illicit distilling, grain from Tiree was ferried to Ireland to be converted into whisky.

A recording from the archives of the School of Scottish Studies in Edinburgh also features the island of Tiree, and provides oral confirmation of a ploy which was regularly undertaken by illicit distillers. The interviewee was octogenarian Donald Sinclair, and the interview was conducted by Eric Cregeen in October 1968:

'This old neighbour of mine, he had a small pot of his own and the pot was leaking, and here comes this day an exciseman, and he would pay any man that would show him where a pot still was and this man says to him, "Well, could show it to you, but I'm afraid – I don't like to do it."

"Well," he says, "you show me the pot and I'll smash the pot and I don't ask who the pot belonged to."

"So," he says, "I went with him and I showed him my own pot that was leaking and he told me to smash the pot and so I did, and he gave me £5 for my work. That got me a new pot and a few pounds in my pocket."

That's the way he had him deceived and he was none the wiser.'

Martin Martin was writing about the Outer Hebridean island of Lewis in *A Description of the Western Islands of Scotland* (1703) when he described three types of whisky being made in the outer islands, all apparently distilled from oats rather than barley, since oats was the most common cereal crop on Lewis. The first was the 'common *usquebaugh*', or twice-distilled spirit, while a second sort was known as *trestarig* (from the Gaelic *treas-tarruing* or 'triple-strength'). Triple-distilled whisky was common in the Highlands and Islands at the time, and indeed Talisker from Skye, a big, powerful malt, was triple-distilled until 1928, though triple-distillation is more usually associated with delicate Lowland malts such as Littlemill, Rosebank and Auchentoshan.

Martin wrote of Lewis that 'The air is temperately cold and moist, and for the corrective the natives use a dose of *trestarig* or *uisgebaugh*'. He described *trestarig* as 'aquavitae, three times distilled, which is strong and hot'. Jamieson's *Dictionary of the Scottish Language* defines *trestarig* as 'a kind of ardent spirit distilled from oats', and its origins are ascribed to Lewis.

Martin also noted the existence of a fearsome spirit which was distilled no less than four times for maximum strength. It was *usquebaugh-baul*, and Martin wrote 'at first [it] affects all the members of the body; two spoonfuls of this last liquor is a sufficient dose; and if any man exceed this, it would presently stop his breath, and endanger his life'.

In the years before the 1823 Excise Act, in Stornoway on the Isle of Lewis the local smugglers had an arrangement with one particular excise officer, by which his 'blind eye' was worth 15s for every 10-gallon cask he failed to observe passing by. He was reckoned to make up to £250 per year – more than twice his official salary.

In *A History of the Outer Hebrides* (1903) W.G. Mackenzie observed 'It was no uncommon thing for even the Excise officers to be asked, when they were treated to a glass, which whisky they preferred, "Coll" or "Gress", both of which farms had celebrated stills.' Lewis landowners routinely accepted whisky as rental payments, and oats were distributed by the tenant farmers for their workers to distil with.

⁂

At Garenin, near Carloway, on the west coast of Lewis, 'black houses' were reconstructed by the Garenin Trust during the second half of the 1990s, following archaeological surveys in the area. A landscape survey was conducted by teams from Edinburgh University's Department of Archaeology during fieldwork carried out in 1994 and 1995. Three sites of illicit stills were identified close to the shore, and local 'folklore' recalled distilling taking place in the area. Indeed, when one still site was discovered, locals suggested that a second one should be situated not far away. Apparently there was a mill nearby, which would have supplied grain – probably oats – while a spring running into the sea provided fresh water.

The first distilling site to be discovered by the archaeologists was described as being a D-shaped stone-built enclosure located above the sea-cliffs, a mile from Garenin village. Archaeologists were unsure what it was, until Garenin natives told them. This was supported by their finding of burnt peat and glass that was probably the remains of spirit bottles and demi-johns. The second, some 200 metres away, was of turf construction, while a third probable still site was identified to the north of the existing two.

⁂

The old island skills of concealment of spirits that dated back to the heyday of illicit distilling came to the fore again in 1941, when the *SS Politician* was wrecked off the coast of Eriskay, and some 12,000 bottles of whisky were looted from its cargo of 24,000 cases by islanders. Compton Mackenzie fictionalised the events in his 1947 novel *Whisky Galore*, made into a highly successful film two years later. In the film, a visit by the excisemen sees a baby being lifted up in its cot while bottles are slipped beneath the covers, and other bottles are secreted in the gutterings of croft-houses. In his novel, Mackenzie wrote, 'Peat-stacks became a little larger than they usually were at this time of year. Ricks suggested that the cattle had eaten less hay than usual this winter. Loose floorboards were nailed down. Corks bobbed about in waters where hitherto none had bobbed. Turf recently disturbed was trodden level again as carefully as on a golf-course.'

Edinburgh University's School of Scottish Studies has been conducting and recording interviews with a wide range of residents, principally in the Highlands and Islands, and usually in Gaelic, since 1951. The School publishes the magazine *Tocher*, in which some of the interviews have appeared, often with accompanying English translations. A number give a unique and fascinating insight into the subject of illicit distilling.

North Uist features in a 1968 interview, where the last whisky-makers were said to have operated in the far north-west corner of the island, on the slopes of Beinn Scolpaig. Their equipment was abandoned in nearby Loch Scolpaig when they gave up distilling. Another recording made in the same year with Andrew Nicolson of Grimsay, North Uist, by Angus John MacDonald tells the story of two encounters between illicit distillers and the Lochmaddy-based excise officer Alexander Carmichael, who was also a keen Gaelic folklorist:

> Now then, I would like to tell you a story about a man who was called Alasdair Bàn, in the island of Grimsay, North Uist. Apparently he was good at making whisky at that time. I remember my father speaking about the man. My father was about eight years old at the time of the story I'm going to tell you. My father was born in 1860.
>
> This day Mr Carmichael had come to the district for the Customs and Excise, and he had decided to catch Alasdair Bàn. And he had picked a bad day for doing this – he came over Carinishford, nearly getting drowned in the process, and arrived at Alisdair Bàn's house where they hadn't expected that sort of person to come. But Alasdair Bàn was still there, and he told Carmichael he was happy to welcome him to his humble home and he was sorry he {Carmichael} was so wet and cold.
>
> 'And, good man,' he said, 'before you go to the trouble of searching the house, I would like to give you a dram of good whisky to warm you, and perhaps give you a little pleasure.'
>
> And he did this. He gave him a glass, and before it had gone down [his throat], Carmichael's eyes were closing and he asked for a place where he could lie down. And he got this on the bench in Alisdair Bàn's house, with a lovely Highland bed cover they had spun themselves, and carded and woven too, put over him. And he slept for four hours.
>
> When he woke up anything that was in the house had been put out of the way where neither he nor anyone else would find it. And the black pot, as they called it, [the still] which was a bit away from the house at Abhainn an t-Searraich, had been taken apart by the old man, Alisdair Bàn MacDonald, and thrown in the loch in front of the door. And this had all been done by the time Carmichael woke up, and Alisdair Bàn asked him to search the house and he did that. He

even went under the beds, in the end, on his knees but he saw nothing there – there wasn't anything there, it was all away. And he said he was sorry he had troubled him . . .

'But next time,' he said, 'I'll catch you.'

'Oh,' said Alisdair Bàn, 'there won't be a next time, my friend. Next time it's to the grave we'll be going, and I'm sure I'll be first to go – I'm old anyway.'

But a short time after that Carmichael was crossing the ford to Benbecula. And there was a house in Gramsdale then, an inn called Gramsdale House – the walls are still to be seen – and . . . He was going towards the house and he had found that drink was being supplied to the house by some of the people who were secretly making whisky at their homes. And he met a brother . . . of the man whose house he had searched some days before – a fine old man at that time, Archie son of Lachlan MacDonald, the brother of Alisdair Bàn.

He [Carmichael] took the jar of his [Archie's] back and he was going to take it to Carinish, but Archie, son of Lachlan caught him by the throat and gave him a good going over and knocked him unconscious. And he carried him on his back to Dead Woman's Island, to the Caigeann [half-way across the North Ford], and he [Carmichael] lay there until the next tide went out, and then he went quietly on foot to Lochmaddy. And he took the packet boat [out] next day, and Carmichael was never seen in Uist again.

There you are then.

Whether an experienced gauger like Carmichael would really have fallen for one of the oldest tricks in the illicit distillers' book is open to question, but certainly taking a 'drap o' the cratur' is the cause of their undoing in many popular stories.

The following tale of a sympathetic gauger was recorded in 1963 with Angus MacLellan of Frobost in South Uist by Donald A. MacDonald.

Peter MacPherson, he was my grandmother's brother and he lived north at Loch Carnan. He was busy distilling whisky and unfortunately his neighbour went off and informed against him. He went to the gauger. And the gauger came with him to Peter's house. Peter wasn't up. And the gauger shouted to him: 'Are you still in bed, Peter?'

'Well, yes,' Peter said to him. 'I realise it's time I was up when you have come as early as this.'

Peter got up and came through. Peter realised well enough that he had been informed against and . . ."Sit down there for a wee minute," said Peter. Peter had the cask in the barn full of whisky. He went and got a jug and went off out and started to take some [whisky] out of the cask and put it into the jug. And the other man knew that Peter had gone to see to the cask and he went out after him. Peter was in the barn and had closed the door and the gauger came to the door.

'Open the door, Peter.'

'Oh, hang on a wee minute,' said Peter.

'Open the door or I'll break it in.'

And, 'Oh dear, dear! Can't you take it easy?'

The gauger went and just put his shoulder against it and broke open the door. Peter went and threw something over the cask. And he had quite a lot in the jug.

'Take a seat on this,' said Peter.

The gauger went and sat on the cask and Peter started to pour a dram for him. And after a bit . . . When Peter had poured them a dram or two the gauger said, 'Oh, I realise, Peter, that they have been telling lies about you, thinking that you were distilling whisky.'

'Oh, right enough,' said Peter. 'I'm not distilling whisky, but I always like to keep a little in the house for myself.'

'Oh well, that's all right, then,' said the gauger . . . The gauger went away.

And a week after that the gauger met Peter.

'So, Peter,' he said. 'How are you getting on?'

'Oh, well enough,' said Peter.

'Oh, well,' said he, 'though I was sworn to tell what I might see,' said he, 'I didn't have orders about what I might sit on,' said he. 'But try and take care!'

The fertility of Lismore in grain, renders it a centre of illicit distillation, for which the facilities are also greatly increased by its extent of sea coast, and the consequent ease with which the manufactured commodity can be exported; while the vicinity and population of all the surrounding shores, offer a ready market for the sale of the produce.

– John MacCulloch, A Description of
the Western Isles of Scotland (1819)

The island of Mull features in a number of recordings in the archives of the School of Scottish Studies, and the following is Alec MacDougall of Treshninsh, Mull, interviewed in July 1967:

My great-grandfather and his two brothers, it was from Ireland that they first came here, up to Lagganulva, and they made whisky there [probably in the late eighteenth century]. They had a lot of good whisky, and they couldn't get it sold at all here: they had to go to Ireland. They left Laggan yonder at nightfall, and they went out through the Sound of Iona, until they were out of sight from everywhere before day broke, and they got to Belfast. They sold the whisky – they got a shilling a bottle for it and they would get flour and stuff like that too. Anyway, they were back in Lagganulva on the morning of the third day – three of them, with a rowing-boat.

Then they came to Treshnish, and the sons started making whisky – my grandfather and his brother [probably in the early nineteenth century]. They were working at it for a long while, and they couldn't get it sold. There was a man in Coll, he was buying it, whatever way he managed to get it away to Ireland. They had a lot of whisky this day and information had been laid that they had it. But they picked a wild day to go to Coll with it, because that way there was less likely to be a boat or anything around to see them.

What should happen but, when they were out half-way to Coll, she came in sight round Caliach Point, the [revenue] cutter, after them. They fired a shot [from the cutter] to see if she would stop. They couldn't turn back, the sea was so rough, so what they did was let her run for Tiree, to get clear of the trouble. They got to Tiree, they ran her into a geo there, and the Tiree people came down to them, masses of them. They realised at once what was happening. They picked up the whisky and went off with it, and hid it somewhere. Then another squad came and lifted the boat out of the water and put her up behind the other boats. The cutter arrived anyway, and sent a boat ashore: they ransacked the whole place but they didn't find the whisky. They found the boat, still wet, up behind the other boats: they took the boat with them to Campbeltown anyway, but I don't believe they ever laid hands on the whisky.

The island of Mull and another sea adventure are at the centre of a tale told by Angus Henderson of Tobermory to Alan Bruford in January 1967.

When they used to make a lot of whisky throughout all the Highlands, they made a lot in Ardnamurchan, and they used to come over to Tobermory quite regularly to sell their whisky. There was one particular night, or early morning, that they came over with a coble from Glenborrodale or Glenbeg, or some place in that part of Ardnamurchan anyway. And they came into the beach at Tobermory, and some of them went ashore to find out what the innkeepers wanted from the casks they had. And day was just breaking, so they didn't notice that the King's cutter, as they used to call it, was anchored there. They left this young lad, Alisdair Crùbach [Lame Alisdair]: he was a cripple, he had dislocated his hip when he was a boy and it had never been put right. He was the son of Alisdair Henderson. And he was watching [?] the beach there, and he noticed a whaleboat with four, or maybe eight oars leaving the gaugers' boat, and he put out his oars and set off out of the harbour mouth before they could get everything in order. But they were not hurrying, knowing well enough that they could catch him up very easily if they needed to. But he kept on behind his pair of oars until he was out level with the Stirks. And [it seemed] as if he were going to give up – they came close enough to him anyway, and he stood up in the boat. They said something to him, but he jumped into their boat, and took an oar and thereupon began furiously knocking the planks out of the boat until he had put the bottom out of her altogether. They had to jump out into the sea, but he dived and swam to his own boat, and made off as fast as he could over to the Glens on the other side.

They got the boat ashore, and the whisky taken out and hidden. The rest of them had been left in Tobermory, no doubt. But next morning they [the gaugers] went across with another boat, over to that coast, to have a look anyway, and they saw this coble and asked whose it was.

'It just belongs to the township, it's not for anyone in particular, just belongs to the township.'

'And has it been out?'

'It hasn't moved from here, not for weeks: as far as we know nobody at all has had it out.'

And they never discovered how Alisdair Crùbach had tricked the gaugers.

Donald Morrison was interviewed in 1974, and his account refers to Mull during the first few decades of the nineteenth century. Again there is a link between illicit distilling on the island and Ireland.

My grandfather was making it, – over, just beside the people I'm talking about, the other side of the stream. And he had it, he had stones down at the bottom and then he piled it up with sods and put some sticks below, you see, and it was like part of the hill. There was a wee opening at the end where you could crouch in. They were making it at night in winter-time.

Once the whisky was made,

you had to hide it, bury it, or put it out under the sea water if there was a sandy beach, or the like o' that . . . and cover it with sand and put a stone on the top of it, a small stone. This was the mark so you could get it. When the sea would come in, you see, it would smooth the sand and you couldn't mark it without the stone being on the top of it. [Then you would] take it up again and send it to Ireland. Uisken was a great place for that.

A song relating to illicit distilling was recorded from Colin Fletcher of Torloisk in Mull, by Alan Bruford in July 1967. The original is in Gaelic, and once more features Mull and Ireland. Some sources consider that the party had gone to Ireland to buy whisky, though in view of the variety of accounts of going to Ireland to *sell* Mull-distilled illicit whisky, this seems unlikely. The skipper of the boat had to be left behind in Ireland as he was ashore when the revenue cutter approached. According to Alan Bruford, editor of *Tocher* when the song was published in issue 2 (1978), the 'yellow [-haired] lad' may be the boat itself, though it could surely also be the abandoned skipper.

Alas for you, yellow lad,
You are sought after today!
Alas for you, yellow lad.

We put the lofty masts on her
Two days before we left Ireland.
We put the new sails on her
So that we got a good turn of speed from her.

We hoisted her anchors
In Belfast in Ireland.

Cutters and gaugers
Were persecuting us together.

English powder and lead
Were making a rattling on her planking.

Passing the Mull of Oa
We drank to one another.

Passing the Mull of Kintyre
The spray was splashing on her.

We were in Lochaline
Before most of them were up.

We drank the health of the skipper
Who wasn't there to hear us.

And we drank the health of the boat
That had brought us safely from Ireland.
It would have been a hard fate if it had happened
That we were all lost.

7

CENTRAL AND EASTERN SCOTLAND

Illicit whisky features in Robert Louis Stevenson's poem 'Atholl Brose', with the still in question being located near the village of Blair Atholl in Perthshire. This area was home to many illicit distillers, and the addition of honey, cream and oatmeal to their raw spirit must have done much to increase its palatability.

> Willie and I cam doun by Blair
> And in by Tullibardine;
> The rye were at the riverside,
> An' bee-skeps in the garden;
> I saw the reek o' a private still –
> Says I 'Gude Lord, I thank ye!'
> As Willie and I cam in by Blair,
> And out by Killiecrankie.
>
> Ye hinny bees, ye smuggler lands,
> Thou Muse, the bard's protector,
> I never kent what rye was for
> Till I had drunk the nectar!
> And shall I never drink it mair?
> Gude troth, I beg your pardon!
> The neist time I come doun by Blair
> And in by Tullibardine.'

So little was it practised in the Perthshire Highlands that a tenant of my grandfather's was distinguished by the appellation of 'Donald Whisky', from his being a distiller and smuggler of that spirit. If all existing were to be named from this traffic, five of the most numerous clans of the country conjoined could not produce so many of one name. In the year 1778, there was only one officer of excise in that part of Perthshire above Dunkeld, and he had little employment. In the same district, there are now eleven resident officers in full activity, besides Rangers (as they are called) and extra officers sent to see that the resident officers are doing their duty; yet, so rapidly did illicit distillation increase, that it would seem as if the greater the number of officers appointed, the more employment they found for themselves; and it is a common, and, I believe, a just remark, that whenever an officer is placed in a glen, he is not long without business.

– Colonel David Stewart of Garth, Sketches of the Character, Manners and Present State of the Highlanders of Scotland *(1825)*

Highland Perthshire certainly became a popular location for illicit distilling. A number of stills were situated in the remote area beyond Loch Broom, to the north-east of the hamlet of Tullymet, south-east of Pitlochry. The old blacksmith at Tullymet, Alex Cameron, spent time as a boy transporting illicit whisky distilled near his home at Tormald, close to the Broom burn, down to the inns of Tullymet and Ballinluig. Further afield, Coupar Angus was the destination for much of the illicit whisky made in Highland Perthshire.

The Loch Broom distillers came up with a clever way of disguising the dam they built to provide a place for steeping their barley – a tell-tale feature for which gaugers would always be on the lookout. When not in use, they covered it with planks of wood and then put turf on top of those, finally herding in sheep to graze on them.

After the 1823 Excise Act, there were up to a dozen small-scale legal distilleries operating within quite close proximity to the River Tay in the 15-mile stretch between Kenmore at the head of Loch Tay and the point near Logierait, where the Tay and the Tummel have their confluence. One was Auchnagie, at Tullymet, which later belonged to the Dewar family, before they constructed their much larger distillery at Aberfeldy in 1896/98.

The story is told of one local, who lived at Tullymet, who managed to get past the excise officers and siphon spirit from casks in the Auchnagie warehouse. He hid small bottles of this spirit in various places in the neighbourhood, and local legend has it that the occasional bottle has been discovered among the stones of dry-stane dykes even in quite recent times. The same man was always accompanied on his trips for a dram at the Ballinluig inn by his pet goose.

Alexander Stewart's *A Highland Parish – or the History of Fortingall* was published in 1928. Fortingall is close to Loch Tay, in Perthshire, and Stewart's reminiscences go back to the 1860s. Writing of smuggling and poaching cases, he observed that

> even the magistrates who tried such cases often refused to take a serious view of them. At the beginning of the nineteenth century such offences were tried by the courts of the Justices of the Peace. At Weem, where the local court met, there was often a long list of poaching and smuggling cases before the magistrates; but Francis Mor, the chief of the Macnabs, who usually presided, as a general rule, let the delinquents off lightly.
>
> In those days the people stood loyally by each other. If an Excise

officer appeared in any glen messengers were sent to the neighbouring hamlets to warn the occupants of the turf and stone bothies that were dug in the sides of the mountain burns for distilling the spirits. The result was that the capture of men or materials were few and far between.

In transporting the products of their labours to market, special precautions had to be taken to prevent discovery. For this purpose women, being less liable to be suspected than men, were often employed. They carried the whisky in tin vessels on their backs. These they covered over with shawls, and, in order to obviate suspicion, they usually carried light baskets with some lace or ribbons in them. On many occasions the carriers travelled by night and wended their way through unfrequented mountain passes. On other occasions spirits were concealed in wool bags or in the bottom of carts, covered over with other goods. In one instance the device was used of carrying the whisky in a cart in which was placed an apparently feeble old man lying on a bed of straw, as if he were in the last stages of illness. On the road to Perth the conveyance was met by a party of Excise officers. The latter suspected nothing, and, moved with pity for the old bed-ridden man, asked the driver of the cart what ailed him. To this he replied that he was suffering from the *duig-leisg*, which they took to be the name of some dreadful malady, but which in reality is the Gaelic phrase for 'back laziness'.

There are few surviving songs about the perennial battle between smuggler and gauger in Scotland, but one fine example is a ballad about what became known as 'The Battle of Corriemuckloch'. Corriemuckloch is a hamlet halfway between Crieff and Aberfeldy in Perthshire, located by the modern A822 road, just south of Amulree. In the early nineteenth century this area of Breadalbane was a hotbed of smuggling, and large quantities of whisky made around Loch Tay were regularly transported via Aberfoyle to Glasgow, at times in convoys made up of sixty or more ponies.

The ballad concerns an epic encounter between a band of smugglers from Bohespic, near Tummel Bridge, and the local excise officer, supported by six dragoons from the Scots Greys, stationed in Auchterarder. The conflict occurred as the smugglers were making their way to Crieff via the Small Glen and Amulree with a large festive consignment of spirit to fuel the Hogmanay celebrations. It took place on 21 December 1823.

In his 1881 book *Crieff: Its Traditions and Characters*, Duncan McAra gave an account of the 'battle', in which he told of the smugglers being warned by their scouts that there were an exciseman and troopers on the road ahead. They decided to hide their casks of whisky in the nearby moss, and proceeded to ambush the soldiers under cover of darkness, injuring one in the ensuing melee, before making off, leaving their whisky behind. According to McAra, 'The smugglers never looked after their barrels, being, it was supposed, afraid that the Excise were continuously on the watch. They were, however, gradually removed by parties who considered that their lying in the moss did not improve their contents. One of those who had an active hand in securing the barrels is still alive, and pursuing his avocation as a member of the "gentle craft" in Comrie Street, Crieff.' McAra noted that even when writing his book, the 'Battle of Corriemuckloch' was 'still the principal theme of smuggling reminiscences'.

December, on the twenty-first,
A party of the Scottish Greys
Came up our lofty mountains steep
To try and Highland whisky seize,
With sword and pistol by their side,
They thought to make a bold attack
And a' they wanted was to seize
Poor Donald wi' his smuggled drap.

Chorus
Dirim dye a dow a dee,
Dirim dye a dow a daddie,
Dirim dye a dow a dee,
Poor Donald wi' his smuggled drap.

The gauger loon drew up his men,
And soon poor Donald did surround;
He said 'your whisky I must seize
By virtue of the British crown.'
'Hip, hip!' said Donald, 'not so fast,
The wee bit drappie's a' our ain;
We care not for you, nor your horse,
Nor yet your muckle bearded men.'

Chorus

The Highland chields were soon drawn up,
With Donald chief to give command;
But a' the arms poor Donald had
Was a good oak stick in ilka hand.
Brave Donald smartly ranged his men
Where a stane dyke was at their back;
And when their sticks to prunock [pounding] went
Wi' stanes they made a bold attack!

Chorus

But ere the action's brunt was o'er
A horseman lay upon the plain,
And Sandy then to Donald said,
'We've killed ane o' the bearded men.'
But up he got and ran awa',
And east to Amulree he flew,
And left the rest to do their best,
As they had done at Waterloo.

Chorus

When Donald and the lads struck fast,
The beardies had to quit the field;
The gauger's men were thumpit weel
Ere driven back and forced to yield.
'If e'er ye come this gate again
Ye filthy, ugly gauger loon
If e'er ye come through Almond's glen,
Ye'll n'er see Auchterarder toun.'

Chorus

When the battle's din was o'er,
And not a horseman to be seen,
Brave Donald to his men did say,
'Come, sit ye doun upon the green.
And noo, my lads, ye just shall taste
A drappie o' the thing we hae.'
'My troth,' quo' Donald, 'they did get
A filthy hurry doun the brae.'

One of the flintlock pistols used by a member of the Scots Greys in the battle was given to the seventh duke of Atholl in 1874, and is now displayed in the entrance hall of Blair Castle in Perthshire.

Differing accounts of the encounter survive, with Donald Dow of Strathtummel giving a version to Tony Dilworth in 1954, which is preserved in a recording in the School of Scottish Studies archive. Dow said that the band of smugglers was led by his ancestor Thomas Dow, who was alerted to the presence of the gauger and dragoons by the smell of cigars, a very unusual odour in that part of the countryside. Dow proceeded to kill the captain of the dragoons and two or three other soldiers, though there is nothing to suggest that anyone died at Corriemuckloch. In Dow's version, it was Thomas Dow's sword that was presented to the duke of Atholl, rather than a pistol.

There are numerous tales of gaugers being caught off guard while 'relaxing' with the spoils of their day's work. Two concern the Foss

Inn, located near the south-west end of Loch Tummel, west of Pitlochry, in Perthshire. The first involves a seizure of spirit and two ponies from one Ewan Fletcher, who operated a still in a glen close to the mountain of Schiehallion. The gaugers duly paused at the Foss Inn for refreshment before continuing to their base in Pitlochry, and while inside an obliging local farmer offered them the hire of his cart to take the casks of spirit back to Pitlochry. He was so obliging that he bought another round of (legal) drinks for the officers while his men transferred the casks from the ponies to the cart. What the officers didn't know was that the friendly farmer was married to a cousin of Ewan Fletcher, and in the best tradition of such stories, Fletcher switched the casks for ones filled with water, while the farmer was entertaining the gaugers in the Foss Inn. It was not until they returned in triumph to Pitlochry late in the evening that the deception was discovered.

The Foss Inn must have been a regular watering hole for the Pitlochry gaugers, for the second anecdote concerns a local smuggler by the name of Donald Cameron, whose confiscated still was taken into the inn by the officers. They carefully locked themselves in their bedroom along with the still, thinking that their prudence would keep the 'evidence' safe.

According to Alexander Stewart in *A Highland Parish*:

> The smugglers not only contrived ingeniously to keep themselves and their stills and other distilling utensils out of the hands of the Excise officers, but some of them even made daring attempts to recover their utensils after they had been seized by the excisemen. Donald C–, one of the boldest of smugglers, had his bothy at the side of a burn behind Schiehallion. It was discovered by the excisemen, and they removed his whole distilling plant to the little inn in Foss, where they decided to put up for the night. In order that the booty might be perfectly secure, it was deposited in the bedroom where they themselves were sleeping. Then with locked doors and, as they supposed, well secured against any would-be intruder, they slept soundly, oblivious of danger. But Donald was determined that they should not get away with his gear. They occupied an upper room, but it had an end or gable window. To this window, Donald, in the dead of night, made his way with the aid of some planks. He quickly unfastened it, entered the room, threw the excisemen's shoes through the window, and with a jingling noise made off with his precious wares. The gaugers, as the excisemen were usually called, though wakened by the noise, spent some little time searching for their shoes, so Donald was some distance ahead of them. The search for their shoes proving vain, they gave pursuit in their stockings' soles, but Donald proved too fleet for them. Before his pursuers could make up on him, he was able to reach a peat hollow, where he hid his gear, and the Excise officers were never able to find it. When he took them

out of this hiding place, he sold them to another man and forsook the illicit trade once and for all.

A story concerning the smuggler William Jackson from near Alyth in Perthshire appears in a newspaper cutting (possibly from the *Dundee Advertiser*) in the Lamb Collection of Dundee City Library. The cutting dates from the late nineteenth century, and the writer recalled that 'in the northern portion of Forfarshire and the eastern division of Perthshire a brisk trade was carried on by men who set the excise laws at defiance, and occasionally fought with and defeated the troopers who were sent by the Government to assist the excise officers in rooting out the traffic and apprehend the transgressors'.

Writing of the Angus town of Forfar and the surrounding area in the early nineteenth century, the newspaper columnist ('JMB') noted:

One of the most successful and daring of the Excise officers in that district was the late John Corbet, Esq., afterwards Collector of Excise in Dundee, who died in Broughty Ferry about 25 years ago. Mr Corbet as a gauger was noticed in the newspapers and periodicals of the day as the greatest opponent of the smugglers, and most fortunate in finding out their hidden haunts among the hills to the north of Forfar. In Perthshire, however, the smugglers had greater scope for their talents in evading the revenue, the mountainous nature of the country affording better facilities for carrying on the illicit manufacture than in Forfarshire, and several clever men managed to avoid for years coming into hostile contact with the authorities. One of these was a man named William Jackson, a young man of powerful frame, who occupied a cottage and pendicle near the town of Alyth. This man is still alive and hearty, is 79 years of age, is in comfortable circumstances, and occupies a pendicle of land near to the town of Meigle. Old Jackson is delighted to tell of the good old times when he 'brewed his peck o' maut', and succeeded in evading the parties sent out to apprehend him, and laughs in his sleeve when he narrates the circumstances of his only having been caught once. The circumstances were these: Bill had a snug distillery in a den or gorge between two hills, access to which was disguised by broom and heather and grass, and from which he could espy any person approaching. Close by was a moss, which in some places was deep in silt, and at others was passable by certain tracks not known to strangers. One day a number of horsemen were seen approaching, some of which were recognised as mounted Dragoons. These must have learned the locality of the still, for they galloped fast to get it surrounded without being observed. There being no time to hide anything, Bill and his mate had at once to betake themselves to flight into the moss. The troopers halted at its edge, but one more daring than the rest dismounted, and commenced to chase the two men. Now in the moss were tufts of grass covering small islands, and between them were pools covered with green scum like grass. Bill and his companion jumped from one clump of grass to another to escape, but the Dragoon ran after them, and straight plunged up to the waist among glaur, which at once stopped his career, and he had no resource but to fish himself out the best way he could, while they cleared these obstacles, and ultimately landed at the other side of the moss, whence they proceeded up a hill and hid themselves, but from which they could see what was doing below, which was the total dismantling of the still, and carrying away the implements and two kegs of whisky which had just been run off.

Bill, being personally known to the gauger, expected to be looked after for punishment. He took care not to sleep in his own house, but kept in communication with his mother and brother, so as to have the crop, which was getting ripe, secured for the winter use. However, early one morning the house was surrounded by Dragoons, and the officer had a warrant to apprehend Jackson; but they were disappointed, for, after searching everywhere, their man could not be found. Shortly after a summons of indictment before the Sheriff Court was served at the house, and Jackson resolved not to attend the Court, as he found on inquiry that in that case a decree in absence would be for a fine or imprisonment for a definite period, whereas, if he appeared in Court, a decree could be passed for an indefinite period, or, in other words, till the fine be paid; so the result was that he was fined £50, or six months' imprisonment. On learning the result of the Court Jackson made up his mind that he would not pay, but go to jail whenever he found that the crop was all in, and provision made for his family during the ensuing winter. On this being obtained he observed that the straw thatch on his house was in bad order, and he commenced repairing it; but while he was thus employed he espied a horseman coming up the hill, who proved to be a sheriff-officer, who, after the usual greeting, asked Jackson to come down and speak to him. Jackson, suspecting that the officer intended to apprehend him, asked if such was not the case, when he learned that it was so. Well, Jackson came down, and desired the officer to show his warrant, which he proceeded to do, but was much crestfallen to find that he had forgotten to bring it with him, so Jackson said that it did not matter, as he had resolved to take the six months' imprisonment, but would not go to prison till he had finished thatching his house, which would take the remainder of the week, and if the officer would return on that day with the warrant he would accompany him to Perth on Monday. This arrangement satisfied both parties, and on the day fixed the officer returned, accompanied Jackson to Perth, and handed him and the warrant to Mr Simpson, the jailer, who placed him in a room in which were confined a Perth writer, detained for debt, a shipmaster imprisoned for smuggling foreign tobacco, and sundry other jolly fellows, and he there spent the most enjoyable six months of his life. At that time jailers were at liberty to sell liquors to the prisoners (*i.e.*, porter and ales, but not spirits), and his friends sent in plenty of good food, and all that had to be done by him was cook it. The six months ended when his labour was required in putting the new crop in the ground, and on counting up all things, considered he had fared as well as if he had been at home.

———※———

Illicit whisky destined for the city of Dundee was transported in pony-trains from as far away as Lochaber. Often these pony-trains stopped in the smuggling centre of Auchterhouse, now virtually a north-western suburb of the city, close to the Sidlaw Hills. There the contents of the smugglers' 5- or 10-gallon casks would be poured into smaller containers for safer distribution in Dundee, often by villagers rather than by the smugglers themselves, who might just have looked a little conspicuous. The villagers acted as agents for regular customers in the nearby towns and cities, and were known as 'bladdermen' or 'blethermen', as they often transported the whisky in bladders.

Bladders were flexible, and fitted neatly beneath a lady's long dress, though one Dundee smuggler by the name of Geordie Fleming wore an exceptionally tall hat which concealed a bladder of whisky! Additionally, flasks were designed to fit under clothing, and milk churns with false bottoms were constructed in order to smuggle the spirit to its customers.

The whisky was frequently carried into towns and cities by women, and the pretext of searching for concealed whisky made many a lecherous gauger's day. Not surprisingly, the gaugers always seemed to be most suspicious of shapely young women, rarely bothering to subject older females to their body searches. Presumably the best way to get whisky past a gauger was to conceal it beneath the skirts of a fat, malodorous old woman. One celebrated woman courier and distiller, whose own whisky had a great reputation around Dundee, was Jean Anderson, who regularly took whisky into the city in bladders concealed beneath her skirt.

———※———

Fife was also thirsty for the 'proper' stuff from the Highlands, and some pony-trains would by-pass Dundee and head for the village of Invergowrie, which, like Auchterhouse, is now virtually a suburb of the city. From there the casks would be ferried across the Firth of Tay into Fife, for distribution in towns such as Cupar and surrounding villages.

———※———

As well as acting as something of a 'clearing house' for spirits, Auchterhouse also boasted illicit stills of its own. On Sundays, the

Sidlaw Hills were a popular venue for picnickers from Dundee, and it was not unknown for local smugglers to mingle with them, offering to sell them home-made spirit. These offers were frequently taken up with enthusiasm, and more than one Dundonian picnicker had to be helped home by his friends after misjudging the potency of the Auchterhouse product. Reputedly, one smuggler concealed a large 'dog' of whisky shaped like a breastplate beneath his voluminous overcoat, and dispensed it to the picnickers – by way of a small tap at the bottom.

W. Mason Inglis – minister at Auchterhouse in the late nineteenth century – wrote a book published in 1888 called *Annals of an Angus Parish*, many of the anecdotes in which were heard from parishioners who had personal knowledge of the events. In it he told of an incident which took place on 12 March 1813, when excise officers discovered the best part of 100 gallons of whisky in casks hidden in a field near Auchterhouse. Commandeering a horse and cart they set off for Dundee with their spoils, only to be ambushed by three smugglers, to whom the whisky obviously belonged. A battle raged for almost an hour, according to Inglis, during which time one officer received cuts to his head, and one of the smugglers was shot in the neck. Finally, the smugglers made off with three kegs of whisky, which the officers accepted, as it brought the conflict to a close. Tellingly, a group of respectable farmers came along during the fight, but passed on, making no attempt to help the excisemen.

The story is told of an occasion in Auchterhouse when a surprise visit from the gaugers led a villager to lift his small daughter from her bed, put bottles of illicit whisky beneath her, and tell her to follow his lead. The gaugers searched the cottage and found nothing. They turned to the man who was leaning anxiously over the little girl, and she duly moaned on cue. When asked by one of the officers what was wrong with her, the man took his hand and said, 'She has a terrible fever, here, feel for yourself.' Predictably, the gauger pulled away, fearing infection, and rapidly left the house.

The following item appeared in the *Dundee, Perth and Cupar Advertiser* on 26 July 1816. Clearly the writer was not overly impressed with the manner in which the excise officers executed their duty.

> A melancholy example of the pernicious consequences of smuggling as well as the cruelty with which the revenue laws are sometimes enforced

occurred in our neighbourhood on the morning of Saturday last. It also
illustrates the severe pressure of the times; by which too many have
been driven to shifts which in their better days they despised.

William Dick, the tenant of a small farm in the parish of
Blairgowrie, having fallen into arrear with his rent, had resorted to
the wretched course of illicit distillation to enable him to meet his
landlord's demands. He had prepared two bolls of malt, and converted
them into whisky; one half of which he had disposed of at Blairgowrie,
and attempted to bring the other to Dundee, in company with two of
his more practised acquaintances, employed in the same traffic, and
driven to it probably by the same cause. A party of Customhouse
boatmen, – who pretend that they had received accurate information
of the quantity of whisky to be smuggled, the way in which it was to
be conveyed, the number of the smugglers, and the road they meant
to follow, – went out on the Cupar road, to the number of nine, armed
with bludgeons, cutlasses, and loaded pistols. Four of them took their
station at the road leading to Logie Farm; and the other five concealed
themselves inside the southernmost door of Logie policies, about two
hundred yards nearer to Dundee. About three o'clock in the morning,
the smugglers, mounted on horseback, approached the gate of Logie
Farm: The four boatmen crossed the road to seize the whisky; but
the smugglers, suspecting their intention, gave their horses the rein,
and proceeded to Dundee at full speed. The party posted nearer
Dundee, warned by the noise of the horses' feet and the hallooing
of their companions, prepared to intercept them. The smugglers, on
discovering the second party, seemed inclined to retrace their steps;
but seeing the others also approach, and being hemmed in on both
sides, two of them adopted the desperate resolution of proceeding to
Dundee at all hazards. The first who passed was fired at; but escaped
unhurt, although his horse was wounded: Another, who had no whisky,
escaped entirely: But Dick, who by his own account intended to submit,
had not his horse, alarmed by the fire-arms, taken fright, was not so
fortunate, – several shots were fired; one of which wounded his horse
in the chest, another in the hind-thigh, and a third wounded himself
(it is feared mortally) at the small of the back. Dick immediately fell.
The boatmen passed on, jeering the poor man as they passed; and it
was not till half an hour afterwards, that he was able to crawl to the
Upper Pleasance, to the house of John Scott, a carter, – who sent for a
surgeon to dress his wound, and has ever since continued to treat him
with the greatest humanity.

The lad who had no whisky was afterwards seized, somewhere
about the Overgate. On his refusing to accompany the boatmen, they
coolly told him, that they had already shot one of his companions; and
(presenting a pistol) they would, if he resisted, do the same for him.
He of course surrendered; and was kept in custody till about two in
the afternoon.

Pitkethly, who appears to have fired the fatal shot, is in custody; and a precognition of all the circumstances has been taken, with more than usual accuracy and promptitude.

⬞⬞⬞

Close to Kinnaird Castle in the Carse of Gowrie, between Perth and Dundee, is the waterfall, whose name Linn-ma-Gray is a corruption of the Gaelic for 'waterfall of my darling'. Smugglers used it as cover to make whisky and stored the finished spirit under the cliffs of the waterfall. Warned off by excise officers who had discovered what was going on, the smugglers left their distilling equipment and casks of whisky hidden. Sadly for them, during a particularly dramatic thaw of snow the waterfall swelled to twice its usual size, and the torrent flushed out all the paraphernalia of distilling and the casks of spirit, which smashed on the rocks as they were swept downstream.

⬞⬞⬞

The Perthshire and Angus glens were popular routes from Speyside to Dundee and Fife. They included Glenshee, Glenisla, Strathardle and the eastern Strathmore glens of Clova, Esk and Prosen. Convoys of illicit whisky came from as far afield as the Highlands of Lochaber and Badenoch. Glenisla, which runs north-west from Kirriemuir in Angus, was also a centre for illicit distilling, especially for markets in Dundee and Fife. Many smuggling routes from the Highlands passed through the Sidlaw Hills, and knowing this only too well, the excise service had bases in Alyth, Blairgowrie, Coupar Angus and Meigle.

⬞⬞⬞

Decoys were an important part of the battle between exciseman and smuggler, and in most illicit distilling communities there was usually no shortage of fleet-footed youths who would take off into the heather from a croft or village at the approach of gaugers, apparently to warn a group of distillers. The gaugers would follow, but, of course, the youths would be heading away from the still, and someone else would unobtrusively go and warn the distillers while the pursuit was in progress.

Well-known third-generation illicit distiller David Ogilvie of Rashiebog, Glen Quiech in Angus was born in 1796, and when in his nineties he was interviewed by a Dundee newspaper reporter. He recalled an occasion on which he sent off his young helper from the distilling bothy as gaugers approached with a sack on his back filled with old pots and pans, the sound of which intimated to them that he was carrying off the valuable worm. They followed him for miles as he ran across terrain he knew very well, while Ogilvie dismantled his still and hid all the evidence of distilling. The boy lost the gaugers, and when they returned to the point further down the glen where they had begun their trek they were deeply embarrassed to find the sack – complete with contents – dumped beside their horses!

Inevitably, with the lucrative markets of Glasgow just a few miles to the south, the Campsie and Kilpatrick Hills north of the 'Highland Line' became a hotbed of distilling in the early nineteenth century, particularly as many Highland folk with a fondness for good whisky moved to the city to find work. At times dragoons were called in from Glasgow and Stirling to help suppress the trade.

According to Mrs Eliza Fletcher (1770–1858), 'Balfron was a most lawless village. It was illicit distillation that demoralised the district. The men of the place resorted to the woods or the sequestered glens among the Campsie Hills and there distilled whisky, which their wives and daughters took in tin vessels in the form of stays buckled round their waists to sell for a high price in Glasgow.'

Smuggling across the Highland Line was a major problem for the authorities, as reported by *The Courier* (London), 14 July 1804:

When the smugglers have a large smuggling adventure ready, about Callander, Crieff, or any where on the borders of the line, having established a telegraphic communication betwixt Stirling and these places, a person is stationed at Balangich, the hill at the west end of Stirling Castle, who, having watched the motions of the Excise Officers, and seen and found out what road they take, he gives a certain whistle, a sign, which is heard and transmitted by other persons stationed at proper distances all the way, and by these means they communicate the information in a very few minutes from Stirling to Callander, or any like distance. Having obtained this notice, they then dispatch two or three of their worst horses, with two anchors upon each; these go directly in the way of the Officers and when they fall in with them, make a great feigned resistance, but at last after a great deal of ado, they are taken and carried off by the Officers in triumph, who congratulate themselves on being very successful, and return home very pleased with their night's excursion, but while they are so occupied and amused, the smugglers run down twenty, thirty, or forty times this quantity with perfect safety by other roads.

8

THE NORTH

The most famous smuggling story associated with the north of Scotland concerns an incident that took place at the Bogroy Inn, a hostelry at Kirkhill, west of Inverness, which still provides accommodation and refreshment for travellers.

Apparently a group of excise officers arrived at the inn one evening with a cask of illicit whisky which they had seized earlier in the day. Requesting a room for the night, the officers proceeded to lock the cask in their room, before going back downstairs to eat. The owners of the confiscated cask were watching events unfold from a discreet corner of the inn, and they asked one of the maids to go and find out exactly where in the room the cask was placed. Armed with this information, they proceeded to drill up through the floor and the base of the cask, catching the contents in another barrel. Meanwhile the excisemen were eating their supper, content in the knowledge that their booty was locked safely out of harm's way.

In *Smuggling in the Highlands* (1914) Ian MacDonald noted that 'An augur hole was shown to me some years ago in the flooring at Bogroy Inn, where the feat was said to have been performed, but I find that the story is also claimed for Mull. Numerous clever stories are claimed for several localities.'

The Bogroy Inn also features in a second smuggling tale. During an excise raid at Glassburn in Strathglass an inexperienced gauger ran his cutlass through a wicker-work barn door which could not be opened, inadvertently stabbing a smuggler in the chest as he did so. The injured man was John Chisholm, or Ian Mor Garvaig in the Gaelic, and as the excise officers made a hasty exit, fearing for their lives, one of them was trampled and kicked by some of the furious smugglers. He was carried to the nearby Bogroy Inn, but died of internal injuries.

MacDonald recalled, 'Ian Mor, who only died a few months ago, showed me the scar on the wound on his chest. He was another man who had gained nothing by smuggling.'

The previous week a party of revenue men were compelled to retreat from Strathglass. They put up at a public house at Comar, and were warned that if they did not immediately return home, 'after what they had already destroyed', worse would happen to them. Mr Macniven, who was in charge of the party, disregarded the warning and next morning set forward. About two miles beyond the public house a smart fire commenced from the upper grounds, and on arriving in a narrow pass of the road, his further progress was stopped by about twenty men, armed with muskets and arrayed within gunshot. The Revenue party, consisting of ten men being armed only with pistols and short cutlasses, had no alternative but to retreat from the determined purpose of slaughter shown by the smugglers, and retired accordingly from the unequal contest; nor is it of any avail for the Revenue officers to attempt a seizure in that quarter until powerfully and efficiently armed.

– The Inverness Courier, *April 1827*

Strathglass lies to the north-west of the Cromarty Firth, which the River Glass enters near Evanton, and the glen was still proving a thorn in the side of the excise service eight years after the *Courier*'s report. The same newspaper noted, 'On Wednesday a party of the *Atlanta* Revenue cutter, consisting of an officer and four men, while discharging their duty in Strathglass, were attacked by a band of smugglers, about 14 in number, and driven back with great violence.'

Inverness excise officer Colin Munro was involved in an incident in 1820, described in a petition by Patrick Andrews to the Inverness sheriff depute:

Having been informed that smuggled whisky was to be conveyed into that place on the evening of the fifteenth or morning of the sixteenth days of February last, he, accompanied by John McDonald extra-assistant officer and two soldiers, went to Clachnaharry about eight o'clock in the evening of the fifteenth to intercept it, and continued watching till about twelve, when they fell in with two horses carrying three casks of whisky and escorted by eight men – after a considerable struggle with these men the officers succeeded in securing the horses and whisky, and carrying them into the house of William McKay in Clachnaharry – the officers and party were then attacked by twelve to fifteen unknown men – who broke open the doors and windows of the house – and after a violent struggle, during which several articles of furniture and the windows and door of the above house were destroyed, these persons succeeded in retaking the horses and spirits.

As we already know, members of the Scottish clergy did not always take a scrupulously anti-smuggling line, but Ian MacDonald reminisced about a man of the cloth who crossed the line from turning a blind eye to smuggling, and even warning his flock when gaugers were approaching, to becoming a distiller and smuggler himself.

The minister in question was Alisdair Hutcheson, of Kiltarlity, a dozen miles south-west of Inverness. Hutcheson turned to smuggling in order to bolster his meagre stipend, but was finally caught red-handed with his illicit whisky hidden in a cart-load of peats on the outskirts of Inverness. The gauger who apprehended him was so surprised that a minister was smuggling that he let him go, on the solemn undertaking that he would never distil again. The gauger had received a tip-off regarding Hutcheson's activities from Inverness publican James Shanks of the Star Inn, who thought he was being charged too much by Hutcheson for his spirit. He omitted to tell the gauger that the smuggler in question was also a minister. The gauger asked the minister to deliver his contraband to Shanks as arranged and then proceeded to arrest the publican for its possession!

On 27 September 1816 Maggie Maclennan, Janet Young, Calum Campbell and six other women were charged at Inverness District Sheriff Court with assault on a revenue officer, and mobbing and rioting. During an encounter near Redcastle, just north of the Beauly Firth on the Black Isle, Maclennan had been injured by the revenue officer in question, John Proudfoot. The women charged had prevented Proudfoot from removing two sacks of malted barley which he had discovered at the side of the road. As Maclennan had spent two weeks in bed recovering from her injuries, she escaped with a fine, while Janet Young, Calum Campbell and a further four women were each jailed for thirty days.

When I was a boy there were stories, which I have not been able to verify, of smuggling being carried on in the vaults and dungeons of Urquhart Castle [on the shores of Loch Ness], which we youngsters were afraid to enter and explore. Similar stories, and better founded perhaps, have been told about Castle Campbell, the haunted Castle Gloom near Dollar. These and numerous stories show over what an extensive area of Scotland, and in what diverse places, smuggling was at one time prevalent.

– *Ian MacDonald*

George Ross of Morangie Farm, near Tain in 1703 owned 'an acquavitae pott with its ffleake and stand' – according to an inventory of his possessions. In 1746 some fifty individuals, including a number from Tarlogie, were indicted for distilling 'in secret places'. Excise records show that stills were discovered under beds, beneath piles of peat, heaps of clothing, and even in latrine-closets. Today the Tarlogie Spring provides water for Glenmorangie distillery.

In *Echoes of the Glen* (1936) Colin Macdonald recounted the following tale.

> Just over a hundred years ago there lived on the Heights of Strathpeffer one John Macdonald. He was then about forty years of age. For many years John had kept two smuggling bothies going alternately. One was in *Coire Bhothain* and the other at the *Leth-allt* near *Cnoc na Bainnse*. He always played a lone hand, thus avoiding the usual pitfall of the smuggler – a babbling confederate. So that not a breath of suspicion blew his way, and all might have continued well had not a gamekeeper by an unlucky chance one day actually walked through the roof of the *Coire Bhothain* bothy and discovered John at his hobby. He was an unfriendly gamekeeper that; he lodged information with the authorities at Dingwall.
>
> After trial John was duly sentenced to be detained for a period of six weeks as an unwilling guest of His Majesty King William IV. John's wife walked to Dingwall every other day bringing food for the prisoner. A fortnight went by without incident. Then John had a brain-wave. The old jailer was well known to favour the cup that cheers; in fact he was possessed of a chronic and insatiable thirst – and on that John gambled – and won.
>
> During the remaining four weeks of the sentence there was observed a gentleman's agreement whereby every evening after dark John's cell door was unlocked. John then proceeded by a quiet route to the *Cnoc na Bainnse* bothy and there worked strenuously and in complete safety until returning dawn warned him it was time to make for his prison again; which he did – bringing with him in liquid form the price of the old jailer's complicity.
>
> As John's son put it to me, 'The safest smuggling my father ever did was that time he was in Dingwall Jile.'

The area around the towns of Dingwall, at the head of the Cromarty Firth, and Beauly, at the western extremity of the Beauly Firth – were long noted for illicit distilling. In 1766 and 1767 there were eleven recorded detections of illicit distilling around Beauly. Five distillers are mentioned by name, and one was caught no fewer than four times!

Strathconon – south-west of Dingwall – was a noted hotbed for illicit distilling, and by 1820 it was estimated that more than 1,000 gallons of illicit spirits were being produced there each week. Such was the scale of smuggling, and so determined were its participants to continue the trade unhindered, that the strath was virtually a no-go area for excise officers.

Naturalist, sportsman and writer Charles St John spent some time living by the River Oykell in Sutherland after leaving his desk job at the Treasury in London in 1830. His classic *The Wild Sports of the Highlands* (1846) included an account of being taken to shelter in a whisky-maker's bothy during a storm in Glen Oykel by his ghillie Donald while on a stalking expedition.

As it got dark, the weather suddenly changed, and I was glad enough to let Donald search for the bearings of a 'whisky bothie' which he had heard of at our last stopping-place. While he was seeking for it the rain began to fall heavily, and through the darkness we were just able to distinguish a dark object, which turned out to be a horse. 'The lads with the still will no be far off,' said Donald. And so it turned out. But the rain had increased the darkness so much, that we should have searched in vain if I had not distinguished at intervals, between the pelting of the rain and the heavy rushing of a black burn that ran beside us, what appeared to me to be the thrill treble of a fiddle. I could scarcely believe my ears. But when I communicated the intelligence to Donald, whose ears were less acute, he jumped with joy. 'It's all right enough, sir; just follow the sound; it's that drunken devil, Sandy Ross; ye'll never haud a fiddle frae him, nor him frae a whisky-still.' It was clear that the sound came from across the black stream, and it looked formidable in the dark. However, there was no remedy. So grasping each the other's collar, and holding our guns high overhead, we dashed in, and staggered through in safety, though the water was up to my waist, running like a mill-race, and the bottom was of round slippery stones. Scrambling up the bank, and following the merry sound, we came to what seemed a mere hole in the bank, from which it proceeded. The hole was partially closed by a door woven of heather and looking through it we saw a sight worthy of Teniers. On a barrel in the midst of the apartment – half hut, half cavern – stood aloft, fiddling with all his might, the identical Sandy Ross, while round him danced three unkempt savages; and another figure was stooping, employed over a fire in the corner where the whisky-pot was in full operation. The fire, and a sliver or two of lighted bog-fir, gave light enough to see the whole, for the place was not above ten feet square. We made our approaches with becoming caution, and were, it is needless to say, hospitably received; for who ever heard of Highland smugglers refusing a welcome to sportsmen? We got rest, food, and fire – all that we required – and something more; for long after I had betaken me to the dry heather in the corner, I had disturbed visions of strange orgies in the bothie, and of my sober Donald exhibiting curious antics on the top of a tub. These might have been the productions of a disturbed brain; but there is no doubt that when daylight woke me, the smugglers and Donald were all quiet and asleep, far past my efforts to rouse them, with the exception of one who was still able to tend the fire under the large black pot.

During the early years of the nineteenth century, the Marquis of Stafford's factor in Helmsdale, on the east coast of Sutherland, was James Loch. Loch estimated that some 300 stills were operating in the area around Helmsdale, and that their make was routinely shipped south, such was the quantity of spirit involved. Barley, noted Loch, was at a premium in the area for food as it was all being purchased for illicit distilling.

In a letter dated 15 May 1816, Loch wrote to Patrick Sellar, who was to become notorious as one of the principal architects of the Highland Clearances, 'while any population is left in the interior here, they will continue whiskey smugglers and of course sheep stealers . . . there is still a strong predilection to protect the offender from the cadger among all ranks and the skill displayed in cheating the Revenue is regarded rather as a proof of praiseworthy dexterity than as a crime to be punished'.

After visiting Clynelish distillery at Brora, eleven miles south of Helmsdale, some seventy years later, Alfred Barnard wrote,

> In the early part of the present century the inhabitants of the county of Sutherland, who up to that time had lived in scattered hamlets in the interior, were, by the proprietors, moved down to the coast, where allotments were provided for them, and in 1819, with a view of affording a ready market for the grain produced on the newly cultivated land, the Marquis of Stafford, afterwards first Duke of Sutherland, founded the Distillery now under notice.

Carrying out hoaxes on excise officers must always have been popular sport, but one late example occurred in April 1888. The Brora excise supervisor undertook a large-scale, detailed search for illicit distilling activity on the evidence of apparently reliable information received from a resident of the Crask area on the duke of Sutherland's estate. The operation involved many men, and their quest took them as far as Altnaharra, some thirty hard miles from their starting point at Brora. Needless to say, there was no illicit still – at least not in the area where they were searching.

A native of Skerray, near Bettyhill, close to the north coast of Sutherland, insisted that distilling survived in the area around Armadale until the 1920s, while to the south-west, in Strath Oykell, an old woman hid a bottle of illicit whisky under her pillow while feigning illness during an excise raid. The gaugers' suspicions were aroused, but they took away the stone hot water bottle at her feet!

Illicit distilling underwent a revival on the north Sutherland coast during the Second World War, when RAF tradesmen at a radar station near Melvich applied their varied technical abilities and abundance of spare time to building a still and producing whisky, which was drunk on the base and also changed hands among the local population.

Some of the more remote, bleak, inland areas of Caithness were ideal for illicit distillation. There were a number of stills on crofts and small farms in the country where the modern A9 road cuts inland from Latheron en route to Thurso and the ferry port of Scrabster.

One was at the now abandoned settlement of Badryrie, to the east of Loch Stemster, where the MacGregor family distilled during the later nineteenth century, but the most celebrated was operated around the same time by the notorious smuggler George Sinclair, a couple of miles away at Benachielt.

Sinclair was renowned throughout the far north as an illicit distiller, but when a party of excise officers led by Supervisor Dawes raided his croft on 18 December 1880 their search for spirit and distilling equipment was fruitless. This was not due to the fact that Sinclair had decided to abandon the trade, but rather because he had transferred his distilling operation to another nearby croft the previous day.

After the raid, the Sinclair family proceeded to sue the excise service for damage done to property, including potatoes and corn. The detailed court reports of proceedings during the summer of 1881, as chronicled in the *John O'Groat Journal*, make fascinating reading. Various Sinclairs testified to their innocence and to the harshness of the excise operation. Much to the chagrin of Dawes and his fellow gaugers, George Sinclair won the case and was awarded substantial compensation.

As one of Europe's leading herring ports during the nineteenth century, it was probably inevitable that the Caithness 'capital' of Wick would acquire a reputation for the excessive consumption of alcohol. In his contribution to the *New Statistical Account of Scotland* (1840) the Rev. Charles Thomson wrote, 'At all seasons of the year, whisky is drunk in considerable quantities, but during the fishing season enormous potations are indulged in. It may seem incredible, but it has been ascertained, that, during the six weeks of a successful fishing, not less than 500 gallons a day were consumed.'

Thomson, of course, had his own religious agenda, and it seems highly unlikely that, even with the annual influx of thousands of fishermen and gutters, anything like 3,500 gallons of whisky were drank per week, but there can be little doubt that serious quantities of alcohol were being consumed.

One legacy of Wick's reputation for hard-drinking was a receptiveness to the concept of temperance among many local people, long after the herring industry had begun its terminal decline. Wick was officially 'dry' from May 1922 until May 1947 – eleven years longer than the period of Prohibition across the Atlantic.

Inevitably, during its dry period, Wick copied the practices of New York and Chicago, and a number of shebeens were established. As many as twenty operated at one time, along with two 'mobile' shebeens, one of which, according to leading Caithness historian and author Iain Sutherland, was 'a horse drawn van which signalled the availability of its special wares by having the whip stuck vertically . . . the most daring of all operated in a restaurant, whose regulars knew that when the fancy silver teapot was in use, that its contents had been brewed some considerable time previously. And not in India or China either' (*Vote No Licence*).

Two illicit distilling enterprises were also developed. One was discovered when the chimney of the house in which the still was located caught fire, and the fire brigade arrived before the hot distilling plant could be taken apart and hidden. The distiller claimed in court that he only made whisky for personal consumption, to calm his nerves, but this did not prevent the court from convicting him.

The second illicit operation is much more thoroughly documented, thanks to the efforts of Iain Sutherland. It was run in The Hill of Newton, just south of Wick, by William 'Willag' Thomson, who worked with his uncle, James Thomson, and cousin George Gunn. Gunn, or 'The Dhuloch' as he was better known locally, was a First World War hero, who had won the Military Medal and the Croix de Guerre. He had been trained as a trench camouflager, a skill that was to prove invaluable during the family distilling venture. When the business was eventually rumbled in 1939 it was not due to clever detective work by the excise officers, but as the result of 'information received'.

According to Sutherland,

> By the time Willag Thomson was tried in 1939, there had been a war between the Caithness rural distilling industry and the Gaugers, for 115 years, as subtle as any conducted by modern, rival, intelligence agencies. It had been fought across a wide arc of the county, from Newton through Sarclet, Whaligoe, Clyth, Ben a Cheilt, Houstry, round to Westerdale, Shebster and Reay, with the nerve centre at Ben Alisky where the three miles clear view in any direction made surprise impossible.

Thomson and his associates worked two stills, one of which has never been recovered. They operated next to the family peat bank in the remote area of Tannach, south-west of Wick, with the still being hidden in a wood-lined bunker constructed by Gunn, using his trenching expertise. A Primus stove was used for heating purposes, so there was no smoke to give away the location of the operation. The still was large enough to make up to forty-five bottles of whisky per week, and Thomson grew his own barley, malting it in the barn of the family farm, a couple of miles from the still. The desired mature whisky colour was obtained by stirring singed sugar into the clear spirit.

One of the greatest difficulties the distillers had was in locating containers in which to distribute their spirit, and sauce bottles were used as 'half-bottles', selling for around 5/-, while 'full bottles' – at 10/6 – had sometimes previously contained bleach. In addition to individual customers, the still serviced many a dance and other social function in the Wick area during the years before the Second World War.

Inevitably, the local excise officers knew what was going on, but were unable to catch the distillers in possession of any incriminating evidence. As Sutherland puts it,

> the coolness of their quarry added insult to defeat. On one occasion they left in their car accompanied on the pipes by Willag who was playing *Will ye no come back again?* An informant saw to it that they did and Willag and the Dhuloch were charged. After a pathetic defence in which his lawyer asked for clemency on the grounds that Willag, who was 38 at the time, was an orphan, he was fined £200, or 4 months, and The Dhuloch was fined £25 for breaking the bottles containing the evidence. There was enough residue in one to convict them. Willag had no intention of paying the fine and went to serve his sentence dressed in plus fours.

In his 1948 book *Over The Ord*, Herbert Sinclair reproduced photographs of two Wick stills. One is quite primitive, apparently capable of turning out no more than two gallons of spirit per week, and was seized just before the Second World War 'less than a hundred yards away from the old Pulteney Distillery in the heart of the Backside of Pulteney'.

The second belonged to Willag Thomson, and is altogether more impressive and professional. Sinclair declined to name Thomson as the still's owner, but wrote 'When I saw him on Bridge Street this summer, I asked, "How's the water up Newton way?"

"Ah, very dry, Mr Sinclair, very dry."

'A dry reply.'

Sinclair went on,

Ordinarily, if you heard tales about the illicit making of whisky, you would think people were talking about the days of eighty years ago, when snow lay heavily on the ground, and when there was no chance of the excisemen getting through the roads on horseback. For there were men of 'spirit' then, as there are men to-day, would dare take a risk to get the 'real Mackay,' even when Old Pulteney whisky could be had by the gallon for so many shillings. Are there any adventurers in the county to-day? I would not know; and if I did, I wouldn't say.

The following story was recorded for the School of Scottish Studies archive from Mrs David Gunn of John O'Groats in 1971, concerning the small and now deserted island of Stroma, off John O'Groats in the Pentland Firth.

My great-granny, a woman Kirsty Banks frae Stroma – she wesna supposed to be very clever, but faith! She hed all her wits boot her. They used to dae a bit o distillin in that time, on their own of coorse, and wan time they hed a browst ready, fan they heird 'at 'e excisemen were comin. Noo she'd hedden a stillborn bairn no long afore 'at, an 'e excisemen kent 'at. And they'd no time til hide 'e malt. So she telt 'e bairns til make up a bed til her in 'e kitchen, and til put 'e malt in 'e bed, and she wes lyin on 'at fan 'e excisemen came in. And she telt them 'at she'd hidden a stillborn bairn no long afore 'at, and she wisna feelin very weil, but 'e bairns wanted her in 'e kitchen, til guide them and tell them fat til do. And 'e excisemen kent that was true, they kent she'd hedden a bairn. So they searched 'e rest o the hoose, but they didna touch 'e bed, and they got off wi' it.

The most famous smuggler in Orkney was the minister Magnus Eunson (see 'In From The Cold'), but a second claimant to the title of leading Orcadian smuggler was another authority figure, the provost, Thomas Traill, who held the office from 1792 to 1812. Along with his son and son-in-law he dealt with numerous illicit distillers based on the islands of Burray, Fara, Flotta and Swona.

David Work, from the Orkney island of Shapinsay, told the next anecdote to a researcher from the School of Scottish Studies in 1971. Similar versions occur regarding Speyside, confirming Ian MacDonald's assertion that 'numerous clever stories are claimed for several localities'.

Away afore this [1914–18] war, the folk here, they used to make a lot o malt and they brewed home-brewed ale: some o them had stills here, and they made whisky oot o this home-brewed ale. I mind hearing a story wan time aboot an exciseman comin to the hoose looking for this contraband, this whisky, and the man was oot aboot, he didna go in till the exciseman geed in the hoose. He got a big knife then, he came in sharpin this big knife on a sharpin stone, and he says to the exciseman: 'Did anybody see you comin in here?'

'Oh no. Nobody saa me comin in.'

'Oh weil, there nobody see you gaan oot other,' he says.

The man just cleared oot an wance!

9

URBAN STILLS

The illicit distilling of Scotch whisky was not confined to the Highlands. There were 400 unlicensed stills in Edinburgh in 1777, when the number of licensed stills was only eight. In 1815 a 'private' distillery of considerable size was found under an arch of the South Bridge in the Scottish capital. The only entrance was by a doorway situated at the back of a fireplace in the bedroom of a house adjoining the arch. Water was obtained from one of the mains of the Edinburgh Water Company which passed overhead, and the smoke and waste were got rid of by making an opening in the chimney of an adjoining house and connecting it to a pipe from the distillery. In the mid-nineteenth century a yet more scandalous instance of the Scottish aversion from paying duties occurred in Edinburgh when a secret distillery was found in the cellars under the Free Tron Church.

– *Aeneas Macdonald,* Whisky *(1930)*

During the 1760s, it was estimated by the Edinburgh excise officer John Scott (*A paper on the means of suppressing smuggling in the distillery of Scotland,* 1784) that 'private' distillers were making around half a million gallons of whisky per year, which was ten times more than was legally distilled.

Interestingly, Scott wrote 'the smuggling distiller finds it most convenient to carry on his illegal trade in the towns because . . . he is there best concealed and finds the most ready and extensive market for his spirits'.

The story of the Free Tron Church distillery, as recounted by Macdonald, was actually first recorded by Hugo Arnot in his 1779 *History of Edinburgh.* Around the same time that the Free Tron Church was catering for spirits of a different sort to that intended by the ecclesiastical authorities, a large illicit still was also discovered in Marionville, between Leith and Portobello, and another close to the centre of Leith. In Aberdeen one was operating in premises just a few doors from the Custom House.

The anonymous contributor to the *New Statistical Account of Scotland* who wrote about Liberton, to the south of Edinburgh city centre, in March 1839 voiced his disapproval of the local population's drinking habits, as was customary in most entries, wherever the location. Nearby Colinton boasted fourteen public houses at the same time – 'a number much greater than is required for the real wants of the people'.

> *Alehouses* – There are 32 shops for the sale of spirits in this parish [Liberton], which is just thirty too many, and the effect is as pernicious as possible . . . some of the publicans are very respectable people, and the blame chiefly rests with those who let and licence so many houses of that description. No ale-houses are allowed to exist by the proprietors or tenants on the estates of Niddry, Mortonhall, Moredun or Brunstane.

How times change . . .

One subject, interviewed in 1956 for the School of Scottish Studies archive, recalled that as a youngster living near Edinburgh he saw old men tumbling down the hill on their way home from a still which was located near a loch, though he does not specify the exact location. He remembers seeing a very large copper pot and a worm which had nine coils to it. The distillers hid their utensils in the loch, and a local miller did the malting for them. A bottle of whisky cost 1/- to buy, but it was known that if you went to buy a bottle you could drink as much as you wanted free of charge while making the purchase.

During the 1930s, when illicit distilling had a brief resurgence, an Edinburgh medical student was found guilty of making whisky in his lodgings. By and large, however, while examples of convictions for illicit distilling in and around Glasgow during the first half of the twentieth century are numerous, the good people of Edinburgh seem to have been remarkably law-abiding in this respect. 'We always preferred claret anyway,' says one Edinburgh librarian, 'but the Glaswegians liked their dram.' Pressed as to the real reason why Edinburgh's citizens so rarely appeared in court for whisky-making, the librarian replied crisply 'too douce'!

Aberdeen was once home to three legal distilleries, and Alfred Barnard wrote the following, after visiting the Granite City's Strathdee distillery while researching *The Whisky Distilleries of the United Kingdom*:

> The Distillery was built in 1821 by Mr. Henry Ogg, father of the present proprietor . . . Previous to the year 1820 the whisky consumed in

Scotland was almost entirely made by Highland smugglers, who distilled it in bothies in the glens among the hills. The Upper Dee and the Upper Don were noted for the production of illicit whisky. The evasion of the Excise Laws was not generally looked upon as immoral in those days. The popular sympathy with the smuggler in his warfare with the gauger is shown in the ballads and songs of the day, and notably in the poems of Burns, who laments his own degradation in having 'turned a gauger.' In Aberdeenshire the trade was conducted by the smugglers with great boldness. There was many a battle or running fight between them and the officers, in which the casualties were sometimes serious and occasionally fatal. The whisky was brought down from the mountains, usually during the night, on the pack-saddles of ponies or small horses, in single file, to the number of six or a dozen, the halter of the second being tied to the crupper of the first and the third to the second, and so on. The owner usually rode the first horse, and his friends scouted behind and before to give warning of danger from either direction. Sometimes the whisky was captured, and sometimes the smugglers escaped with their booty.

To remedy these evils, the Government resolved, about the year 1820, to encourage distilling under legal authority, and the erection of Distilleries was suggested to the brewers of that period. Strathdee, one of the first Distilleries in Aberdeenshire, was erected by Mr Ogg, the principal partner of the Ferryhill Brewery, and about the same time the Devanha Distillery was established by the owners of the brewery of that name.

Strathdee, on Great Western Road, survived until the Second World War, when, in common with most distilleries, production was suspended. At the end of the war, it did not reopen. Devanha had already closed, in 1915, while Aberdeen's third distillery, Bon Accord, in Hardgate, operated from 1855 to 1910.

Traditionally, Glaswegians obtained their illicit whisky from the hills to the north of the city, as well as by sea from Kintyre and the Isle of Arran, but significant quantities were also distilled within the city itself. In 1815 a Glasgow newspaper carried the following report:

On Monday night, Mr Anderson, supervisor of Excise, and two of his officers, discovered an illicit still of nearly 50 gallons between Union Place and Mitchell Street. Two men were working it, whom they detained, while they proceeded to destroy utensils and raw materials. The still was charged with low wines at the time, which the officers allowed to flow into the street. One of the smugglers set fire to the spirit, and escaped in the confusion. The fire was extinguished, and officers demolished tuns and had gone some distance with the worm etc, when the fellows who had escaped returned with about 12 of their gang, and soon recovered possession of their utensils. The officer who was knocked down was severely cut on the head. This is only one instance of the audacity of the smugglers. It has been calculated that from three to five hundred illicit stills are at work in this city and vicinity.

Glasgow's Saltmarket was a favoured area for illicit distilling, with ten stills being seized there in the month of January 1815 alone. The *Glasgow Herald* of 9 May 1843 reported the detection of a still and 20 gallons of illicit whisky at 115 High Street Glasgow. Two distillers were subsequently each fined £30.

During the first half of the twentieth century the hub of Glasgow's illicit trade was Shettleston. In their excellent book devoted to the seemingly inexhaustible subject of Glasgow and drink – *The Bevvy* – Rudolph Kenna and Ian Sutherland suggest that this was because miners, who made up a fair proportion of the population of the area, received allowances of free coal which would have been used to heat stills.

According to Kenna and Sutherland, 'One hapless citizen, confronted by police and gaugers, was asked to account for the equipment in his house – and announced "It's an Irish musical instrument".'

They also noted that 'From the eighteenth century until at least the 1920s, Eaglesham Moor, to the south-east of Glasgow, seems also to have been a favourite hiding place for illicit distillers. Stills of up to 500 gallons capacity were regularly uncovered during the nineteenth century'. A 500-gallons still is not a small object, so the smugglers' camouflaging techniques must have been very good indeed.

The occasional illicit still was discovered in Glasgow as late as the inter-war years, and in 1926 a newsagent from Glasgow was arrested at a still he was operating in Ayrshire, where he made whisky to sell in his shop. The following year a tinsmith was charged with possession of a still. He admitted in court that he had also been making similar ones for his friends.

In 1928 one Joseph Brady of Bridgeton was caught in possession of 'a complete still, properly connected up and in the process of making whisky'. The whisky sold at 8/- a bottle, two-thirds of the market price for legal whisky. In *They Belonged to Glasgow* Kenna and Sutherland tell the story of Edward Hilley, of Bonnar Street in Bridgeton, who when charged during 1934 with fraudulently obtaining gas by tampering with his meter said in his defence 'I needed the gas for the still, which was for making whisky'. Two years after that particular misdemeanour, Gorbals labourer Michael Flannery of Waddell Street was convicted of operating a still in his home. Wartime whisky shortages even led to members of the eminently respectable Antediluvian Order of Buffaloes

in Bridgeton being fined £3 per member for drinking illicit whisky in
their lodge during 1944!

~~~

Kenna and Sutherland produce some interesting figures to illustrate
how illicit distilling is no longer financially rewarding. In 1948, such
was the scarcity of whisky after the war that bottles changed hands in
the cities and towns at Christmas for £4, and around that time the
official price was over a pound – or 20 per cent of a working man's
weekly income. Half a century later a bottle of blended whisky could
be purchased for £8, while the average wage was £300 a week – not
much more than two per cent of income.

~~~

The last significant seizure of illicit whisky in Glasgow took place
during the 1960s, when a distiller in the Gallowgate was caught using
a twin-tub washing machine as a mash tun. For some time, twin-tubs
had been popular in urban areas for purposes other than washing
clothes, and Fiona Murdoch of the Whisky Shop in Dufftown notes
'They look perfectly innocent but I've been told that their stainless steel
drums are perfect for whisky-making. They have a built-in heater for
the mash, and most of the pipework to transfer the liquids from one
process to another is in place. The only extra item needed is a worm.'
    Also during the 1960s illicit whisky found its way into Glasgow in
the luggage of several students returning to their studies after vacations
spent at home. 'Home' in this instance being villages on Upper Deeside.
The whisky was reported to have been of very good quality.

~~~

Two stills which are now on display in the Whisky Museum in
Dufftown on Speyside were discovered in Glasgow. One is of simple
design, being made from a milk churn, with a pipe leading to a
condenser fixed to the top of the vessel. The still was confiscated by
Customs & Excise officers in 1943, and is thought to have been used to
make a whisky or poitin-like spirit.
    The second is based on a metal beer keg, and was confiscated after
Customs & Excise received a tip-off from a member of the public. The
still, which was working when seized, has an intricate arrangement of
pipes, and in places basic condensers have been fashioned by inserting
a metal pipe into the larger plastic pipe. The alcohol passed through
the metal pipe, with cooling water surrounding it in the plastic pipe. As
a second, smaller, barrel was discovered during the raid it seems likely
that two-part distillation usually took place. There are two immersion

heaters fitted into the base of the still, used to heat the wash to boiling point before it left the still under pressure to pass through the condensing pipes. The resultant alcohol would be collected in a basin or jar. As with the other, simpler, Glasgow still, whisky or something closer to Irish poitin would have been made from cereal or potatoes.

Victorian Glasgow had hundreds of shebeens, or unlicensed drinking dens, and their popularity and numbers grew as the effects of the temperance movement were increasingly felt. In particular, this followed the passing of the Forbes-Mackenzie Act in 1853, which prevented Scottish licensed premises from operating after 11 p.m., and banned Sunday trading completely. It was not just in Glasgow that shebeens thrived, as David Barrie noted in his *The City of Dundee Illustrated* (1890):

> There are lots . . . in Dundee and in all large towns, and also all over the country parishes . . . If the shebeeners were sent to prison for long terms without the option of a fine, which they almost invariably pay, their trade would soon disappear. It is no uncommon case for a fine of £30 to be paid down in court rather than submit to go to gaol. This is not to be wondered at, if, as is credibly said, the shebeeners can make from somewhere about forty to fifty percent. of profit on their sales, and never be bothered with Excise people about monies for licences . . .

Shebeening was a lucrative business, and it was estimated that in the heyday of the shebeens during the 1860s, a proprietor could take as much as £80 on a Sunday. In 1859 more than 600 shebeen-keepers were convicted, and many of their premises were supplied with illicitly distilled whisky. In 1862 John Lynch of World's End in Finnieston received a fine of £12 10/- for having an unlicensed still in his house, doubtless intended to supply local shebeens.

In one shebeen in King Street, raided by the police in 1893, it was reported that 'The inspector went to the gas pipe, turned it full on, and the liquid came pouring out. The spirits were concealed in the wall and the gas pipe attached to the jar.'

A number of shebeens flourished even in the post-war new housing schemes of the city, and lasted until the mid-1970s, when reform of licensing laws and the increasing availability of cheap supermarket and off-licence whisky rendered them superfluous.

Much of the legally distilled whisky consumed in cities and towns across Victorian Britain was adulterated with various, often alarming, substances to increase the element of profit for the vendors. Concerns in Scotland culminated in a celebrated piece of investigative journalism undertaken by Dr Charles Cameron, editor of the *North British Daily Mail* during the early 1870s. He arranged for thirty samples of 'whisky' to be surreptitiously collected from a variety of drinking establishments and had them analysed. The result was that only two turned out to be pure whisky. Many had been watered, while others contained a variety of additives, including methylated spirits, turpentine and even sulphuric acid, while some consisted entirely of 'finish', a kind of varnish used by manufacturers of hats. How attractive the make of even the most primitive, tin, Highland 'sma' still' seems by comparison!

The story broke in September 1872, and was widely greeted with incredulity and horror. Sadly, as whisky was just one of many drinks and foodstuffs which were routinely adulterated around the time, the authorities found it most convenient to dismiss the report and no action came about as a result of Cameron's work. Curiously, this aspect of the history of the whisky industry rarely rates a mention in print, though it is the subject of a meticulously researched book by Edward Burns, called *Bad Whisky*.

During its crusade against drink adulteration the *North British Daily Mail* received a letter from a former Glasgow shebeener by the name of Tom O'Neil, who was born in the city's Saltmarket, and was active around the mid-nineteenth century. The letter was published on 13 November 1872. It was subsequently published as a pamphlet under the title *Doings of a Notorious Glasgow Shebeener.*

At one point O'Neil describes purchasing whisky during the 1860s from an illicit distiller:

> He unbuttoned his monkey jacket, and I saw a pair of tin stays upon him, at least it was liker that than anything else. It was a vessel of tinplate, made to go round the body, for all the world like a pair of corsets, and fastened behind at two places. When he came into the kitchen he looked a man of 16 or 18 stone in weight, but when he had taken his stays off I would say he was barely 10 stone. I said: 'Where's the stuff?' He replied: 'It is here. Bring a jar.' I brought a five-gallon jar, and he unscrewed a little cap from the top of a pipe at one corner of the stays, and poured out its contents into the jar. There was a little over the fill of the jar, which he and I discussed, and then he went away. After he was gone, I proceeded to reduce the stuff with two gallons of water . . .
>
> The following week the man came back – without the stays this time – and asked if I wanted any more.
>
> 'In the name of thunder, what stuff was yon you gave me?'
>
> 'It was some of my own making,' he replied, 'didn't you know that I made it.'

'Indeed I did not.'

'Well then come over with me to Rose Street [in the Gorbals] and I'll let you see.'

I went over the water with him to Rose Street, and into a house up two stairs. I saw nothing on entering that would give you an idea that such things were made there, but presently he pulled up two boards on the floor, and showed me a portion of the works of his still, and a pipe that conveyed the smoke from his fire up the chimney a short way. I asked him what he would do in the event of the authorities coming to the door, demanding admittance. 'I'll show you,' he said – and opened the window and just outside of it I saw a rope hanging down from above, which rope he caught hold of. Jumping out, he swung himself into another close.

He also confessed to me that the chief ingredients he distilled were molasses and sour beer . . .

The following extract is taken from J. Livingston's Victorian song *Glaisca Whisky*, inspired by the publicity surrounding the adulteration of whisky, as publicised in the *North British Daily Mail*:

The pooshin stuffs the doctors sell [pooshin = poison]
You scarcely can get ony,
But Glaisca whisky bears the bell,
It's flavoured wi' sae mony;
An' pooshin sellin's sae fenced roun',
To buy it is but risky;
But ye may cut throats, hang, or droon,
When primed wi' Glaisca whisky!

The traditional song *Donal' Don* features a somewhat unsavoury Dundee-based smuggler. The description in the song of Donal's complete disregard for even rudimentary personal hygiene does nothing to make his whisky seem appetising.

Wha hasna heard o' Donal' Don,
Wi' all his tanterwallops on;
I trow, he was a lazy drone,
And smuggled Hielan' whisky, O.

When first he cam' to auld Dundee,
'Twas in a smeeky hole lived he,
Where gauger bodies cou'dna see,
He played the king a pliskie, O. [pliskie = trick]

When he was young an' in his prime,
He lo'ed a bonny lassie fine;

She jilted him, and aye sin' syne
He's dismal, dull, and dusky, O.

A bunch o' rags is a' his braws, [braws = best clothes]
His heathery wig wad fricht the craws;
His dusky face and clorty paws [clorty = dirty]
Wad fyle the Bay o' Biscay, O.

He has a sark, he has but ane, [sark = shirt]
It's fairly worn to skin an' bane,
A' loupin', like to rin its lane, [loupin' = leaping]
Wi' troopers bauld and frisky, O.

Whene'er his sark's laid oot to dry,
The blockhead in his bed maun lie,
An' wait till a' the troopers die,
Ere he gangs oot wi' whisky, O.

Yet, here's a health to Donal' Don,
Wi' a' his tanterwallops on;
An' may he never want a scone
While he mak's Hielan' whisky, O.'

In 1998 an illicit distilling operation was discovered in the somewhat unlikely setting of the North Tayworks Industrial Estate in Dundee. A locksmith found a still, boiler, and hundreds of empty spirits bottles when he arrived at a unit to change the locks after the tenant fell into arrears with his payments. Not surprisingly, the tenant was never traced.

According to a mechanic who worked out of the neighbouring unit, 'Two men used to come about the place, but they never had much to say for themselves. They seemed to do all their work at night, and they never seemed to take any deliveries during daylight hours. Now I can understand why.'

During the period of prohibition in the USA, there was a decline in traditional moonshining standards, with cheap corn sugar replacing grain, though this was still good stuff compared with some of the literally poisonous hooch produced.

A favourite drink on the waterfront in Philadelphia was 'Soda Pop Moon'. Frequently spiked with isopropyl alcohol, it literally paralysed the tongues of drinkers. 'Jake' was ninety per cent alcohol fluid extract of Jamaican ginger, with wood alcohol added for good measure. It too caused paralysis – in the hands and feet, and it was estimated in 1930 that more than 15,000 people across the USA had been paralysed by Jake. Scotland was not immune to the perils of illicit alcohol, either. In 1949 eight people died in Blackhill, Glasgow, after drinking what was essentially industrial alcohol at a Hogmanay party.

The author Charles MacLean recalls a bizarre event which illustrates the lengths to which thirsty men would go to get a drink.

> My father was a medical officer in the navy during the Second World War and at the end of the 'German war' he was based at Rosyth dockyard on the Firth of Forth. Half a dozen German U-boats were being held there, with their crews on board, and my father was called because on one boat they were making a kind of schnapps from torpedo cleaning fluid! One of the sailors died and two or three were temporarily blinded.

There is probably more illicit distillation taking place in urban Scotland today than there is in rural areas. It has become increasingly difficult to find truly remote rural places in which to distil, with ever-increasing numbers of ramblers and hill-walkers always likely to stumble on anything suspicious taking place. Paradoxically, busy urban areas offer greater anonymity to the would-be distiller, as in the example of the Dundee industrial estate distillers described above.

The same situation applies to Ireland, where in addition to the old poitin strongholds of the rural west and north-west – the counties of Donegal, Tyrone, Derry, Mayo and Galway – much illicit distilling now occurs in towns and cities. Today, poitin is as likely to be made in the centre of Belfast as it is in its old remote, Donegal stronghold of the Inishowen peninsula.

Illicit whiskey was distilled during the 1960s in the science laboratories of Queen's University in Belfast, and one Belfast-based former illicit distiller was interviewed by John McGuffin for his book *In Praise of Poteen*. The distiller, Ben Lorimer, tells McGuffin how at one time he had a regular order for a dozen bottles of his poitin from a South Belfast police station, and how, when he was arrested for illicit distillation, he was only charged with possession of two bottles. No doubt this helped him to get away with a modest fine, but Lorimer muses about what the police did with the other eight gallons of spirit he actually had in his house when apprehended!

Ireland's prisons have traditionally been a fine example of ingenious poitin-making, using Burco boilers as stills, with lengths of copper piping stripped from wash rooms fashioned into primitive worms, while yeast and potatoes were smuggled from the prison kitchens. Usually the spirit was only distilled once, since to give it a second run would almost certainly be pushing your luck too far. Drinking the 'singlings' led to extraordinarily severe hangovers due to the presence of fusel oil.

'Prison poitín' was certainly made in the Curragh Internment Camp during the Second World War, because Brendan Behan recalled drinking it there, and during the 1970s and '80s Long Kesh was also a centre for poitín manufacture, not to mention the women's jails in Armagh and Limerick. In July 1992 *The Daily Telegraph* carried a news item which noted that 'An investigation was launched at the Maze prison in Belfast yesterday into how Loyalist inmates managed to make alcohol at the jail.'

In the USA, too, while the southern states of Georgia, Kentucky, North and South Carolina and Tennessee remain strongholds of moonshine, illicit distilling has moved into the cities. US revenue authorities estimated during the mid-1970s that more than 60 per cent of all illicit whiskey was produced in urban areas.

10

IN FROM THE COLD

Both in Scotland and Ireland the smugglers may be looked upon as pioneers of the Whisky trade. To them is largely due the superior quality of the Fine Old Malt Whisky that is made in these days, and the 'Sma' Stills', and 'Illicit Potheen' may be said to be the foundations upon which the vast Whisky Distilling interests were founded . . . no men understood better the localities where they could turn out good spirit, and this fact may be seen to this day, when we find many of the oldest distilleries existing upon sites which have been well known to have been chosen by smugglers of old as places where the purest mountain streams, flowing over moss and peats, could be used to distil and produce spirits of the finest descriptions.

– *Alfred Barnard*, The Whisky Distilleries of the United Kingdom *(1887)*

When he toured the distilleries of Scotland during the mid-1880s Barnard often talked to distillers whose fathers or grandfather had operated illicit stills in the years before the 1823 Excise Act, and in some cases, the years afterwards. Indeed, Barnard is an excellent source of material relating to the illicit origins of distilleries that were operating legally at the time of his visits, some of which survive, while some have now passed into history.

From the mid-1820s onwards, many smugglers decided to try their hands at legitimate whisky-making, and a dozen legal distilleries were opened in the Aberfeldy area of Perthshire alone by formerly illicit distillers who had operated in the hills and glens of the area. On Deeside, Lochnagar distillery was built by local smuggler James Robertson of Crathie, while at Fettercairn, in Kincardineshire, Alexander Ramsay of Fasque converted a corn mill into a distillery, and installed James Stewart as its tenant. Stewart was an ex-illicit distiller from between Fettercairn village and nearby Clattering Bridge. There are numerous other examples of landowners deciding to set up legal distilling operations, and it made sense for them to employ experienced illicit distillers such as James Stewart.

The 1823 Excise Act stimulated a great deal of distillery construction, and those plants which have survived to this day include, in addition to Lochnagar and Fettercairn, Aberlour, Ben Nevis, Cameronbridge, Glendronach and Macallan. An astonishing twenty-seven new distilleries appeared in Campbeltown between 1823 and 1837, while six were built on Islay between 1824 and 1830, including the now silent Port Ellen.

Below are featured some distilleries with roots planted firmly in the old smuggling days. Unless otherwise stated, all quoted material is by Alfred Barnard.

ARDBEG (Port Ellen, Isle of Islay)
(*Operated by Glenmorangie Distillery Co. Ltd*)

The Ardbeg Distillery is situated on the south-east coast of the island, in a lonely spot on the very verge of the sea, and its isolation tends to heighten the romantic sense of its position. It was established in the year 1815, but long previous to that date it was a noted haunt of smugglers. For many years the supervisors had been searching for this nest of illicit traffickers without success; most of the band were known by sight, and endeavours had long been made to catch them when out in their boats. At length, the spot where they carried on their nefarious practices was discovered, but the band was too strong for an open attack; however, one day, when the party were absent with a cargo of whisky, a raid was made and the place destroyed after a seizure of a large amount of the

illicit spirit. As it was impossible to procure other vessels, and finding their occupation gone, the whole band was scattered, and most of them migrated to the Kintyre shores. The site of their operations was shortly after occupied by the founders of Ardbeg distillery who chose it on account of the water, the chief characteristics of which are its softness and purity.

Ardbeg was working in 1794, when the business, in the hands of Alexander Stewart, was sequestrated. John MacDougall was distilling there from 1815, and his family had been distillers and farmers in the area for many years.

AUCHTERMUCHTY (Fife)
(*Operated from 1829 to 1926*)

'The Distillery has been in the hands of the Bonthrones, father and son, for nearly a century,' according to Barnard. The distillery had started production in 1829, and was, in fact, operated by the Bonthrone family until its demise. The Bonthrones were large-scale maltsters, as well as millers and brewers in Fife at various times, and before the construction of Auchtermuchty distillery, almost certainly took part in illicit distilling operations. Barnard wrote

> The Ochil and Lomond Hills were in former times the resort of smugglers, both male and female, and Mr. Bonthrone's brother, as late as the year 1828, supplied them with malt, which was carted by night to the foot of the hills, and fetched away by the smugglers under cover of the darkness. The celebrated 'Lady Miller', a most daring and masculine woman also kept an illicit still in these hills, and for a great many years evaded the law. Mr. Bonthrone was well acquainted with her, and told us some stirring tales of her doings.

AULTMORE (Banffshire, Speyside)
(*Operated by John Dewar & Sons Ltd*)

Aultmore distillery was established in 1895, and is located off the Keith to Elgin road, a couple of miles from Keith. The distillery draws its water from the Auchinderran Burn. The area around Aultmore distillery was once home to four separate illicit ventures, and John Milne's Auchinderran distilling bothy used the same water source as the present distillery. According to local lore, one of the Aultmore smugglers used to preserve his distilling yeast between whisky-making sessions by sticking it to the leaves of birch bushes, which he then placed in the chimney of the house to dry, with the peat smoke preserving the active qualities of the yeast for the next distillation.

BALBLAIR (Ross-shire, Northern Highlands)
(*Operated by Inver House Distillers Ltd*)

Balblair is situated at Edderton in Easter Ross, and was founded in 1790. It is sometimes confused with an illicit operation in the Black Isle village of Balblair, which was working around 1750. Barnard noted that

> All the streams in the district of Edderton are considered suitable for distilling purposes. There is also an inexhaustible supply of peat close by, Edderton being known as the 'Parish of Peats'. In former days the whole neighbourhood abounded in smuggling bothies, and was the scene of many a struggle between the revenue officers and smugglers.

BALLECHIN (Perthshire)
(*Operated from 1810 to 1927*)

Ballechin distillery was situated near Ballinluig, just off the A9 road in Perthshire, a few miles south of Pitlochry.

> As we drive through the parish of Logierait, our worthy coachman, who knows the object of our visit, reminds us that we are in the heart of a district famous from a most remote period for the distillation of whisky. The burns, or small streams, which rise in the peat mosses and bog of Ballechin moor, under the shade of the Fergan range of hills, fall into the Tay, and are associated at every secluded bend and shady corner with the smuggling bothy, where illicit distillation was carried on extensively in olden times. Among the Strath Tay smugglers there were men of remarkable muscular power and shrewd audacity. A surviving remnant of the brotherhood, residing near Ballechin, still tells of a halloween night some forty years ago, when the famous Stewart arrived at a place near Perth with a boatload of potheen. He had sent up to town for assistance to remove the Whisky, when 'lo and behold!' instead of his friends, the revenue officers appeared on the scene. Stewart immediately rowed out mid-stream, but the officers seeing an idle boat followed him. A chase commenced, and the smuggler seeing that he was closely pressed, and that capture seemed inevitable, proceeded to use strategy that he might escape out of their clutches. Pretending to surrender, he invited the gaugers into his boat to take possession, and seized one of their oars to assist them in stepping on board. In a twinkle he had thrown the oar on the top of his potheen barrels, and quickly rowed down the stream, leaving the poor discomfited gaugers with but one oar 'to paddle their own canoe' as best they could. He was soon lost to sight, and landed his cargo safely in one of his hiding-places on the river side. The career of this noted smuggler is a record of unbroken triumph; his last distillation was sold in Leith, and was conveyed thither in a canopied cart, containing a caretaker muffled up

as a patient (with an infectious disease), who managed thus to escape the prying curiosity of the excisemen, and succeeded in disposing of the Whisky at a high price.

BALMENACH (Morayshire, Speyside)
(*Operated by Inver House Distillers Ltd*)

Our way [to Balmenach distillery] was along the Cromdale Burn, and as we proceeded, the range of the Cromdale Hills, some seven or eight miles long, stretched out before us. In days gone by these acclivities were the favourite haunt of smugglers, who chose the locality on account of the numerous hill-streams, whose waters are of fine quality and highly suitable for distilling purposes. At our request, when we reached the Distillery, Mr. McGregor, Jun., took us to see the various haunts of the smugglers, who in days gone by were pretty numerous in the district, and whose romantic history has been the subject of many adventurous tales.

He first directed us to the double-arched cavern, dug deep into the hill, fifty yards from the Distillery, in which at one time a noted band of smugglers carried on their operations, but it has since been demolished. It possessed an underground spring, wherein the little coil or worm which condenses the precious spirit was laid, and at a lower level it dipped into a receiver made out of an earthen jar some two feet high with a wooden lid thereon. The little copper still stood on a furnace made with the loose stones that had fallen from the rock behind, and the mash tun had originally been a wash-tub. The place was totally dark and no light was ever permitted except that which came from the furnace fire. One night the Revenue Officers made a raid on the place, and knowing the desperate men they had to deal with, were all well armed. On their arrival they crept stealthily through the narrow entrance to the cave, following the informer, who knew the place well. Meanwhile the smugglers, unconscious of the close proximity of their enemies, were scattered about the cavern, some sleeping, others smoking, and one or two looking after the distilling operations. One of their number opened the furnace door to replenish the fire, and the momentary flash of light revealed to his comrade the figures of the officers stealing upon them. With great presence of mind he instantly unhooked the pipe which connected the furnace with a concealed chimney in the roof, and then fired off his pistol at the nearest enemy. The noise alarmed the gang who escaped from the cave, under cover of the dense smoke emitted from the open furnace. The officers were dumbfounded, and almost choked, but the informer quickly replaced the chimney-pipe, and as soon as the smoke had dispersed, the officers lighted their lamps from the furnace fire, and proceeded to demolish the place. They broke up the Still, Worm, and vessels, kicked the debris and loose stone into the well, annexed a few kegs of Whisky, and departed with one of their comrades slightly wounded. This scare broke up and scattered the notorious gang, and since that time there has been very little smuggling in this district.

Within two hundred yards of Balmenach, Mr. McGregor showed us another place which, a century ago, was a smuggler's bothy, and one of the largest of its kind in the famous Glenlivet district.

Three Macgregor brothers left the notorious smuggling centre of Tomintoul in Banffshire, during the early 1800s, and settled at Cromdale, not far from Grantown-on-Spey. One became a miller, the second a farmer, while the third, James, began to farm at Balmenach, though whisky-making was far more lucrative for him. It was James Macgregor's son who guided Barnard around Balmenach during his visit. All three brothers had almost certainly been illicit distillers back in Tomintoul – a village described by the writer John Wilson, alias 'Christopher North', in 1815 as ' a wild mountain village where drinking, dancing, swearing and quarrelling went on all the time'.

Soon after the 1823 Excise Act was passed, the local excise officer visited James Macgregor at Balmenach, and after sharing a generous dram with his host and talking about cattle and such like the officer said that he had better do his duty and take a look around the farm. Eventually the two men came to a stone building with a mill-lade beside it. 'What will that be?' asked the exciseman.

'Oh, that'll just be the peat-shed,' replied Macgregor, and the visit continued. Back in the house, another dram was shared and some more farming talk was engaged in. When he rose to leave the excise officer said, 'If I were you, Mr Macgregor, I'd just take out a licence for yon peat-shed.'

The hint was duly acted upon . . .

CARDHU (Morayshire, Speyside)
(*Operated by United Distillers and Vintners*)

Until 1975 this distillery was known as Cardow, but in that year its owners, the Distillers' Company Ltd, decided to revert to the Gaelic *Cardhu* – which translates as 'black rock'. The distillery was originally licensed to John Cumming, who had been born in 1775, and who possessed three convictions for illicit distilling. He took over the lease of Cardow Farm in Upper Knockando in 1813, settling there with his wife, Helen. He took on the farm partly because of its remote location, which made it ideal as a base for illicit distilling.

Apparently, gaugers used to stay with the Cummings when in the area, as there was no local inn. Helen would make supper for her visitors, then raise a red flag over the farm to warn her neighbours that the gaugers were in the area. All the time, illicit distilling was going on under their very noses, masked it is said, by the smells of Hellen Cumming's home baking.

The Cummings smuggled their whisky over the Mannoch Hill to eager markets around the towns of Forres and Elgin, but once the distillery was operating legitimately, it could be openly transported in carts to the port of Burghead, and shipped to Leith. From 1860, the Strathspey Railway carried it south with a rapidity unimaginable just a few years previously.

Helen Cumming was clearly one of those redoubtable 'distilling women', whose contribution to the history of Scotch whisky has never received its true recognition. According to one admirer, she 'possessed the courage and energy of a man, and in devices and plans to evade the surveillance of the gaugers, no man or woman in the district could equal her'.

When Barnard visited, Cardow was owned by John and Helen Cumming's daughter-in-law, Elizabeth. Their son, Lewis, had taken it on in 1839, but died in 1872. Barnard wrote, 'Cardow was established as a licensed Distillery in 1824, previous to which date illicit distillation was carried on both there and in other places in the neighbourhood'. At the time of his visit, a new distillery had recently been completed (in 1884), and equipment from the old distillery was acquired by one William Grant of Dufftown, who opened his Glenfiddich plant at the end of 1887. Cardow was subsequently sold to John Walker & Sons Ltd in 1893 by Elizabeth Cumming's son.

CRAGGANMORE (Banffshire, Speyside)
(*Operated by UDV*)

Cragganmore was built close to the Spey at Ballindalloch in 1869/70,

and was the first Speyside distillery purposely constructed next to a railway line. This was certainly useful for its founder, John Smith, who was so large that he could only travel in a guard's van!

During his tour of Cragganmore, Alfred Barnard was shown by Smith's son, William,

> the Receiving and Ball Room, which contains a Low-Wines and Feints Receiver holding 800 gallons, the Safe, Sampling Safe, &c. This ball room is a low-pitched chamber, and is the remaining and only portion of a smuggling bothy, which was not demolished when the Distillery was built. Mr Smith informed us that a few years previous to the erection of this Distillery, there were as many as 200 illicit Distilleries at work in the Glenlivet district.

DAILUAINE (Banffshire, Speyside)
(*Operated by UDV*)

The name Dailuaine is derived from the Gaelic for 'green valley', and the distillery was founded in 1852. It is located at Carron, to the south of the River Spey, and a few miles south-west of Aberlour.

> A short distance up the glen [from the distillery], by the side of one of the burns, there dwelt in olden times a nest of bold smugglers, and the ruins of one of their so-called bothies was pointed out to us on the Distillery premises. A popular legend has it that the midnight wanderer may yet see evidences of their craft, and that the darker the night and

the wilder the weather the more likely is he to stumble across the
haunted bothy, which is situated in a rocky cavern in a ravine through
which rushes one of the Dail-Uaine Burns. There the Still-fires are seen
weirdly sparkling like eyes of diamonds, and the ghosts of the departed
smugglers busy at their ancient avocations. This discovery was made
one winter's night by a shepherd, who took shelter in a cleft of the rock
from the bleak winds and drifting snow, but he declined to say if he
tasted the ghostly spirit. Some are rude enough to hint that a stiff glass
of Dail-Uaine inspired the vision; far, however, be it from us to doubt
the worthy shepherd.

EDRADOUR (Perthshire, Southern Highlands)
(*Operated by Signatory Vintage Scotch Whisky Co. Ltd*)

The Edradour burn, which flows through the site of the present
distillery, was once the location of a number of illicit stills, with peat
being cut from Moulin Moor to provide fuel for the black pots. The
men who undertook the illicit distilling were mainly local farmers,
who turned their attention to whisky-making once the harvest was
gathered each autumn. The duke of Atholl, who owned vast local
estates, unintentionally provided excellent cover for their illegal
activities when in 1774 he planted fir, larch and spruce trees on no less
than 15,500 acres in the area.

In 1825 the farmers of Edradour and the surrounding district
decided that there were advantages to distilling legitimately, and a
distilling co-operative was set up on the present site, which was leased

from the duke of Atholl. The fact that there were enough farmers with independent distilling skills to make the venture viable so soon after the Excise Act was passed suggests there was quite large-scale local illicit distillation prior to legalisation of the operation.

It is thought that in the early years, each farmer would malt his own barley – as he had done previously, but without the need for secrecy – then take it to the new distillery to use the equipment installed there to turn it into whisky. If this was really how the co-operative worked, it suggests even more strongly that these men were not novice distillers.

FETTERCAIRN (Kincardineshire, Eastern Highlands)
(*Operated by Kyndal International*)

Fettercairn distillery dates from 1824, though prior to the 1823 Excise Act an earlier distillery which bore the same name was located two miles further up into the Grampian mountains. Barnard recorded that 'The Fettercairn Distillery . . . is situated at the foot of the Grampians, where "our fathers fed their flocks" and smugglers made the Whisky. It was the head-quarters of these latter gentlemen, and many a racy tale is told by the villagers of their daring and boldness.'

GLENDARROCH (Argyllshire)
(*Operated from 1831 to 1937*)

Glendarroch distillery was situated beside the Crinan Canal, close to Ardrishaig, in Argyllshire. Barnard wrote, 'It is built at the foot of the Robber's Glen which runs upwards from the banks of the canal into the heart of the hills in the background; this glen was once the haunt

of smugglers, and no more romantic spot could have been chosen for a Distillery'.

GLENDRONACH (Aberdeenshire, Speyside)
(*Operated by Allied Distillers Ltd*)

Glendronach dates from 1826, and is located at Forgue, near Huntly. The distillery is set in a landscape of tall trees, which are home to a long-established rookery. When Barnard toured the plant he noted the 'extensive rookery. It is considered fortunate to have a colony of these birds over a Distillery, as they are said to bring good luck . . .' He makes no mention of the fact that Glendronach was a centre for illicit distilling prior to the foundation of the legal distillery, or that the rookery made it an attractive place in which to carry on illicit distilling. The birds were, indeed, lucky, as they acted as an excellent early-warning system if excise officers – or anyone else – approached the site.

GLENGOYNE (Stirlingshire, Southern Highlands)
(*Operated by Lang Brothers Ltd*)

Glengoyne distillery was first licensed in 1833, but is believed to be considerably older. The distillery site straddles the 'Highland Line', and its output is classified as a Highland malt. Although it is made in the Highlands, Glengoyne matures in the Lowlands, in warehouses situated on the opposite side of the A81 road!

The Campsie Hills around Glengoyne were a hotbed of smuggling in the late eighteenth and early nineteenth centuries. The old blacksmith's shop at the western end of the village of Blanefield, just south of Glengoyne distillery, was said to have been a popular meeting place for Campsie distillers and 'cadgers' from Glasgow who came to buy the spirit to sell in the city. Apparently, the blacksmith was friendly with the local excise officer, who obligingly was never in the vicinity when these alcoholic trysts were taking place. Such open illicit trading was dealt a serious blow when the officer in question drowned in Ebie's Loch around 1820.

In 1886 local historian Guthrie Smith wrote that in the early years of the nineteenth century 'the smoke of 13 illicit stills' was visible in the Blane Valley.

GLENLIVET (Banffshire, Speyside)
(*Operated by Chivas Brothers Ltd*)

The present Glenlivet distillery at Minmore dates from 1858, and is situated close to the confluence of the rivers Livet and Avon, in the

most famous distilling glen in Scotland. It was established by George Smith, who had previously distilled at two other sites in the vicinity. (See 'Speyside'.)

> Formerly smuggling houses were scattered on every rill, all over the mountain glens, and at that time the smugglers used to lash the kegs of spirit on their backs, and take them all the way to Aberdeen and Perth for disposal. Now all is changed . . .

GLENTURRET (Perthshire, Southern Highlands)
(*Operated by Highland Distillers plc*)

> The Glenturret Distillery is said to be one of the oldest in Scotland, having been established in 1775 . . . This work is reported to have

originally been in the hands of the smugglers, who selected the site not only for its convenient slope to the river, but more particularly for the sake of the Turret water, which is said to be as fine as any in the Kingdom, and to contain all the required properties for distilling purposes.

Distilling on the Glenturret site, near Crieff, can be traced back to 1717, when it was a favourite haunt of smugglers, and today the distillery's owners claim that as many as five illicit stills at one time functioned in the immediate vicinity. In addition to the high-quality water mentioned by Barnard, the site was popular with illicit distillers because it was located between two high hills. These provided handy vantage points from which to keep a lookout for approaching gaugers.

GRANDTULLY (Perthshire)
(*Operated from 1825 to 1910*)

Situated three miles from Grandtully, near Aberfeldy, this was 'the smallest Distillery in the United Kingdom', according to Barnard.

It is the most primitive work we have seen. The whole 'bag of tricks' could be put inside a barn, and a child four years old could jump across the streamlet which drives the water-wheel and does all the work of the Distillery . . . In olden days the whole of this district abounded with smugglers' bothies. Our loquacious driver was the grandson of a notorious smuggler, and pointed out to us as we passed, a farm-house perched on the top of a hill, which was the scene of the smuggler's nefarious practices. On the face of this hill, and just under the farm-house kitchen, was a spacious cave, entered by a small opening made by a dried-up water-course. This they blocked up with stones and pieces of rock, leaving an opening of a few inches wide for the water to trickle through from a spring, which they diverted from the other side of the hill, and brought through the cave. They then burrowed an entrance from a distant thicket, for ingress and egress, and carried a flue from the furnaces some seventy yards underground to the farm-house chimney. Here for years they made the whisky, whilst their confederate lived in the farm-house pretending to till the land, but always on guard. In an evil day for them, one of their number, out of revenge, peached to the revenue officers, who made a raid upon the place in the middle of the night, broke up the still, tubs, and worm, and took away a few kegs of whisky. Three only of the smugglers were at work at the time, who were just making up the furnace for the night, when a comrade rushed in and informed them that the officers of justice were close upon them. However, as the night was very dark, all four managed to escape, and fled to America. Ten years after, having repented of their crimes, they returned to their native country, settled down, married, and became respectable members of society; and our jolly driver quaintly reminded us that if his grandfather had not done this he would not have been there to drive us.

HIGHLAND PARK (Orkney Islands)
(*Operated by Highland Distillers plc*)

. . . the site whereon the Distillery now stands, was the place where the famous Magnus Eunson, carried on his operations. This man was the greatest and most accomplished smuggler in Orkney. By profession he was a U.P. Church Officer, and kept a stock of illicit whisky under the pulpit, but in reality he was a 'non-Professing' distiller. This godly person was accustomed to give out the psalms in a more unctuous manner than usual if the excise officers were in church, as he knew that he was suspected, and that a party of the revenue officers, taking advantage of his absence, might at that moment be searching his house. A singular story is told of this man. Hearing that the Church was about to be searched for whisky by a new party of excisemen, Eunson had the kegs all removed to his house, placed in the middle of an empty room, and covered with a clean white cloth. As the officers approached after their unsuccessful search in the church, Eunson gathered all his people, including the maidservants, round the whisky, which, with its covering of white, under which a coffin lid had been placed, looked like a bier. Eunson knelt at the head with the Bible in his hand and the others with their psalm books. As the door opened they set up a wail for the dead, and Eunson made a sign to the officers that it was a death, and one of the attendants whispered 'smallpox'.

Immediately the officer and his men made off as fast as they could, and left the smuggler for some time in peace.

The site of Eunson's first still is not known, though it seems likely that it was near Holm, south of Kirkwall, which was such a popular location with illicit distillers that the track from Holm to Kirkwall was dubbed 'the whisky road'. This road passed by the Cattie Maggie spring, and presumably its pure water appealed to Eunson, who ultimately moved his distilling operation to the site.

Despite his ingenuity, Eunson could not escape the attentions of the excise officers indefinitely, and in 1813 he was caught in possession of illicit whisky and prosecuted. Interestingly, the trial was apparently stopped at an early stage, and Eunson was not convicted. One of the officers who had arrested Eunson was John Robertson, who just happened to purchase the 'High Park' land on which Eunson had his still, prompting speculation about some sort of 'arrangement' between the two. Robertson, in partnership with Robert Borwick, opened the first legal distillery on the site, though Highland Park has long claimed its date of establishment as 1798.

INCHGOWER (Banffshire, Speyside)
(*Operated by UDV*)

Inchgower distillery is situated near the fishing port of Buckie, and was a comparatively new concern when visited by Barnard, having been established in 1871. It is one of the few working distilleries in Scotland to have been owned by a local authority, being purchased by Buckie

Town council for £1,000 in 1936. Two years later they sold the venture to Arthur Bell & Sons of Perth for four times its purchase price.

> As we drive along our coachman points out a farmhouse on the high ground, opposite the Distillery, where lived McPherson, a noted smuggler, who for many years evaded the law, but was at last captured with several kegs of whisky in his possession which he was carrying in his cart, concealed in trusses of straw, to the sea-shore. He was heavily fined and in default of payment imprisoned. The fine would have been remitted had he revealed to the judge the Still from whence it was procured. As a matter of fact it was the product of an illicit Still at Aultmoor Glen, at the back of the Bin Hill, a regular smuggler's haunt, and these men used the same water as that now in use at the Distillery.
>
> The Still was worked in a cavity in a hill side, the entrance to which was covered up with turf and heather, and might be passed a hundred times and yet never be seen. It was an accident which disclosed the secret. Some Highland cattle were being driven home, when one of them strayed from the track and putting its foot in a hole displaced a large piece of turf, disclosing to the eyes of the farmer, who was up to every dodge of the smugglers, McPherson's well-kept secret and the means of securing the offered reward. On reaching home he communicated with the revenue officers, who proceeded to the place, dismantled the Still and vessels, broke up the Worm, and brought away several kegs of whisky. McPherson and his associates, having heard of their approach, took to their boats and escaped.

Lagavulin (Port Ellen, Isle of Islay)
(*Operated by UDV*)

> Lagavulin is said to be one of the oldest Distilleries in Islay, the business to a certain extent having been founded in 1742. At that period it consisted of ten small and separate smuggling bothys for the manufacture of 'moonlight', which when working presented anything but a true picture of 'still life', and were all subsequently absorbed into one establishment, the whole work not making more than a few thousand gallons per annum. The term 'moonlight' used always to be applied to illicit Whisky in contradistinction to that which paid duty, which was termed 'daylight'. A century ago smuggling was the chief employment of the crofters and fishermen, more especially during the winter, and many were the encounters which took place between them and the Government officers. Up to the year 1821 smuggling was a lucrative trade in Islay, and large families were supported by it. In those days every smuggler could clear at least ten shillings a day, and keep a horse and cow. Early in the century the buildings were converted into a legal Distillery . . .

In fact, there were originally two legal distilleries on the site, one founded by John Johnston in 1816, the second established by Archibald Campbell a year later. By 1837 the two distilleries had been amalgamated under a licence held by Donald Johnston.

LOCHHEAD (Campbeltown, Argyllshire)
(*Operated from 1824 to 1928*)

> . . . we walked to Lochead [sic], another of the few old-fashioned distilleries, remnants of the romantic smuggling days. It is built on the banks of the Lochead Burn and close to the Kinloch Park, and was there erected in 1824. As you enter the enclosure you observe an air of antiquity round and about you. There is a small swift stream running through the works into the sea, and a large burn outside. What was once a cluster of old houses, and an ancient mill, with doubtless several illicit stills, is now a licensed Distillery; and time has indeed dealt leniently with its old stone walls and fences. The establishment has now absorbed the whole four corners of a block covering two and a half acres of ground.

MILTONDUFF (Morayshire, Speyside)
(*Operated by Allied Distillers Ltd*)

Miltonduff distillery, to the south-west of Elgin, stands on land once owned by the Benedictine Priory of Pluscarden. The ruins of Pluscarden Priory are not far from the distillery, and its monks were noted brewers, using water from the Black Burn to make their ale.

On a New Year's Day in the fifteenth century, an imposing ceremony occurred on the grounds where now stands Milton Duff. It was the occasion of blessing the waters of the Black Burn, previous to its being used by the Benedictine Monks of Pluscarden. Attended by its priors, palmers, and priests, an aged abbot proceeded to the banks of the stream, where, kneeling on a stone with hands outstretched to heaven, he invoked a blessing on its waters, and ever after the life-giving beverage distilled therefrom was christened 'aqua vitae', the rivulet being to this day held in high repute and veneration by the natives. We were shown the stone on which the abbot is said to have knelt; it bears an indistinct date, and is built into the wall of the Malt Mill . . . The works, which now cover two acres of ground, were mostly rebuilt as far back as the year 1824, by Pearey and Bain; but previous to that time the site was occupied by the descendants of a band of smugglers, of whom many interesting tales are told. At one time there were as many as fifty illicit stills in the Glen of Pluscarden, and there are those living who remember some of them in operation. In this well-known establishment some of the oldest fads and methods are in use, and the ancient style of stills and utensils as carried on by the smugglers, have also been continued. These gentlemen, who were the pioneers of whisky making, well knew in what locality the best water was to be found, hence their choice of Pluscarden, and the erection of 'sma' Stills' by the score on the banks of the Black Burn.

According to legend, when a party of excise officers was seen to be approaching, a flag was hoisted on one of the three hills that enclosed the glen and made it such an attractive place for illicit distilling. It was in Pluscarden that the famous story of 'Mrs Watson and the Gauger' was set, though a similar tale is claimed for several other locations around Scotland, including Orkney. Apparently, an excise officer spent the night waiting and watching at a croft where illicit distilling was clearly taking place. Early the following morning he approached the house and was confronted by Mrs Watson, who was a large lady, while the officer in question was of modest build. On entering the house he discovered that equipment from the previous evening's distilling remained in place. 'Did anybody see ye come in here?' asked Mrs Watson. Perhaps naively, the officer replied in the negative. 'And naebody'll ever see ye gang oot,' she said menacingly. The gauger fled, left Pluscarden, and was replaced by an officer who always obligingly announced his intended visits well in advance.

ORD (Ross-shire, Northern Highlands)
(Operated by UDV)

When it was founded in 1838, Ord was one of no fewer than ten licensed distilleries in the parish of Muir of Ord, Ross-shire. According to the *New Statistical Account of Scotland*, in 1840 'distilling of aquavitae' was the only 'manufacture' of the area.

> The Distillery which is erected on the slopes of a gentle hill . . . is supplied with fine water from the Glen Oran and two lochs in the hill of Knockudas . . . The Oran rivulet, which proceeds from the glen, rattles along, close to the roofs of some of the buildings, and the quality of the water is said to be superior to any in the district . . . Glen Oran has, for more than a century, been the favourite resort of smugglers, and even to this day they carry on their illegal business, and every now

and then a bothy is unearthed. The site of the Distillery itself was a smuggler's bothy, early in the [nineteenth] century, but it was not until the year 1838 that it was turned into a legal Distillery.

RIECHLACHAN (Campbeltown, Argyllshire)
(Operated from 1825 to 1934)

From the remotest days of antiquity distilling was carried on in the neighbourhood of the Distillery, if not on the very same spot. In the year 1815 there was only one legal Distillery in Campbeltown, but nine years after several others were erected, all on the plan of the Old Pot Still or Smuggler's Kettle, Riechlachan being among the number.

Riechlachan, situated in the distilling heart of Campbeltown, off Longrow, somehow continued in production as its Campbeltown rivals fell by the wayside. When it closed in 1934, only the present-day survivors Glen Scotia and Springbank remained in operation.

ROYAL BRACKLA (Inverness-shire, Speyside)
(Operated by John Dewar & Sons Ltd)

Brackla distillery was established in 1812 by Captain William Fraser, and in 1835 became the first to be granted a Royal Warrant.

The Cawdor Moss is just above the Distillery, and running through it is the famous Cawdor Burn, which, after passing through a deep rocky ravine beautifully wooded within the park surrounding the ancient castle of Cawdor, splashes past and flows into the Nairn. This burn, which supplies all the water to the Distillery, was in remote days used by the noted Tarrick and other smugglers, whose illicit stills abounded on its banks.

ROYAL LOCHNAGAR (Aberdeenshire, Eastern Highlands)
(Operated by UDV)

The Distillery was built in the year 1825 by one John Robertson of Crathie, an old smuggler, and it came into the hands of Mr. John Begg in the year 1845.

As Ross Wilson observed in *Scotch: Its History and Romance* (1973),

During the smuggling period the remote glens along the foothills of the Grampians were ideal for illicit distilling and smuggling. The whole area at the foot of Lochnagar – of Byronic fame – became famous for the quality of its whisky. With the settlement of 1823 an enterprising

young man named John Begg thought it a pity to allow the experience of the old distillers to go to waste.

STROMNESS (Stromness, Orkney)
(Operated from 1817 to 1928)

In the little old-fashioned Still house are to be seen two of the 'sma' old pot stills', each holding 300 gallons. One of these, a veritable smuggler's Still of a peculiar shape, is the quaintest we have seen in our travels, and was formerly the property of a noted law-evader; its body is shaped like a pumpkin, and is surmounted by a similarly shaped chamber one fourth the size, to prevent the goods boiling over, through which the neck passes to the head of the Still.

Orkney's third legal distillery (along with Highland Park and Scapa), Stromness was renamed Man O'Hoy during the latter years of the nineteenth century, and its malt whisky was labelled Old Orkney. The original pair of stills at which Barnard marvelled was displayed in the distillery yard. After its closure, the distillery was demolished to make way for local authority housing.

TAMBOWIE (Dumbartonshire)
(Operated from 1825 to 1914)

This old-fashioned Distillery, situated as it is in the country of Rob Roy, brings us back to the old smugglers' days, for this place was actually the scene of their illicit exploits, and the cave cut out of the solid rock, wherein they carried on their nefarious practices, is converted into and now used as Stores.

Tambowie was located a couple of miles from Milngavie, to the north-west of Glasgow, and was ultimately destroyed by fire in 1914. According to local lore, people converged on the burning distillery from miles around, carrying containers of any kind in which to salvage the whisky, and there were many drunken 'sessions' in the woods close to the distillery during the nights following the blaze.

BIBLIOGRAPHY

Arnot, Hugo (1779) *History of Edinburgh*

Barnard, Alfred (1887) *The Whisky Distilleries of the United Kingdom*, Harper's Weekly Gazette

Barrie, David (1890) *The City of Dundee Illustrated*

Beaton, Angus John (1906) *The Social and Economic Condition of the Highlands of Scotland Since 1800*

Behan, Brendan (1962) *Brendan Behan's Island*, Century Hutchinson Publishing Group Ltd

Bond, Keith (1996) *Still Life – Memoirs of an Exciseman*, Jimmy Brown

Bradley, Edward (1861) *Glencreggan*

Brander, Michael (1974) *The Original Scotch*, Hutchinson & Co Ltd

Brown, Gordon (1993) *The Whisky Trails*, Prion Books

Burns, Edward (1995) *It's a bad thing whisky, especially Bad Whisky*, Balvag Books

Burns, Robert (1867) *The Complete Works*, William P Nimmo

Campbell, J.R.D. (1994) *Clyde Coast Smuggling*, St Maura Press

Carswell, Catherine (1930) *The Life of Robert Burns*, William Collins & Sons

Cooper, Derek (1982) *The Whisky Roads of Scotland*, Jill Norman & Hobhouse Ltd

Craig, Charles (1994) *The Scotch Whisky Industry Record*, Index Publishing Ltd

Dabney, Joseph Earl (1974) *Mountain Spirits*, Bright Mountain Books

Donovan, Prof. M (1830) *Domestic Economy*

Gillespie, Malcolm (1828) *The Memorial and Case of Malcolm Gillespie*

Glen, I. (1970) *A Maker of Illicit Stills*, (published in) Scottish Studies

Grant, Elizabeth of Rothiemurchus (1898) *Memoirs of a Highland Lady*, John Murray Ltd

Gunn, Neil, (1935) *Whisky and Scotland*, George Routledge

Guthrie, Thomas (1874) *Autobiography of Thomas Guthrie DD*, Daldy, Isbister & Co

Hart, F.R. & Pick, J.B. (1981) *Neil M Gunn – A Highland Life*, John Murray Ltd

Jamieson, John (1808/09) *Etymological Dictionary of the Scottish Language*

Johnson, Dr Samuel (1755) *Dictionary of the English Language*

Kania, Leon W., (2000) *The Alaskan Bootlegger's Bible*, Happy Mountain Publications

Kellner, Esther (1971) *Moonshine – Its History and Folklore*, Weathervane Books

Kenna, Rudolph and Sutherland, Ian (2000) *The Bevvy*, Clutha Books

Kenna, Rudolph and Sutherland, Ian (2001) *They Belonged to Glasgow*, Neil Wilson Publishing Ltd

Leyden, Dr John (1800) *Journal of a Tour in the Highlands and Western Islands of Scotland*, W Blackwood & Sons

Lockhart, Sir Robert Bruce (1951) *Scotch*, Puttnam

McAra, Duncan (1881) *Crieff: Its Traditions and Characters*

MacCulloch, John (1819) *A Description of the Western Isles of Scotland*

MacCulloch, John (1824) *The Highlands and Western Isles of Scotland*

Macdonald, Aeneas (1930) *Whisky*, The Porpoise Press

Macdonald, Colin (1936) *Echoes of the Glen*, Moray Press

MacDonald, Ian (1914) *Smuggling in the Highlands*, Eneas Mackay

MacDonald, J. (1811) *General View of Agriculture of the Hebrides or Western Isles of Scotland*

McDowall, R.J.S. (1967) *The Whiskies of Scotland*, John Murray Ltd

McGuffin, John (1978) *In Praise of Poteen*, The Appletree Press Ltd

McGuire, E.B.(1973) *Irish Whiskey*, Gill & Macmillan Ltd

McHardy, Stuart (1991) *Tales of Whisky and Smuggling*, Lochar Publishing Ltd

MacLean, Charles (1997) *Malt Whisky*, Mitchell Beazley Ltd

Mackenzie, Sir Compton (1947) *Whisky Galore*, Chatto & Windus Ltd

Mackenzie, Sir Osgood (1921) *A Hundred Years in the Highlands*, Geoffrey Bles

Mackenzie, W.G. (1903) *A History of the Outer Hebrides*

Martin, Martin (1703) *A Description of the Western Islands of Scotland*, Andrew Bell

Mitchell, Joseph (1883/4) *Reminiscences of My Life in the Highlands*

Morewood, Samuel (1824) *An Essay on the Inventions and Customs in the Use of Inebriating Liquors*

Morrice, Philip (1983) *Schweppes Guide to Scotch*, Alphabooks Ltd

Morton, Tom (1992) *Spirit of Adventure*, Mainstream Publishing Co Ltd

Moss, Michael & Hume, John (1981) *The Making of Scotch Whisky*, James and James Ltd

The New Statistical Account of Scotland (1845), various contributors, W Blackwood & Sons

O'Neill, Tom (1872) *Doings of a Notorious Glasgow Shebeener*

Philipson, John (1991) *Whisky Smuggling on the Borders*, Society of Antiquities, Newcastle upon Tyne

Phillips, J. Gordon (1897) *The Origin of Glenlivet Whisky, With Some Account of the Smuggling*, (published in) The Distillers' Magazine and Spirit Trade News

Postlethwayt, Malachy (1751) *Universal Dictionary of Commerce*

Robb, J. Marshall (1950) *Scotch Whisky – A Guide*, W&R Chambers Ltd

Ross, James (1970) *Whisky*, Routledge & Kegan Paul Ltd

Sillett, Steve (1965) *Illicit Scotch*, Beaver Books

Simpson, W.D. (1942) *The Book of Glenbuchat*

Sinclair, Herbert (1948) *Over the Ord*, Herbert Sinclair

Sinclair, Sir John (ed.) (1791-9) *The Statistical Account of Scotland* (29 vols)

Smith, Adam (1776) *An Inquiry into the Nature and Causes of the Wealth of Nations*

Smith, Gavin D. (1993) *Whisky – A Book of Words*, Carcanet Press Ltd

Smith, Gavin D. (1999) *Scotch Whisky*, Sutton Publishing Ltd

Smith, Gavin D. (2000) *Whisky Wit & Wisdom*, The Angels' Share

Smith, George (1738) *A Compleat Body of Distilling*

St John, Charles (1846) *The Wild Sports of the Highlands*, John Murray

Steadman, Ralph (1994) *Still Life With Bottle*, Ebury Press

Stewart, Alexander (1928) *A Highland Parish – or the History of Fortingall*

Stewart, Col. David (1825) *Sketches of the Character, Manners and Present State of the Highlanders of Scotland*

Sutherland, Iain (n.d.) *Vote No Licence*, Iain Sutherland

Walsh, Maurice (1926) *The Key Above The Door*, W&R Chambers Ltd

Walsh, Maurice (1940) *The Hill is Mine*, W&R Chambers Ltd

Townsend, Brian (1993) *Scotch Missed – The Lost Distilleries of Scotland*, Neil Wilson Publishing Ltd

Wilson, John (1842) *The Recreations of Christopher North*

Wilson, Neil (1985) *Scotch and Water*, Lochar Publishing Ltd

Wilson, Ross (1959) *Scotch Made Easy*, Hutchinson & Co Ltd

Wilson, Ross (1973) *Scotch – Its History and Romance*, David & Charles Ltd

Worth, W.Y. (1705) *The Compleat Distiller*

The Courier
The Daily Telegraph
The Dufftown News and Speyside Advertiser
Dundee, Perth and Cupar Advertiser
The Glasgow Herald
The Inverness Courier
The John O'Groat Journal
The London Scotsman
North British Daily Mail
The Northern Scot
The Press & Journal
The Scotsman
The Scots Magazine
Tocher
West Highland Free Press
Whisky Magazine – issues 1–25

INDEX